T3-BRJ-832

A CENTURY OF MIRACLES

A CENTURY OF MIRACLES

Christians, Pagans, Jews, and
the Supernatural, 312–410

H. A. Drake

OXFORD
UNIVERSITY PRESS

BR
180
.D73
2017

OXFORD

UNIVERSITY PRESS

Oxford University Press is a department of the University of Oxford. It furthers
the University's objective of excellence in research, scholarship, and education
by publishing worldwide. Oxford is a registered trade mark of Oxford University
Press in the UK and certain other countries.

Published in the United States of America by Oxford University Press
198 Madison Avenue, New York, NY 10016, United States of America.

© Oxford University Press 2017

All rights reserved. No part of this publication may be reproduced, stored in
a retrieval system, or transmitted, in any form or by any means, without the
prior permission in writing of Oxford University Press, or as expressly permitted
by law, by license, or under terms agreed with the appropriate reproduction
rights organization. Inquiries concerning reproduction outside the scope of the
above should be sent to the Rights Department, Oxford University Press, at the
address above.

You must not circulate this work in any other form
and you must impose this same condition on any acquirer.

Library of Congress Cataloging-in-Publication Data
Names: Drake, H. A. (Harold Allen), 1942– author.
Title: A century of miracles : Christians, pagans, Jews, and
the supernatural, 312–410 / H. A. Drake.
Description: New York : Oxford University Press, 2017. |
Includes bibliographical references and index.
Identifiers: LCCN 2017010324 | ISBN 9780199367412 (hardback) |
ISBN 9780199367436 (epub) | ISBN 9780199367443 (online content)
Subjects: LCSH: Church history—4th century. |
Constantine I, Emperor of Rome, –337. | Christianity—Influence. |
Religions—History. | Miracles. | Supernatural.
Classification: LCC BR180 .D73 2017 | DDC 270.2—dc23
LC record available at https://lccn.loc.gov/2017010324

1 3 5 7 9 8 6 4 2

Printed by Sheridan Books, Inc., United States of America

"But stories take place in societies, otherwise they cannot exist."

Iain Pears, *Arcadia*

For Logan and Vivi
nepotes dilectissimi

CONTENTS

Illustrations   *xi*

Acknowledgments   *xiii*

Abbreviations   *xv*

Introduction   1

1. Historians and the Miraculous   7

2. Theodosius's Miracle   27

3. Constantine's Miracle   49

4. Miracle Doctors   75

5. The Miracle of the Cross   93

6. Jews in Miracles   115

7. Miracle in the Desert   135

8. Miracles on Trial   157

CONTENTS

9. Failed Miracles   181

10. Alaric, Augustine, and the End of a Century
    of Miracles   199

11. Epilogue: The Story of Titus   219

Notes   235
Primary Sources   265
Bibliography   269
Index   307

ILLUSTRATIONS

1.1 Roman orgy scene from C. B. Demille's
"Manslaughter" (1922). 24

2.1 Mosaic of St. Ambrose, San Ambrogio, Milan (early
fifth century). 32

2.2 Gold solidus of Theodosius I (r. 379–395). 35

2.3 Peter Paul Rubens, "Theodosius and
Ambrose" (1618). 36

3.1 Constantine's Dream and Vision. Ninth-century
manuscript illustration. 52

3.2 Christogram or staurogram? 53

3.3 Coin of Constantine with chi-rho emblem.
Ticinum, 315. 54

3.4 Gold coin of Constantine and Apollo-Helios.
Ticinum 313. 62

3.5 A halo phenomenon. 63

3.6 Constantine crowned by God. Gold medallion. 69

5.1 Map of Jerusalem in the first century. 97

5.2 Coüasnon's plan of Constantine's Church of the
Holy Sepulchre. 100

5.3 Detail of Jerusalem in the sixth-century Madaba mosaic. 101
5.4 Coin of Helena, minted in Antioch. 106
5.5 Icon of Helena and Constantine with cross. 108
5.6 Helena finds the cross. 110
6.1 Helena throws Judas into a well. Fifteenth-century woodcut. 117
6.2 Solar chariot in mosaic floor of a fourth-century synagogue. 124
7.1 Saint Antony beaten by the devils. Painting by Stefano di Giovanni (1392–1450). 138
7.2 Santa Julitta. Twelfth-century fresco. 143
8.1 Dispute of Silvester and the rabbis. Thirteenth-century fresco. 158
8.2 Emperor Julian "the Apostate." 162
8.3 Silver coin of Octavian (the future emperor Augustus) showing the golden statue of the goddess Victoria (Victory). 173
9.1 Model of the Second Temple in Jerusalem, as restored by Herod the Great. 191
10.1 Honorius receives news of the fall of Rome. "The Favorites of the Emperor Honorius" by John William Waterhouse, 1883. 201
10.2 Fresco of St. Augustine, c. 600 CE. 206
11.1 Image of Daniel the Stylite, from the eleventh-century Menologion of Basil II. 220

ACKNOWLEDGMENTS

A number of friends and colleagues have been kind enough to read drafts of all or part of this book. It is a pleasure to acknowledge the suggestions of David De Giustino, Abby Dowling, Bart Ehrman, Martin Henry, Michael O'Connell, Joe W. Leedom, Nelson Richards, Jeffrey Burton Russell, Chris Sandner, Mark Smith, and Miriam Raub Vivian. Mike Proulx "test marketed" chapters with his graduate students at the University of North Georgia, and they responded with thoughtful and detailed critiques. Amanda Burr, Lauren Hardman, and Nathan Scales have great careers ahead of them.

I owe special thanks to Tim Vivian for trying to make me seem literate, and to Kyle Smith for teaching an old dog some new tricks.

I must acknowledge as well one critic whose advice I sorely miss. Tom Sizgorich's untimely death in 2011 deprived not just me but the whole choir of late antiquity scholars of one of its most angelic and profound voices.

Needless to say, these friends have not been able to catch all of my mistakes, nor could they talk me out of all my idiosyncrasies.

ACKNOWLEDGMENTS

I thank with special fondness my colleagues in the original University of California late antiquity group—Emily Albu, Susanna Elm, Claudia Rapp, and Michele Saltzman—for decades of friendship and encouragement, and for allowing me to be what Susanna once called "our token male."

This book was little more than a thought in the back of my head when I mentioned it to Stefan Vranka at Oxford University Press, who proceeded to do everything an author wants from an editor. He pushed, prodded, and occasionally punched, and was a frequent source of inspiration when my own muse fell silent. And, although I have tried, I have yet to find the limit to the patience, enthusiasm, and expertise of Stefan's assistant, John Veranes. My anonymous readers also made a number of suggestions of ways to navigate a subject that turned out to be much trickier than I thought it would be.

Santa Barbara, California

ABBREVIATIONS

Ag. Gal.	Julian, *Against the Galilaeans*
Catech.	Cyril of Jerusalem, *Catechesis*
CCSL	Corpus Christianorum, Series Latina
CSEL	Corpus Scriptorum Ecclesiasticorum Latinorum
civ. dei	Augustine of Hippo, *De civitate Dei* (*City of God*)
DI	Lactantius, *Divine Institutes*
DMP	Lactantius, *De mortibus persecutorum*
Ep.	*Epistles* (Letters)
GCS	Die Griechischen christlichen Schriftsteller der ersten drei Jahrhunderte
HE	*Historia ecclesiastica* (Church History)
LC	*Laus Constantini* ("In Praise of Constantine")
LCL	Loeb Classical Library
Life	Eusebius of Caesarea, *de vita Constantini* ("Life of Constantine")
obit. Theo.	Ambrose of Milan, *De obitu Theodosii* ("On the Death of Theodosius")

ABBREVIATIONS

OC	*Oratio Constantini ad coetum sanctorum* ("Oration to the Saints")
Pat. Gr.	Migne, *Patrologia Graeca*
Pat. Lat.	Migne, *Patrologia Latina*
PL	*XII Panegyrici Latini* (*Latin Panegyrics*)
SC	*De sepulchro Christi* ("On Christ's Sepulchre")

Introduction

The fourth century of our Common Era was a time of rapid and unprecedented religious change. At its start, Christians were a minority in the Roman Empire, enduring what came to be called the Great Persecution. At its end, they were a much larger minority, putting the final touches on what was about to become a Christian Roman Empire. It is a change that had profound consequences for Jews and for that congeries of local religious practices we now label "paganism."

This book is about two miracles that shaped the course of that century—one at its start that was witnessed by the emperor Constantine the Great, the other a miraculous windstorm at its close that saved the army of another emperor, Theodosius I. My aim is to demonstrate that more than coincidence is involved in the timing of these miracles. Because Christians were the winners in both contests, these events convinced them that their God wanted Christianity to be the sole religion of the Roman Empire.

Other events in between these two miracles served to reinforce their belief. These include discovery of wood identified as the True Cross, the emergence of a regimen that could turn gifted individuals into channels of divine energy, and a discourse that increasingly relied on an argument of divine favor to prove one's case. All have been the subject of numerous scholarly studies, but they have not heretofore been made the focus of a single inquiry. Not all of these developments were in themselves miraculous, but when filtered through the lens of the two imperial miracles, they reveal a unique combination of circumstances that allows this period to be thought of as a century of miracles.

Underlying them all was a belief during this century that supernatural support was available to individuals who gained divine favor. That belief might well be called the governing idea of this century, and it is the reason this book does not end with Theodosius's miracle in 394 but instead continues down to the year 410. In that year, a barbarian army sacked the city of Rome, ending an eight hundred–year run that saw this little settlement in central Italy rise to control of the entire Mediterranean and much of continental Europe. It is a date now often used for the fall of Rome as a whole, but its specific importance here is that, given this governing idea, it amounted to convincing proof that the Christian God was not up to the job of protecting the empire.

Or so it should have. Seen from the perspective of the fourth century, Christianity's ability to survive this signal failure, and many others even more severe that followed, is the great unanswered question of the age: after a century of bragging about the power of their God, how were they able to dodge responsibility for this disaster?

A CENTURY OF MIRACLES

This is a topic that calls for a little light housekeeping, which is the aim of chapter 1. Historians have an uncomfortable relationship with miracles and a problem with The Truth. The result is a narrative about the fourth century that has changed over time. Before throwing miracles into the mix, these cobwebs need to be swept away.

That chore accomplished, we can start addressing the paradox of Christian power. Chapter 2 does this, appropriately enough, by taking a paradoxical starting point: Theodosius's miracle at the end of the century, instead of Constantine's at its start. One of the historian's most dangerous gifts is hindsight. Knowing where a story ends makes it all too easy to project that ending onto the beginning. So it is with the history of the fourth century, where it is easy to assume that the narrower and more rigid form of Christianity that prevailed under Theodosius at the end of the century was already the only type of Christianity available when Constantine converted at its start. Starting in this unorthodox manner is a way to lay bare those changes so that in ensuing chapters we can be more aware of what it was that changed.

The story of this century is, at its most basic level, a story of a change in the meaning of what it meant to be a Roman. An important marker of this change is the power and leverage over public affairs that came to be exercised by Christian bishops. Two figures who are inextricably entwined in the Christian imagination of later centuries—the emperor Theodosius I (r. 379–395) and Bishop Ambrose of Milan (bp. 374–397)—show how bishops had emerged as power brokers over the course of this century. In a funeral oration for Theodosius that he delivered in 395, Ambrose attributed the emperor's last victory, only months before his death, to his overwhelming piety. Ambrose's career was devoted to bringing emperors under the authority of bishops, at least in religious matters, and making piety the virtue to celebrate served to further that goal.

Theodosius's miracle was the last of this century. It was also an echo of the first, Constantine the Great's miraculous Vision of the Cross, traditionally placed in the year 312. After more than 1,700 years, the question of what he saw, when he saw it, and what it means is as fascinating as ever, despite distinct shifts in our understanding and evaluation of what happened. Chapter 3 takes us back to this event. Just because it is so fascinating, it is easy to forget the role of Late Roman political ideology as it was understood and presented at the time. There is also the matter of how Constantine himself understood this event. Accounts differ, but the emperor's own plan seems to have been to build an image of himself as the "Man of God," a phrase that resonated in both Christian and imperial vocabulary.

This image bridged Constantine's joint role as both a Roman emperor and a Christian ruler, but it posed problems for Christian thinkers. Their efforts to deal with it are the subject of chapter 4, which looks at the way this event was framed for future ages by two contemporaries of Constantine: the "Christian Cicero" Lactantius, in the West, and the Father of Church History, Eusebius of Caesarea, in the East.

Chapter 5 turns to another miracle, the story of Constantine's mother, Helena, and the discovery of Christendom's most sacred relic, the cross on which Jesus had been crucified. Ambrose's account is the earliest we have for this story, but it is clear that elements of it were in circulation earlier. Christians had always venerated the cross as a symbol of their belief, but the cult of the cross exploded with the spread of fragments from what pious believers identified as the genuine article.

Christian thinking about miracles, as about so much else, depended heavily on Jewish roots. But as with so much else, here too Jews found their own history usurped and turned against them. Miracle stories both shaped and reflected Christian attitudes toward the Jews. In chapter 6 we will consider the introduction of a Jew into the Helena legend and what his portrayal reveals about the complicated relationship of Christians with the religion that, on the one hand, validated their faith, but on the other rejected its premises.

Chapter 7 focuses on the creation of an even more influential story, one that promoted a movement to abandon earthly cares for a life of seclusion and prayer. Attributed to Bishop Athanasius of Alexandria, the *Life of Antony* also triggered the start of a new genre, the saint's life, or "hagiography." As part of the legacy of the Age of Reason, with its tendency to undervalue religious experience, the monastic movement gets blamed for draining the empire of much-needed manpower and financial resources. But the *Life of Antony* demonstrated to contemporaries the immense power that could be channeled through a person who denied the grip of the material world.

This chapter serves as a pivot—away from miracles themselves and toward the way miracle language started to influence the standards of debate. The accession of Constantine's nephew, the emperor Julian (r. 361–363), intensified this trend. Dubbed "the Apostate" because he had "turned away" from his Christian upbringing, Julian revived the detested practice of animal sacrifice. But he opposed his former coreligionists with words as well as deeds, deploying his thorough knowledge of Christian belief with lethal effect. This war of words is the subject of chapter 8. In Julian's wake, other pagan intellectuals tried to convince Christians to let them practice their traditional religions by adopting arguments that Christians themselves had used to gain toleration for their own beliefs. (One of the more striking ironies of this period is the way these belated pagan arguments for toleration have come to support the stereotype of tolerant pagans versus intolerant Christians.)

Julian's ultimate effect was to stoke Christian anxieties and accelerate religious polarization. In the short run, however, he showed how miracle language had started to redefine the terms of debate. Two spectacular failures—his attempt to rebuild the Temple in Jerusalem, which had lain in ruins since the first century, and his death in a vainglorious effort to conquer the

Persian Empire—fed into a narrative that served with the imperial miracles to confirm Christian determination to make their set of beliefs the official religion of the empire. Chapter 9 looks at a string of failures by the old gods (at least in Christian telling) that were as important as their own successes for proving the truth of their message and strength of their God.

By the start of the fifth century, Christians had every reason to believe that they would be protected as well from the danger posed by tribes of Germanic peoples who were roaming through their empire. Instead, one of those tribal groupings captured the city of Rome itself, a humiliation the great capital had not experienced for eight hundred years. By this point, Christianity had become the official state religion, which meant the Christian God was now expected to keep the empire safe. Chapter 10 deals with the fallout from this failure. After a century of boasting, the fall of the city of Rome in 410 should have provided grounds for second thoughts. In fact, it did. But these were dealt with brilliantly in a book that became a cornerstone for Western Christianity—Augustine of Hippo's *City of God*. His book demonstrates the role bishops had assumed as arbiters of miracle. But in the course of refuting pagan claims, it also ended the century of miracles.

In a farewell look at this century, chapter 11 offers another answer to the question of how Christianity was able to survive the disaster of 410. Christians developed a form of storytelling that came to be more important than the miracles themselves. Along with the more eloquent and intellectual works that we still study in our schools, these stories, filled with wonder, are what held the newly Christian empire together.

Chapter 1

Historians and the Miraculous

In the great house of Acadēme, historians are the plumbers. We do a pretty good job of keeping the pipes of information clean and gauging the rate and quality of the stuff that flows through them. Supernatural phenomena are the job of the people on the top floor: philosophers, theologians, maybe theoretical physicists. So the first thing I need to explain is why I, a historian, am writing about miracles.

Actually, my subject is not miracles per se but stories about miracles. Even more, it is about the way people in the fourth century of our Common Era used these accounts to interpret and understand the bewildering changes they experienced. The difference is small, but important. It is often said that miracles are events that can be explained in no other way. True enough. But until a miracle has been turned into a story—by which I mean until somebody has interpreted it and shown its significance—its effects will be minimal. Once that narrative has been established, however, it will reveal a great deal about the people who told and listened to it.

Here is an example:

Sally has been diagnosed with an incurable disease and given three months to live. Out hiking, she accidentally falls into a deep ravine. To her rescuers' surprise, Sally suffered no physical

injuries, and her doctors discover all symptoms of her ter-
minal illness are gone. They say there is no scientific ratio-
nale for what happened. Sally has never prayed to any saint
or deity; in fact, she is an atheist and does not believe such
beings exist.

What does Sally's experience mean? Well, that depends on how you
explain it. Here are some possibilities:

Explanation I. It was a miracle. But why Sally when the prayers
of so many more deserving and pious sufferers go unanswered?
God specifically chose Sally because she is an atheist, to make her
miracle more credible. Additionally, God sent this cure as a sign to
Sally and her ilk to mend their wicked ways.

Explanation II. Many thousands of years ago, alien beings
landed on this very spot to carry out repairs to their spaceship. The
substance they used has healing properties for humans but does not
register on our relatively primitive instruments. When Sally landed
on this same spot, her body absorbed a trace of this substance. That
is what cured her.

Explanation III. a. (shrug); b. "There are more things in heaven
and earth, Horatio, than are dreamt of by your philosophy"; c. There
is an explanation; I just do not know what it is.

Each alternative shapes the meaning of Sally's experience in a
markedly different way.

The first is that of a believer: the lack of a medical or scientific
explanation for Sally's cure proves that it was the result of divine
intervention.

The second might seem too far-fetched to be called "scientific,"
but it is at least an answer that does not require a supernatural
explanation. And this person would be quick to point out that it
is an answer for which there is just as much proof as the believer
can offer.

The third alternative is probably the most common these days; it might be called the agnostic response. This person does not want to accept a miracle on the one hand, but on the other thinks anyone who buys the spaceship story must have sniffed too much model airplane glue as a child. Confident that an alternative explanation will be found eventually, until that happens this person will think Sally was just terribly lucky.

Each answer is in its own way "rational," in the sense that it provides a reason for an inexplicable event. Each also requires a certain amount of faith: in the existence of a divine being, a spaceship, or an as-yet-undiscovered alternative. Each of these explanations, in turn, can reveal a great deal about the needs and aspirations of the people who accepted them. Did you find yourself drawn to one or another of them? Or did you come up with one that you liked even better? If so, what have you just told me about yourself?

The lesson, then, is this: miracles are what they are, but there are many ways to explain them. Moreover, of the three explanations for Sally's cure, only the one that called it a miracle raised additional questions, requiring further explanation of why God acted in this particular way. That explanation will not always be the same. For this reason, once people start talking (or writing) about miracles, those miracles become the kind of stuff historians can work with.

Did any of the miracles in this book actually occur? Don't ask me; I am just a historian. But as a historian, I can tell you that events are shaped as much by what people think happened as by what actually did happen. If the aim is to understand an age in which a great deal that was unexpected happened, we dismiss such evidence at our peril.[1] During the century between 312 and 410, Christians used miracle stories to explain these changes to themselves. We can use them now to understand those same changes.

In particular, stories of two miraculous events, each involving a Roman emperor on a battlefield, show how Christians were able to embed themselves so rapidly in the traditional power structure. For us, these two events will serve as filters with which to sift through other changes—some miraculous, some mundane—that led to this totally unexpected result.

It is quite a story.

AN EMPIRE REVIVED

It is a story about an empire that was shattered seemingly beyond repair in one century only to come back in many ways stronger than ever in the next, about a century where everything was shaken up from top to bottom, and about people who were still trying to figure out what made them "Christians" or "pagans" or "Jews," and whether, like it or not, they were still going to be "Romans."

It was a century that began and ended with a miracle. In the traditional date of 312, the emperor Constantine (r. 306–337) experienced his famous Vision of the Cross, a promise of victory that led him to convert to Christianity. In the autumn of 394 another emperor, Theodosius I (r. 379–395), uttered a prayer that turned the tide of battle against the last organized opposition to a Christian empire. In between these events, other miracles stoked Christian ambitions: Constantine's mother, Helena, discovered the True Cross, and the hermit Antony showed how a life of Christian discipline could endow one with Christ's power to heal the sick and defeat demons. Other miracles exposed the weakness of Christian enemies. Increasingly, the language of miracle entered debate, and yet when this book ends with the dramatic sack of Rome in 410, this failure of the Christian god to protect his new empire caused barely a hiccup in the march toward a Christian state.

All this happened in the fourth century of our Common Era, but the preconditions were set in the third century, which was a crucible for the empire. For the first two centuries of our Common Era, relative stability on the frontiers had allowed Rome's rulers to avoid confronting some basic problems, such as who was responsible for choosing the emperor, how large their military should be and where it would come from, and—most important of all—how much this was going to cost and who was going to pay for it. These questions suddenly became very real when the one thing Roman generals feared most, a two-front war, came to pass with the arrival of new Germanic peoples in the North and the rise of a strong and expansionist Persian Empire in the East. The soldiery had always had a say in the choice of emperor, but now they took a more active role, elevating trusted commanders without waiting for consent from the Senate, even though it was the Senate that, at least theoretically, made that choice.

After half a century of chaos, near collapse was averted only by a series of iron emperors, the greatest of whom was Diocletian (r. 284–305). An extraordinary administrator with a dominating personality, Diocletian realized that, because of the empire's size and the relative slowness of communications, a major part of the problem was that the executive authority only an emperor could provide had to be multiplied. He created a system of power sharing with three colleagues—two senior emperors (Augusti) and two junior emperors (Caesars)—now known as the Tetrarchy. He also reorganized the provinces into smaller and more governable units and introduced a reformed system of taxation that allowed rulers to predict revenue for the first time in imperial history.[2]

Then Diocletian did the unthinkable. In 305, he abdicated power and convinced his colleague in the West to do the same. Both Caesars became Augusti, with two new Caesars to replace them. Diocletian might have intended this form of regular succession to avoid the pitfalls of dynastic succession, but it barely outlasted him. By 324, the Christian emperor Constantine had swept away the last remnants of that system and designated his own sons to succeed him. Of these, Constantius II ruled until his death in 361, leaving the empire to his upstart cousin, Julian. This Flavian dynasty ended in 363 with Julian's death on campaign in Persia. A Valentinian dynasty replaced it. Valentinian I (r. 364–375) sent his brother, Valens (r. 364–378), to rule in the East while he himself successfully campaigned against the northern barbarians. Valens was less successful than his brother: he died in battle in 378 and was replaced by Theodosius I. In the West, Valentinian's sons, Gratian (r. 375–383) and Valentinian II (r. 375–392), succeeded him, but both died at the hands of usurpers, leaving Theodosius the only emperor standing. Before he died in 395, Theodosius raised both his young sons, Arcadius and Honorius, to the purple and set one to rule in the East, the other in the West. From this time on, the two halves of the empire, which theoretically remained united, operated in practice as independent units.[3]

RELIGIOUS FERMENT

Diocletian is also the emperor who unintentionally triggered this century of miracles. Before retiring, he decided he had to deal with the Christians, who had suffered two empire-wide persecutions in 251 and 257 but since then had enjoyed legal protections. In the intervening forty years, Christians rose to the point where they held imperial office in the provinces and even in Diocletian's court. But in 303, the emperor revived state-sponsored persecution.

Diocletian's reasons are still debated, but at least one factor in his decision was the religious assumptions that now undergirded imperial rule. As a key proof of their ability to rule, emperors were expected to show close ties with a potent divine *comes*, or "comrade," who lent cosmic support to their efforts. It was a program that Arthur Darby Nock once charmingly compared to having a private line instead of having to go through a switchboard of deities. (Today, we would make the comparison between using a smartphone and having to go to a computer lab.)[4] To the tidy mind of this extraordinary organizer, Christian refusal to recognize his special connection to Jupiter, the ruler of the Roman pantheon, amounted to treason, and he went about suppressing it with the same ruthless thoroughness that he applied to every problem. This "Great Persecution" foundered almost immediately in the western empire. But in the East, where the bulk of the Christian population lived, it did not finally end until a decade later.[5]

This context of persecution lent additional significance to Constantine's conversion, at the tail end of the persecution. With surprising speed, once Constantine made Christians power players in the empire by providing riches and influence, their leaders soon began to sanction, and even encourage, attacks on heretics, pagan temples, and Jewish synagogues—the beginning of a millennium and a half of violent enforcement of Christian norms.

THE AGE OF REASON

There is a traditional explanation for why this dark turn occurred: the advent of Christianity signaled the start of a long decline from the enlightened standards of Greco-Roman civilization, resulting in the fall of Rome and the superstitious miasma of the Middle Ages. Miracles, if they are worth any attention at all, merely serve to illustrate that decline.

A corollary to this analysis is that these changes unleashed Christianity's inherent intolerance. With unprecedented access to the halls of power, the standard account goes, Christians set about paying back debts to their pagan tormentors with a zeal that led

Theodosius to withdraw support from the gods that had protected Rome for a thousand years and declare Christianity the only legal religion in the empire.

This story line has a distinguished pedigree, one that traces back to the great Enlightenment thinkers of the eighteenth century whose efforts were so instrumental to freeing Western thought from the grip of religious dogma. Among historians writing in English, the best-known exponent of that view is Edward Gibbon (1737–1794), who left an indelible mark on the study of Roman history when he summed up the fall of Rome as "the triumph of barbarism and religion."[6]

To account for the surprising speed with which Christians turned to coercion as a means of spreading their beliefs, Gibbon pointed to Christianity's intolerance of other forms of worship, listing it as the first of his famous five reasons for Christian success, and contrasting it with the tolerant and inclusive practice of traditional polytheism.[7] Whereas the polytheistic pagans could tolerate any number of new deities, he argued, Christians as monotheists could not. Indeed, the God they inherited from their Judaic past ordered them to "have no other gods before me," and their own faith doubled down on this ban by telling them that making the slightest concession to pagan religion, including paying honor to the emperors' imperial cult, would be to lose their chance for a spiritual afterlife.

Gibbon's thesis makes a certain a priori sense—Christians, after all, did deny the old gods, and they certainly manifested a robust intolerance in the decades following Constantine's conversion. For the leaders of the eighteenth century's Enlightenment, locked in battle with a church that too often stood in the way of free thought and rational inquiry, the intolerance argument made more than a priori sense. It accounted for a rapid descent into superstition, bias, and corruption that they could trace in a direct line from Constantine to their own day.[8]

There are two profound weaknesses in this classic narrative. The first is that it ignores the fact that the use of force amounted to a stunning reversal of what had been, until then, an adamant Christian position that true belief could not be coerced, and that violence should be endured, not reciprocated ("turn the other cheek"). As late as the period of the Great Persecution, and perhaps even later, a council of bishops meeting in Spanish Elvira (near modern Granada) forbade Christians from attacking pagan temples, on the grounds that such actions were never undertaken in the Gospels nor approved by the Apostles.[9] The intolerance narrative directs attention away from this tradition of opposition to coercion, and it accordingly fades from view.

The usual response, if this earlier Christian attitude is taken into account at all, is a cynical one: Christians argued that way only because they were too weak to do anything else; toleration is "a loser's creed."[10] That conclusion might very well be correct, but if so, it means the argument has shifted ground—from principles and inherent qualities (whether intolerance or the opposite) to other factors that have nothing to do with Christianity as a religion, but maybe everything to do with Christianity as a social and political force. However much Christians might have been predisposed to resort to coercion, we cannot take it for granted that they would simply throw away their principles without coming up with a good reason.[11]

The second problem has to do with the characterization of religion in general, and Christianity in particular, as "irrational" and "superstitious." Historians now are more aware than ever before that deciding whether a given action is "rational" or "irrational" depends on value judgments that are not always consistent. For this reason, anthropologists long ago abandoned such terms in favor of an approach that looks at the role and function of religious systems in a given society. The value of such an approach for this period was demonstrated in 1971 by Peter Brown, who looked at the seemingly "irrational" behavior of fifth-century "pillar saints"—men who spent their lives living atop slender columns—and decided they actually were helping hold together a society in the throes of social and cultural change.[12]

Miracle stories are a means to take Brown's insight one step further. As the different explanations of Sally's cure at the beginning of this chapter showed, these stories are never simply bare-bones accounts. They come with a set of attendant circumstances—the situations in which they occurred, for instance, or the way actors responded and the consequences to those responses. Such details point to a lesson the hearer or reader was meant to derive from the account, and in this way they amount to interpretations; without these interpretations, the meaning of the miracle is much less clear.[13]

Just as miracles were a way for people to think about and understand their circumstances, so studying these accounts is a way for us to enter into communication with an age that thought very differently about the way the world worked.[14] In the fourth century, the interpretation of miracles was supplied by Christian leaders, the bishops, a group uniquely situated to take control of these stories. The interpretation they increasingly favored was that God wanted Christianity to be the religion of the empire, by force if necessary.

Miracle tales in this sense are a bridge. These stories helped people at that time understand the rapid changes in their fortunes that they were experiencing, and reading them can bring us closer to the world as they saw it.[15] The battlefield miracles with which the fourth century opened and ended gave unique potency to these stories, for all of them were refracted through the lens of these imperial events. In a word, for Christians, the string of miracle stories served to underscore the truth and power of their God and, in effect, helped them understand this dizzying change in their fortunes. As such, they offer us a fresh way to understand both the growth of Christian power and the increasing use of coercion that followed in its wake.

DIFFERENT MIRACLES

Even though pagans and Jews appear in them, all of the miracle stories in this book were told by Christians. It will not be hard to pick out the biases that result (Christians always win, for instance); but this would be a good moment to consider differences in the way these three groups thought about supernatural intervention, since those differences can in turn help isolate the features that made fourth-century miracles unique.

The most obvious difference is that the people we call pagans believed in many gods. Jews and Christians, by contrast, asserted the supremacy of their God. The difference is not merely a matter of number. Ancient polytheists saw gods everywhere; in the late Keith Hopkins's happy phrase, theirs was a "world full of gods."[16] Divine and semidivine beings presided over streams, forests, and mountaintops. Every city had its own traditional gods, and some had particular deities associated with them (like Athena for Athens and Capitoline Jupiter for Rome). These gods were also fairly easy to understand. They were human in appearance, and they had very human emotions. They were interested in humans and were even known to walk among us. More important, they could be persuaded to come to our aid; if offended, they showed their displeasure through what we now call natural phenomena—floods, droughts, earthquakes.

Above all, it was the gods who decided winners and losers in battle—an important role during times of crisis. So it was a good idea to keep these deities happy, and animal sacrifice was traditionally the best way to do that, although by late antiquity this practice was

falling into disuse. Inspecting the entrails of these animals also provided a means to gauge the will of the gods, as did observing the flight
of birds, consulting oracles (sites where a deity was thought to be particularly easy to approach), and consulting books of portents. If "miracle" simply means intervention in human affairs by a supernatural
force, then in paganism miracles were a part of the natural world.[17]

A monotheist's God is far more difficult to get along with.[18] This
God is a transcendent being—not part of nature but above and
beyond nature, responsible for everything that exists. Accordingly,
the distance between this deity and humans is immense; only
through extraordinary effort and training can humans hope even
to glimpse the reality of such a perfect being. But the most difficult
part of this relationship is figuring out why this God sometimes
acts in ways that do not seem to accord with his followers' needs or
even, as in the Sally example, their sense of fair play. But if God is all-
powerful and only willing to do good things, then these actions have
to be for a good purpose, even if that purpose is not always clear.

So here is one important difference: a polytheist's miracles do
not have to be explained—they are part of the natural order of
things; a monotheist's miracles do.[19] Jews passed on to Christians
this concept of miraculous intervention, but by late antiquity there
was a difference in the way the two understood it.

Jewish history is filled with examples of miraculous interventions, illustrated especially by the events of Exodus.[20] But through the
prophets and rabbis, Jews had come to understand that the greatest
of all miracles was Torah, which preserved the record of God's covenant and the conditions it bound them to.[21] Hence, Jews no longer
expected their God to intervene simply when it would be convenient
for them. To this day, the unique combination of intimacy derived
from Torah and resignation based on experience informs the best
Jewish humor (as when the milkman Tevye in the *Sholem Aleichem*
stories sighs, "With God's help, I starved to death"; or Golda Meir's

sardonic "Let me tell you something that we Israelis have against Moses. He took us forty years through the desert in order to bring us to the one spot in the Middle East that has no oil."[22])

Fourth-century Christians, on the other hand, shared an important premise with pagans. They saw life on earth as the reflection of a cosmic order, where a fight between good and evil was taking place. This cosmic tie bound events here on Earth with those taking place in the higher realm of the universe. Christians shared as well a belief that their God, like the pagan gods, was prepared to intervene in this sphere on their behalf. Fueling this belief was a string of successes, beginning with Constantine's miracle in 312 and continuing in an unbroken chain down to Theodosius's miracle in 394.

This is the significant difference in the role miracles played in the fourth century. During this century, Christians were dizzy with success, and they enthusiastically embraced the idea that God was now sending their way the miracles recorded in scripture. It is not the occurrence of miracle accounts in the fourth century that makes them unique. Miracle stories began with Genesis, and belief in miracles certainly continued long after the fourth century ended. Rather, what makes the miracles of this century stand out is the way that they were held up as proof that God wanted the religion of the empire to be Christianity.

COLD WAR DICHOTOMIES

In a certain way, the biggest change in our understanding of the fourth century was the end of the Cold War in the twentieth. It is now clear that the dichotomies of that era, separating everything into black and white, good and evil, intensified an already-prevalent scholarly bent to see the fourth-century conflict as a matter of "life and death," a struggle from which only one winner could emerge.

Historians as much as everybody else are influenced, sometimes consciously but mostly unconsciously, by their cultural environment, their *habitus*.[23] (Any historian who says otherwise would not be a good person to buy a used car from.) As one historian has pointed out, the Cold War environment facilitated the idea "that great ideologies can polarize the collective imagination by dividing the world into power blocs."[24]

The creation of a monolithic Christian orthodoxy did not begin with the Cold War, nor did the construction of a mirrorlike pagan "other" in its likeness.[25] But for obvious reasons, this stark, black-and-white approach was highly compatible with the contrast between classical reason and Christian superstition favored by the rationalist narrative. Under this paradigm, the religious ferment of the fourth century was read as a life-and-death struggle between Christianity and paganism—binary opposites from which only one winner could emerge. The approach still has its adherents, but late antiquity scholars have shown greater interest in the wide swath of overlapping pagan, Christian, and Jewish interests closed off by this approach. Using a more variegated palette, these scholars have drawn attention to interests and attitudes common to all sides—a permeable region where the heart of late antiquity beat strongest.

With more shades at our disposal, we can see these common beliefs and practices more clearly. As these chapters will show, for instance, classical ideas about government and the duties of state officials play a role in the behavior of Christians after Constantine that was at least as large as, and conceivably larger than, any played by that religion's allegedly inherent intolerance. A broader understanding of what constitutes "rational" behavior can be similarly informative. Here is where miracles have a role to play.

In thinking inspired by the Cold War, miracles were thought of as weapons that Christians could use against their pagan enemies. But scholars are now more likely to see them in a more positive light, as "the voice of Hope"—a means for Christians to see the positive effects of the changes they were experiencing.[26] For Christians in the early fourth century, a miracle was simply the most rational way to explain the stunning reversal in their fortunes that followed upon Constantine's victory. Ensuing miracles persuaded both elites and commoners that the healing prayers of an emaciated pillar saint provided better understanding of their world than Aristotle's comfortable syllogisms.[27]

New scholarship and new thinking during the past half century have provided grounds for concluding that much of what used to be attributed to Christian influence was actually a case of Christianity being swept along by more general currents.[28] It is worth asking whether the same might also be true for the coercive turn Christianity took in the aftermath of Constantine's conversion. The popular view is that emperors persecuted Christians unceasingly throughout their history, right up to the moment of Constantine's victory. But prior to the panoply of crises that the empire faced in the third century, most emperors were indifferent to the fate of this new sect; such persecutions as occurred were sporadic and localized.[29] One reason for the beginning of state-sponsored, empire-wide persecutions in the third century appears to have been a heightened sense of the need for divine support that developed during this stressful period.[30] Since Christians were, in this case, the victims, their own adoption of coercive tactics in the fourth century might also best be thought of as another instance of wider political and religious trends not captured by too narrow a focus on Christianity itself.

WHO'S WHO? A LESSON IN LABELS

The biggest casualty of the binary thinking encouraged by the Cold War was the range of religious belief that did not fit into the Christian versus pagan paradigm. This included Christians who coexisted comfortably with the old gods, pagans who believed in a single Supreme God, and Jews who expressed themselves in ways that did not conform to rabbinic teaching. In effect, Cold War thinking defined out of existence a period when religious identity was much more fluid than it became.

Without an approach that takes this permeable mass of Christians, pagans, and Jews into account, these names become labels, and the problem with labels is that they easily become one-dimensional: they take the characteristics of a certain type that existed within each group and make them normative for the whole. The problem is particularly acute when scholars project the hardened attitudes of later ages back onto the earlier part of the fourth century. The effect is to blur boundaries that over the course of this century hardened along lines that are more familiar today, and thus make us miss an opportunity to understand how this hardening of boundaries occurred and what its effects were.

It is still commonplace, for instance, to use militant, aggressive opposition to pagan idols as the litmus test for sincere Christian belief. Those who held a more conciliatory position are described as, at best, "semi" or "token" Christians, Christians whose conversion somehow did not take or was incomplete.[31] By default, this approach leaves only the most coercive and belligerent Christians for us to ponder, which is a little like allowing only warmongers, or else maybe street demonstrators, to count as "Americans." The point is not to pretend that such Christians did not exist, much less to deny that they did indeed come to dominate Christianity in the ensuing centuries. It is, rather, to look for a solution that not only explains the turn to coercion but also explains why a previous commitment to freedom of belief was so readily abandoned. Without doing this, we forego a valuable opportunity to add some historical insight to the study of the ways that groups once considered extreme manage to capture control of a movement.[32]

In the case of Jews, the problem is not just that the label normalizes rabbinic Judaism, but that modern readers interpret it as solely a religious identity. As chapter 6 will show in more detail, Jews in the Roman Empire did not limit themselves to this one facet of their identity. In fact, just as it is often said that pagans did not know they were pagans until the Christians told them, it now seems that Jews did not start to define themselves as primarily, if not exclusively, a religion until pressure from Christians in this century led them to.[33]

Unquestionably, the one term that stands in the most desperate need of rethinking is "pagan." Originally neutral in meaning, the term *paganus* in Latin simply meant a rustic or farmer—someone who lived in the countryside. But it took on overtones from the stereotype of these country cousins, becoming synonymous with "hick" or "rube" in English. In the fourth century, Christians started using it to denote all those Romans who still clung to the old gods of Greco-Roman culture. From there, pagans took on all the lurid traits that we now associate with the label, especially the lusts and physical indulgences that Christians increasingly denied themselves. Hollywood has done the rest (Fig. 1.1 is an early example). Thanks to the "sword and sandal" Roman movies produced to counter "godless Communism" in the 1950s, "pagan" now pretty much universally signifies the only people in antiquity who were having any fun.

What makes this particular stereotype so damaging is not just that it suppresses the highly moral tone of late Roman paganism but even more that it ignores the popularity of belief in a "Supreme Deity" in the same circles. This common ground—what might even be called a lingua franca of vaguely monotheistic language reflected by such terms as "Supreme God" or "Highest Power" and

Figure 1.1. The infamous Roman orgy scene from C. B. DeMille's "Manslaughter" (1922) encapsulates the connection in the popular imagination between "paganism," immorality, and the Fall of Rome. With barbarians at the gates, Rome's pagans are lustful, languorous, and so depraved that they are (shudder) ruled by a woman. Photo courtesy of the Cecil B. De Mille Foundation.

frequently visualized in terms of a ubiquitous Sun God—is one of the most important religious currents of the fourth century.[34] Even worse, the term leaves the impression that there was a single, cohesive body of belief and practice that can now be labeled "paganism," whereas in fact Christians simply created "paganism" out of whole cloth to have something like themselves to fight against.

What we need is a term that will embrace the spectrum of pagan belief and practice, without the stereotype. But scholars have struggled to find an agreeable alternative. "Polytheists" has the advantage of keeping Jews out of the category, but it also defines out of existence the very group of pagan monotheists we are trying to preserve. "Hellene" is currently popular and has the advantage of being a term that both Greek intellectuals and their Christian adversaries employed. But it works only for the eastern half of the empire, while excluding the original pagans—rustics who did not participate in this high culture.[35] I have used "traditional religions," but in addition to being a clumsy phrase to keep repeating, there was nothing traditional about the pagan monotheism of the late empire. Moreover, as anthropologists are quick to point out, "traditional" often serves as code for "primitive" and "savage," and thus puts us right back where we started.[36]

In *The Last Pagans of Rome*, Alan Cameron has made the highly original argument that "pagan" came into use in the fourth century not as a slur but as "a neutral, nonspecific term" that Christians could use in polite company, much the same way that "gay" emerged in the 1970s as an alternative for the more baggage-laden "homosexual."[37] Cameron's analysis has not been universally accepted,[38] and it cannot in any case wash away the centuries of negative accretions that have grown onto the term, but it is sufficient for me to remove the scare quotes from "pagan" for the rest of this book, so long as you keep in mind that I am using the term in this neutral and unsystematic sense.

Because labels have played such an outsized role in the history of this century, the next chapter uses the final miracle of this century as a means to reflect on the changes that took place.

Chapter 2

Theodosius's Miracle

On September 6, 394, the forces of the emperor Theodosius I were on the verge of a rout, having been set upon by the army of a usurper before they were fully deployed. At this critical moment, the emperor leapt from his horse, strode to the front of his battle line, and, stretching his arms heavenward, cried out, "Where is the God of Theodosius?" As if on cue, a sudden windstorm blew in the eyes of the enemy and turned the battle in Theodosius's favor. What had started out as a disaster for one side turned into a rout of the other. Here is the way the Church historian Theodoret described the moment about half a century later:

> When both sides had begun to discharge their weapons . . . [a] violent wind blew right in the faces of the foe, and diverted their arrows and javelins and spears, so that no missile was of any use to them, and neither trooper nor archer nor spearman was able to inflict any damage upon the emperor's army. Vast clouds of dust, too, were carried into their faces, compelling them to shut their eyes and protect them from attack. The imperial forces on the other hand did not receive the slightest injury from the storm, and vigorously attacked and slew the foe. The vanquished then recognised the divine help given

to their conquerors, flung away their arms, and begged the emperor for quarter.[1]

This battle, at the Frigidus River (probably the Vipana in what is now western Slovenia), was the final victory of the last emperor to rule over both halves of the Roman Empire, and the miracle he produced serves as an appropriate bookend for a century that began with another miracle, Constantine's famous Vision of the Cross, which will be discussed in the next chapter.

It must seem odd to begin at the end like this, but miracles of this sort—divine interventions on behalf of a Christian emperor—were something Christians had not had much need to contemplate before this century began, and the story of Theodosius's miracle is an opportunity to gauge how much the stories they learned to tell can help us understand the changes that occurred between these two battlefield miracles.

Like so many of the stories in this era, the story of Theodosius's miracle is one that only got better with the telling. Eventually, it came to be seen as the final victory of Christianity over a determined pagan opposition, but that is not the way it began.[2]

We first hear of Theodosius's miracle some six months after the event in a much more restrained account by Bishop Ambrose of Milan. The occasion was a sad one, for Ambrose was commemorating the death of that same emperor. Theodosius died on January 17 of the new year, little more than four months after this signal success, leaving rule of the empire in the hands of his two young sons, the teenaged Arcadius in the East and in the West the ten-year-old Honorius, who now stood by Ambrose at the altar.[3]

Speaking on February 25, after a customary mourning period of forty days, Ambrose told the story of Theodosius's prayer near the beginning of his eulogy. Speaking of "what victories the faith of Theodosius gained for you," Ambrose reminded the congregation of the recent battle, in which many of those present would have participated:

> When, because of the problems of the terrain and the hindrance of the camp followers, the army was falling into the battle line too slowly, and through the delay in joining battle the enemy's cavalry was seen to be charging, the emperor leapt down from his horse and, advancing alone before the line, cried out, "Where is the God of Theodosius?" He was saying this as one already close to Christ. For who possibly could say this except one who knew himself to be united with Christ? By his cry he put heart into everyone, by his example he moved everyone to arms, a man undeniably advanced in years, but mighty because of his faith.[4]

Ambrose makes no direct mention here of the ensuing windstorm, but he seems to allude to it a few sentences later when he reminds soldiers who were at the battle that, like the prophet Elisha in Samaria, Theodosius's faith blinded his enemies: "You have surely heard, you soldiers who were surrounded [during the battle of the Frigidus], that wherever there is perfidy, there also is blindness. So the army of unbelievers deserved to be struck blind."[5] The dignitaries of court and army in attendance could not have missed the point of this reference.

Ambrose did make a more direct reference to the windstorm a month later, in a sermon he preached on Psalm 36 ("the transgressions of the wicked"). Here, the bishop calls to mind the way a sudden wind at the Frigidus "tore their shields from the hands of the faithless and turned all their spears and missiles back on the army of the sinner."[6]

Ambrose's focus in 395 was on the late emperor's piety, but as the story took on additional layers of meaning, it turned into a confrontation between the old gods and the new one. By the time the Christian scholar Rufinus wrote, about a decade later, Theodosius's opponents are said to be intent on restoring the gods that Theodosius and fellow

Christian emperors had taken away. The leaders of this army were the barbarian general Arobogastes, his hand-picked emperor Eugenius, and the Roman senator Virius Nicomachus Flavianus, famous for his devotion to the old gods. While Flavianus bloodied his hands with sacrifices seeking support of those gods for their cause, Arbogast set up a statue of Jupiter wielding a thunderbolt of solid gold, and their army marched forth under the banner of Jupiter's powerful son and helpmate, Hercules. More ominous yet, in Rufinus's account, Flavianus and Arbogast now leave Milan vowing to defrock Ambrose's clergy and dragoon them into their armies when they return, and also to use Milan's basilica as a stable for their horses.[7]

It is thus small wonder that scholars already conditioned by Cold War polarities to see the fourth century as a battle to the death between Christianity and paganism turned the Battle of the Frigidus River into the death knell of a "pagan revival," ending a century of struggle. Now, however, all of the factual details and preconceptions that powered that interpretation have come under much closer scrutiny.[8] One prerequisite of this narrative is so obvious that it is easy to overlook: if the recipient of the miracle is pious and honorable, his or her opponents must by default be the opposite, enemies of everything that is good and just. This imperative works well enough when that opponent is a pagan, and even better if the opponent is a heretic—a Christian who did not conform to what became the orthodox position.

But what if that opponent is also an orthodox Christian? Such is the case with Eugenius, the upstart emperor whom Theodosius faced at the Frigidus River. The template did not make provision for such an eventuality, so storytellers had to improvise. Usually, they did so by simply ignoring the fact and tainting Eugenius with guilt by association. When they do mention his own faith, it is in terms that rarely were questioned by subsequent generations: Eugenius's Christianity was "unsound" (*ouk hygiōs*), in the words of the fifth-century Church historian Sozomen, a judgment rendered by his nineteenth-century translator as "by no means sincere," the term now used to question the bona fides of any Christian who did not conform to the now-expected standard of behavior toward other religions.[9]

What earned Eugenius this scorn was the fact that he made common cause with such pagans as Arbogast and Flavian. Stories that he promised to restore state subsidies that had been taken away by Gratian and Theodosius may be exaggerated, but Eugenius evidently did not regard pagans as "the enemy."[10] Christians like Eugenius who favored a policy of coexistence have been air-brushed out of the records of this century, and for this reason alone it will be worth remembering that such middle-of-the-road Christians still existed even this late in the century. The Battle of the Frigidus River is no longer seen as the last hurrah of a pagan revival, but it just might have been the final victory of coercive Christians over their more moderate brethren.

BISHOP AND EMPEROR

It is not surprising that Ambrose used the language of miracle to celebrate Theodosius's life. He was speaking at the end of a century of tumultuous change, one that began with a systematic effort to stamp out this upstart faith and that was now ending with Christianity riding high as the sole legal religion of the empire. Theodosius had played a pivotal role in this process. His reign was marked not only by legal disabilities against non-Christians and heretics but also by the spectacular demolition of temples that had stood for centuries as the embodiment of classical civilization. This century witnessed changes so "rapid and far-reaching" that a leading scholar in the field identified the period 380–430 as "the end of ancient Christianity."[11]

One important factor in the more robust form of Christianity that took hold during this century was the vastly increased power now available to bishops, and few of his brethren understood how to make use of that power better than Ambrose (Figure 2.1). Born into an elite Roman household in 339, by 370 Ambrose had risen to the rank of consular prefect, or governor, of Aemilia-Liguria (roughly, modern Piedmont and part of Lombardy), an important province in north-central Italy that housed the imperial capital of Milan. It was in that capacity that he came to Milan in 374 to resolve a dispute over election of a new bishop. To everyone's surprise, except perhaps Ambrose himself, he became the compromise

Figure 2.1. Ambrose as depicted in the chapel of St. Victor in the San Ambrogio Basilica of Milan, early fifth century. From Wilpert 1924, plate 84, 1.

candidate. After a due show of reluctance, he was raised to the epis-copacy as soon as a few messy details (he had never been baptized and had never held clerical office) were resolved in record time.[12]

Ambrose's episcopacy coincided with a unique set of circum-stances that had put Milan at the center of imperial affairs in the West. Although Rome remained the titular capital of the empire, emperors who needed to focus attention on unstable northern frontiers found it too distant for effective communication with these trouble spots and accordingly stayed in Milan when they stayed in Italy at all. Because Milan was never more than an expedient, it had few of the deep patronage links through which authorities exercised control over the local population, and even fewer of the sites, such as Rome's Forum and Senate house, that were essential to the ritual and ceremonial events whereby late Roman rulers displayed their commitment to the rule of law, listened to advice and praise delivered by polished orators, and received acclamations symbolic of universal consent to their rule.

In Milan, Ambrose and his cathedral could supply these needs. Ever since Constantine's day, bishops had been endowed with funds to provide for the poor and empowered to dispense justice outside of the traditional legal framework, and by attending the weekly liturgy emperors could display themselves before an impor-tant constituency.[13] By training and temperament, Ambrose knew how to use the power of his office to capitalize on this need. During his long episcopate, he forced three emperors to bend to his will, setting one precedent after another for the priority of church over state. The most famous of these occurred in a letter to the juvenile emperor Valentinian II, where the bishop blandly asserted that "the emperor is in, not above, the church," thereby denying the oversight role that emperors had played since Constantine the Great.[14] His claim had little immediate impact, but it was long remembered.

But it was in manipulating control over Milan's sacred spaces that Ambrose showed his true genius.

In 385, Valentinian II made a routine request to use one of Milan's churches. Ambrose, suspecting the church would be used for heterodox purposes, and probably also aware that such a move would undermine his own authority with the court, refused.[15] His action touched off a year-long power struggle that reached crisis levels during the Easter season of 386. To prevent the pre-emptive takeover of one of his churches, Ambrose's congregation staged what might well be the first sit-in in Western history, refusing to leave even when troops were sent to clear the area. Ambrose maintained his distance from what legally would have been an act of high treason, but the event nonetheless demonstrated the powerful tie he had forged between himself and Milan's Christian congregation. Thus, by the time Theodosius first came to Milan, in 388, Ambrose had demonstrated unmistakably that the way to gain the support of Milan's populace and achieve a semblance of harmony led through, not around, their bishop.

A military disaster had brought Theodosius (Figure 2.2) to the purple. In August 378, the eastern emperor Valens died fighting Gothic insurgents at the disastrous Battle of Adrianople (now Edirne in the European part of Turkey). With him was lost a major portion of the eastern army's general staff and two-thirds of its best troops.[16] Gratian, ruling in the West with his younger brother, Valentinian II, tasked Theodosius with restoring the eastern frontier, and in 379 made him a co-Augustus. A decade later, in 388, Theodosius was forced to turn his attention westward to deal with a usurper who had put Gratian to death. Theodosius quickly learned that he had to deal with Ambrose as well. On two occasions—one ugly, the other uplifting—Ambrose clashed with Theodosius and forced the emperor to back down.

The first occurred less than a year after he arrived in Milan. It was sparked by events in Callinicum, an important entrepôt on the frontier Rome shared with Persia in the East. Egged on by their bishop, a rioting mob burned the town's synagogue to the ground— an ominous harbinger of the violence Jews would increasingly suffer

Figure 2.2. Gold solidus of Theodosius I (r. 379–395). Photo by Daderot, Wikimedia Commons.

over the next millennium and a half. When the governor's report reached Theodosius, his own belief did not prevent the emperor from enforcing the law and ordering Callinicum's bishop to pay restitution. But Ambrose would have none of it. A hectoring letter that he wrote the emperor is the source of one of his most audacious pronouncements. "But, perhaps, the cause of discipline moves you, O Emperor," he allowed. "Which, then, is of greater importance? When the Church and the law conflict, it is the law, not the Church, which must yield."[17] Theodosius rightly ignored this astonishing claim, but Ambrose was not yet done. At mass the following Sunday, the bishop preached a thinly disguised sermon on the duty of rulers to obey God's ministers, then refused to continue with the liturgy until Theodosius promised not to enforce his order.[18]

A more edifying confrontation, and the one that firmly fixed bishop and emperor in the Christian imagination, came two years later, in 390. It followed a slaughter of rioting citizens in Thessalonika that threatened to destroy the emperor's ability to govern. Treading more gently this time, Ambrose convinced

Theodosius to perform an act of public penance at the cathedral. The event, which saved Theodosius's reputation, as well as his soul, soon became Exhibit A in the struggle between church and state, and another story that only grew better with the telling. In its later versions, a defiant Ambrose confronts the emperor not in a diplomatically phrased letter but at the very door of the church, heroically denying him entry. In the classic painting by Peter Paul Rubens, Theodosius visibly collapses before this display of moral authority (Figure 2.3).

Figure 2.3. Peter Paul Rubens' "Theodosius and Ambrose" (1618), portraying the bishop as he bars the emperor from entering Milan's cathedral, testifies to the grip of this imaginary action on western Christianity. Rubens' patriarchal Ambrose should be compared with the fifth-century mosaic (Fig. 2.1) depicting the bishop of Milan as a much more ordinary-looking individual, robed in more typical attire for a bishop of his age. Rubens' painting now hangs in Vienna's Kunsthistorisches Museum. Photo by H. Drake.

Ambrose is a saint and a Father of the Church, but he was also very much a late Roman man of his class, thoroughly trained in all the rhetorical arts and capable of what one scholar has called "misrepresentation on an heroic scale."[19] New discoveries have shown how carefully he culled and ordered his record for posterity, and this editing alone makes it doubly important to keep in mind that even saints can have agendas.[20]

THE SERMON

Aware of Ambrose's skill, the elite audience of generals and courtiers in 395 must have anticipated the bishop's eulogy of their deceased leader with not a little apprehension. What did he want, and what stunt was he ready to pull to be sure he got it? Certainly it was a surprise to see Theodosius's young heir Honorius standing with Ambrose at the altar: early in their relationship, the bishop had put Theodosius in his place by insisting that only clergy belonged there.[21] But they soon learned the reason for this unusual step: it turned out that a major goal of Ambrose's sermon was to secure the loyalty of the late emperor's army to an heir of such tender years.

Throughout the long history of the Roman Empire, the moment when power was transferred from one emperor to another was a traditional flash point, a negotiation that often took place at the point of a spear. While we hear of no challenges to the succession of Arcadius in the East, the fact that Theodosius's son Honorius was so young, and the situation in Italy still unsettled only months after the emperor's final victory, made succession in the West much more problematic. Ambrose's account of Theodosius's miracle was part of his plan to bolster Honorius's appeal by reminding his generals how much they owed to the late emperor's piety, which they were now bound to reciprocate by a piety of their own.

Rome had a long tradition of public orations delivered at the funerals of prominent individuals, but Ambrose delivered his oration for Theodosius on an occasion that was uniquely Christian, and one over which he had complete control. Internal evidence is sufficient to show that Ambrose delivered his oration for Theodosius during a mass, over which he as bishop presided, and it came during the part of the service in which the bishop ordinarily would explain to the congregation the scriptural readings they had just heard—the homily, or sermon.[22] The fact that this negotiation was conducted during a church liturgy, and that a Christian bishop was inserting himself into the process, testifies to the prominence gained by these prelates during the course of the fourth century.

It is easy, today, to take the sermon for granted, but in late antiquity it was a novel instrument for influencing public opinion. In sheer number, sermons dwarfed any previous means of communication. Brent Shaw has calculated that in North Africa alone, some five million sermons were delivered over a four-decade period of the fourth century. He concluded, "The effect of this relentless and ubiquitous teaching of common people was transformative."[23] Coins certainly matched this number, and a remarkable amount of propaganda could be packed into their legends and images. But it was not just frequency that made the sermon such a potent instrument. Since the meaning of a day's reading was not always self-evident, congregations relied on their priest or bishop to explain it to them in his sermon. In so doing, the homilist could easily show how the reading applied to a current situation in a way that motivated his congregation to act in accordance with his explanation of scripture. Inevitably, such explanations differed, sometimes dramatically, depending on the preacher and the circumstances. On some occasions, even well-known passages could be bent to fit the homilist's objective. The practice is alive and well. In 1997, a British cleric said to his congregation that shoplifting from large chain stores was justifiable because "Jesus said love your neighbor; he didn't say love Marks & Spencer."[24] Somewhere, Ambrose must have smiled.

Two further considerations added to the sermon's potency. First was the bishop's long tenure, which helped forge a particularly strong bond between him and his parishioners, most of whom he was likely to have baptized or instructed in the faith. Without such ties, Ambrose never could have succeeded in his confrontations with the court. Second was the potential conflict between Christians' two most important obligations: one, to love their neighbors and return hatred with love, and the other to resist Satan. Which response did a given situation call for? That was the kind of guidance their bishop could supply. In the fourth century, when opportunities to mold public opinion were limited, the sermon was a uniquely powerful weapon in a headstrong bishop's armory.[25]

Thanks to Ambrose's relentless record keeping, we have a copy of the entire speech, albeit one that might have undergone some editing for publication.[26] The funeral oration as we have it has been divided into fifty-five chapters of varying length—some no more than a sentence or two, others as long as a page, most amounting to a solid paragraph. It fills thirty-three pages in a recent translation, nineteen pages in Latin. The story of Theodosius's miracle comes early in the oration, following an enumeration of Theodosius's virtues (piety, clemency, humility). Directly addressing the late emperor's soldiers, Ambrose reminds them of the many victories the late emperor's piety had gained for them, and it is at this point that he calls to mind the most recent of these, the battlefield miracle. "Thus the faith of Theodosius was your victory," he continues; "let your faithfulness be the strength of his sons." As this concluding line suggests, the point of the story was to convince Theodosius's retainers, and especially his army, that they owed it to the late emperor to support his decision to leave the empire to his sons. In all, Ambrose devoted a good third of his sermon to this purpose.

With this exhortation, Ambrose moved into his main theme, a celebration of Theodosius's piety and the assurance of an eternal reward it had gained him. The reading of that day evidently was Psalm 114 (116 in some editions): "I love the Lord, because he has heard my voice and my supplications." For the first half of the oration, Ambrose used the phrase "I have loved" as the touchstone for his eulogy, putting it first into Theodosius's mouth to illustrate the emperor's virtues of piety, mercy, compassion, and humility, then switching to his own voice and using "I have loved" as a refrain to elaborate on his own pastoral care for the emperor.[27]

Another verse from the same psalm, "I will pay my vows to the Lord in the presence of all his people" (Psalm 114:18), would have suited Ambrose's depiction of the confrontation over Thessalonika:

> He threw to the ground all the royal attire he was wearing; he wept publicly in church over his sin which had stolen upon him through the deceit of others; with groans and tears he prayed for forgiveness. What private citizens blush to do the emperor did not blush to do, to perform public penance.[28]

Ambrose did not quote the psalm, at least not in the version he left for posterity. Perhaps, as is often the case in learned sermons, he thought it would be more effective as an intertext, something his hearers would recall without the need to bring it to mind.[29]

CHURCH AND STATE

While shoring up support for Honorius might have been the immediate reason for Ambrose to tell the story of Theodosius's miracle, it was by no means the only one. For one thing, the care he took to remind the audience (and posterity) of his close ties to the deceased emperor shows that the bishop also had his own legacy in mind. Even more important, the miracle story formed part of a broader aim to map out a theoretical foundation for a reformed empire.

In having the emperor cry, "Where is the God of Theodosius?"—instead of, say, "Where is the God of the Romans?" or "Where is the God of the Christians?"—Ambrose undoubtedly meant for his audience to associate the emperor's miracle with one performed by the prophet Elisha, who used Elijah's mantle to part the waters of the Jordan while crying, "Where is the Lord, the God of Elijah?"[30] But the personal nature of Theodosius's appeal and the ensuing miracle were both integral to the theory of rule that underlay Ambrose's sermon. It was a vision of a Christian empire that relied on such miraculous intervention for its justification.

With this account, Ambrose effectively bound the empire to the cross.

His theory was based on two interlocking propositions. In the first, Ambrose held that God would reward pious emperors and bring them victory, even if outnumbered by their enemy. In the second, he defined pious behavior as rewarding the church and punishing its enemies. Both propositions appear in the funeral oration. To illustrate the former, Ambrose called to mind the biblical Asa, who, like Honorius, "was not fully mature physically" when he became king. Yet, "when pressed by an unending and unnumbered multitude of Ethiopians, [Asa] trusted that with the Lord [on his side], and with only small numbers he could be saved."[31] He made the second condition clear in the same passage, when, before the example of Asa, he called to mind Josiah, who also succeeded his father at a tender age, yet "pleased the Lord because, more than the other kings of Israel, he . . . abolished false religious practices." Just so there would be no mistake, later in the oration Ambrose posed a rhetorical question, asking who could be more pious than

Theodosius, "who got rid of sacrilegious errors, closed the temples, destroyed the images?"[32]

This was Ambrose at his most mischievous. By making support for the church not just the chief but even the only marker of piety, and piety the condition for divine support, he effectively shoved aside all legal protections for any group whose interests conflicted with the church. This is the thinking that underlay his astonishing demand that the needs of the church take priority over a thousand-year-old legal tradition—a prime condition for church–state relations in the West for the next millennium and a half.

Paradoxically, the only way to understand Ambrose's theory is to realize that it had nothing to do with the distinction we now make between the activities of church and state. It rested solidly on accepted thinking in the ancient world that the primary duty of a state's magistrates—people we think of as civil or secular officials—was to maintain the goodwill of deities. This was not an issue that divided Christians and pagans. A distinguishing feature of ancient society was the belief that divine support depended on correct worship.[33]

Thanks in no small part to conflicts such as those in which Ambrose was involved, the Western world eventually developed a very clear distinction between the categories of religious and secular activity, summed up in the twin concepts of church and state. Modern political theory posits that the state is entirely secular, an outgrowth of a figural "social contract" whereby we all rationally agreed to give up some things (such as homicide or speeding) to gain mutual protection from such antisocial behavior. It is strictly a civil organization, with only a tiny overlap with the religious realm, primarily in the ongoing debate over how involved the state should be in enforcing religious injunctions.

The ancient state started from an entirely different set of premises. It was an outgrowth of the family, and the family itself developed out of a need to maintain relations with those divine forces that govern our lives.[34] The chief duty of rulers in the ancient state—any ancient state, not simply those we now call "theocracies"—was to conduct those relations. In that sense, every ancient state was also a church, and there was little, if any, distinction between the priesthood and magistrates whom we now think of as civic or secular. In the Roman Empire, the emperor was not just head of the government and of the military; he was also pontifex maximus, head of the Roman state religion (a title now held by the bishop of Rome). A Venn diagram would illustrate this distinction by showing the modern concept of church and state as virtually two separate spheres, while in the ancient state they would be virtually indistinguishable.

With his programmatic slogans—"The emperor is in, not above, the Church" and "When law and religion clash, it is the law which must yield," Ambrose was not aiming to divorce church and state. Indeed, these pronouncements only make sense in the context of a state that was also a church. His aim was not to break this bond but to reorder the relationship, so that, instead of being a state that was also a church, henceforward it would be a church that was also a state. With this worldview, it was not difficult for Ambrose to argue that the emperor had religious duties and obligations. It was also relatively easy in such an environment to blur the line between civil and religious crimes (something to keep in mind when considering Christian martyrdom in chapter 9).

Ambrose was not the first to put forward a theory of Christian empire. Many of his ideas were already present in earlier thinkers we will encounter in chapter 4. Although Ambrose fits into this tradition, he also represents a significant change in the language of miracle. Where those earlier accounts highlighted the role of the emperor, Ambrose repeatedly emphasizes the bishop's role in maintaining the emperor's successful relationship with the Christian

God. For this reason, even the personal relationship implied in Theodosius's battlefield appeal to "the God of Theodosius" did not confer upon him the independent status that Constantine's Vision of the Cross had won for that emperor at the beginning of the century. Instead, when rebuking the emperor in the Callinicum incident, Ambrose pointedly reminded Theodosius that the same God who had given him victories in the past might not be so willing to do so in the future. Implied by such a threat was that Ambrose would have a say in the matter. Episcopal oversight made Christian emperors more, rather than less, vulnerable to a discourse of persecution than even their pagan predecessors had been.[35]

AMBROSE AND MIRACLES

As bishop, Ambrose had his own share of miracles. They began early in his episcopacy when, according to his secretary and biographer, Paulinus of Milan, he healed a paralytic woman "who touched his garments as he prayed and placed his hands upon her," a scene strikingly reminiscent of one of Jesus's miracles:[36] just as well, for a disturbingly large number of Ambrose's other miracles involved the suffering or death of individuals who challenged his authority. Early in his episcopate, when a rebellious nun grabbed hold of him, Ambrose warned her to beware "lest something befall you," and within twenty-four hours she was dead. This power stayed with him down to his last days, when a slanderer named Donatus "was suddenly smitten with a grave wound," took to his bed, and died.[37]

So, whereas the funeral oration showed Ambrose knew how to love, his miracles showed he also knew how to hate. Ambrose's animosity extended to his understanding of Christianity's core message. In his commentary on Psalm 118 ("His love endures forever"), Ambrose brought up Jesus's command to love enemies in a way that significantly diluted its force. "The Lord Jesus taught us that *it was desirable* to love our enemies," he claimed, "but he also taught us to pursue with hate God's enemies" (emphasis added).[38]

Doubtless the most fortuitous of Ambrose's miracles was his discovery of the remains of two dimly remembered martyrs, badly needed to consecrate a controversial new church.[39] The miraculous discovery was disputed at the time and remains an object of skepticism today, but the important point here is that, once these relics were discovered, Ambrose knew what to do with them. Before naysayers had time to marshal their arguments, Ambrose organized an emotional procession punctuated by miraculous healings of those close enough to touch the remains. Refusing to bow to demands that he wait for confirmation of the finds before installing the martyrs in his new church, Ambrose forged ahead with a ceremony in which he raised the stakes for skeptics by denouncing any who doubted the discovery as heretics.[40]

To supplement his miracles, the bishop used language that nurtured a disquieting sense of victimhood. Repeatedly, in his brief to Theodosius regarding the synagogue at Callinicum, he made the unsubstantiated claim that Jews had destroyed Christian basilicas with impunity. "Your Clemency must consider," he warned, "how many are seeking to ambush the Church, how many are out to find her weak spots. If they find a slight chink, they will drive a pointed weapon through it." This is the thinking that underlay the words he puts in Christ's mouth: "I therefore enabled you to triumph over your enemy, and yet you gave my enemies a triumph over my people!"[41] In Ambrose's mind, the church was surrounded by enemies, just waiting to pounce. It is an ominous sign of what lay in store.

As a carrot to this stick, Ambrose consistently dangled the promise of divine support. His depiction of Theodosius's miraculous

windstorm was by no means the first time he had associated imperial piety with miracles. Such propositions pervade the bishop's
thinking. From the earliest days of his episcopacy, he made a habit
of promising divine support (or retribution) to those in power. Back
in 382, the then-emperor Gratian (r. 367–383) became the first
Roman emperor to refuse the robes (and office) of pontifex maximus, head of the state religion. As if this break with precedent was
not shocking enough, he also cut off financial support for the traditional Roman cults. Ambrose was beside himself with joy. In a
treatise "On the Faith" (De fide) that he wrote at Gratian's request,
the bishop rolled out his repertoire of Hebrew rulers whose faith
had gained them victory in battle and counseled the emperor that
his perfect faith was more important for victory than the valor of
his troops.[42]

Like his views on the role of religion in the state, Ambrose's
promise of divine aid for pious emperors was grounded in ancient
thought, where deities were believed to intervene in human affairs
on a regular basis, especially in response to the needs of a favored
individual. If the favor of a deity could make the difference between
a bountiful harvest and a famine, then it went without saying that
support by a deity was also by far the most important factor in
determining the outcome of a battle, and thus the ruler who had
a relationship with a powerful deity was far more important to the
outcome of that battle than the size of his army.

But as Jews had already learned and Christians were about to
find out, the ways of their God did not always conform to the immediate needs of his worshippers. A year after disestablishing the traditional cults, Gratian lost his army, and his life, to a usurper. In an
exchange that we will look at again in chapter 8, pagan leaders of the
Roman Senate were quick to point out that a famine and his own
death had followed in the wake of Gratian's actions, sure signs that
the gods were not pleased with him. Ambrose had ready answers. In

anticipation of Freud's famous judgment on the cigar, he responded that, in effect, sometimes a famine was merely a famine. As for Gratian's fate, which occurred despite the victory Ambrose had promised, he said, in effect, "Stuff happens."[43]

As his responses show, as far as Ambrose was concerned, nothing was going to be called a miracle without his say so.

Chapter 3

Constantine's Miracle

Whether or not Theodosius's miracle occurred exactly as Ambrose described it in his funeral oration, anyone listening would immediately have connected the account to another battlefield miracle, Constantine's famous Vision of the Cross at the beginning of the century. Just in case someone failed to make the association, later in the oration Ambrose pictured Theodosius and Constantine embracing in heaven, thus creating an appropriate meeting between the emperor who opened the door to Christianity and the one who slammed it shut on everybody else.[1]

It is a tidy picture, but one that has caused no end of mischief. With Constantine's miracle at one end of this century and Theodosius's at the other, it is altogether too easy to assume that, if he could, Constantine would have imposed orthodoxy as ruthlessly as did Theodosius.[2] But between these two reigns there had been a number of radical changes, none more so than what took place within Christianity itself. Since this is a book about miracles, little will be said about the theological disputes that dominate the religious record of this era (no miracles there). But by the end of the century, the hardening of positions that resulted from those debates contributed to a much narrower and less accommodating Christian identity, one that in turn spilled over into the way Christian leaders looked not only at non-Christians but also (as in the case of

Eugenius) at orthodox Christians who could still envision a world filled with other gods.

Constantine's miracle is an opportunity to study this more open kind of Christianity. But to see it, we have to consciously break the bond forged by Ambrose and avoid the assumption that no change had occurred in the interval. In fact, a great deal had changed.[3]

Not all of this confusion is the result of Ambrose's fantasizing. Constantine carries a lot of baggage as well from the religious wars of the European Reformation. The Reformers despised him for creating the worldly and opulent church that they broke from, and the scholars of the Enlightenment built on this negative image by tying him to the monolithic and intolerant church that they fought just as passionately (though less lethally). But the result is that scholars have applied an arbitrary and lopsided model of Christian behavior to the first Christian emperor. According to this model, conversion is the result of a sudden, blinding experience, and the invariable result is a convert devoted to the extermination of paganism.

By this standard, it is easy to cast doubt on the "sincerity" of Constantine's conversion (a traditional parlor game for historians), for time and again he insisted that he was looking for a consensus, a *modus vivendi*, centered on worship of a Highest God (*Summus Deus*) for whom public religion required no further qualifications. To defend his "sincerity," scholars have had to insist that he persecuted whenever he could. Instead of defending Constantine's sincerity in this way, it makes more sense to re-examine the criteria that have been used to define "conversion" and "sincerity."[4] Once this is done, it is easy to see that there is simply no reason to doubt the sincerity of Constantine's conversion, but every reason to doubt the model that has been used to understand his reign, beginning with the miracle itself, traditionally associated with a decisive battle that ended at Rome's Milvian Bridge on October 28, 312.

WHAT DID HE SEE?

To gauge the impact of Constantine's miracle, we first have to figure out what it was that he saw. Toward the end of his reign, the emperor described the event in this way to Bishop Eusebius of Caesarea, who included it in the influential *Life of Constantine* that he wrote between the time of Constantine's death in 337 and his own in (probably) 339:

> About the time of the midday sun, when day was just turning, he said he saw with his own eyes, up in the sky and resting over the sun, a cross-shaped trophy formed from light, and a text attached to it which said, "By this conquer." Amazement at the spectacle seized both him and the whole company of soldiers which was then accompanying him on a campaign he was conducting somewhere, and witnessed the miracle.[5]

This is the best-known version of Constantine's famous vision, but it is not the only one. Around the year 315, another Christian, the rhetorician Lactantius, wrote about a different experience that occurred on the eve of a battle for the city of Rome:

> Constantine was advised in a dream to mark the heavenly sign of God on the shields of his soldiers and then engage in battle. He did as he was commanded and by means of a slanted letter X with the top of its head bent round, he marked Christ on their shields. Armed with this sign, the army took up its weapons.[6]

Constantine went on to win the battle and liberate the city of Rome.

Both accounts place Constantine's experience in the context of a military campaign, but there the similarity ends. The

Eusebian version occurred in broad daylight and was witnessed not just by Constantine but by his entire army; in Lactantius, Constantine was asleep and, presumably, alone (Figure 3.1). But the biggest difference lies in the content of the sign he was given. Eusebius's description is relatively unproblematic: he saw a cross and words associating this emblem with victory. Lactantius's "heavenly sign," on the other hand, has given rise to a variety of interpretations.

The difficulty lies in the phrase translated previously as "a slanted letter X with the top of its head bent round." It is a tricky passage in Latin: *transversa X littera, summo capite circumflexo,* literally, "the letter X transversed (*transversa*) and turned at the very top."

Figure 3.1. Constantine's Dream (top) and Vision. Detail from a ninth-century presentation copy of the Homilies of Gregory Nazianzen commissioned by the Patriarch Photius for emperor Basil I, now in the French Bibliotheque Nationale (Paris Gr. 510, f. 440r). Reprinted by permission.

Three possible interpretations appear in Figure 3.2. The sign on the left is produced by using *transversa* to modify X, which thereby gets "tipped over" or "turned on its side." This interpretation produces a cross whose top has been twisted into the Greek letter rho. It has the advantage of coming closest to the cross described by Eusebius, and it is furthermore bolstered by signs known to have been used by Christians, known as "staurograms," from the Greek *stauros*, a cross. But if Lactantius meant a cross, why did he describe it as a tipped-over letter X, instead of simply as a cross?

In the center is a more literal version, showing the letter X, which itself is twisted into a rho, making it a Christogram, or monogram of Christ, formed by the first two letters in the Greek spelling of Christus (Χριστός). This, too, is a sign with known Christian antecedents, but it requires *transversa* to modify one of the lines of the letter X, rather than the whole character, reading something like "one of the crosslines of the letter X tipped at its top."

Finally, the symbol at the right is a straightforward X (chi) and rho monogram. This is certainly the most familiar of the Christograms; it appears attached to Constantine's helmet in a coin produced by the Ticinum mint in north Italy (the modern Pavia) in the same year that Lactantius wrote his pamphlet

Figure 3.2. Christogram or staurogram? "Tipped over" or "intersected"?

(Figure 3.3).[7] Coins are important resources for Roman historians, because they were a major medium for emperors to send messages to their subjects. Unlike the relatively fixed images on modern coins, those on Roman coins were in constant flux, partly because dies wore out faster in the ancient, hand-held minting process, and partly because of the rapid turnover in rulers (the first thing a new emperor or usurper would want to do would be to acquaint everyone—especially his soldiers, who likely received these coins as pay—with his image). The value of these coins as "propaganda" should not be overestimated; for the most part, their messages were commonplace banalities. Nevertheless, the way these banalities were juggled could tell something about an emperor's goals, or at

Figure 3.3. Silver medallion of Constantine issued by the mint of Ticinum in 315. The emblem atop his helmet (farthest to the left) is badly worn, but traces of a chi-rho symbol can still be made out. Photo by Nicolai Kästner, Staatliche Münzsammlung München.

least about the particular audience for which the coin was minted. (Unlike modern mints, which are in constant operation, ancient mints went to work only when coinage was needed for a specific purpose.) Romans developed a set of symbols and abbreviations that allowed them to cram highly sophisticated messages onto the limited space available. On this silver medallion, for instance, Constantine appears with the message IMP CONSTANTINVS PF AUG, telling everyone that he was a ruler (IMP = *imperator*), that he was both loyal (P = *pius*, duty bound) and fortunate (F = *felix*), and that he held the supreme rank of Augustus.

Although scholars have been focused on the chi-rho emblem on this coin, Constantine's shield, bearing an image of the Capitoline wolf suckling the twins Romulus and Remus, is at least equally important, since it advertised his attachment to the imperial city.[8] On the reverse ("tails"), Constantine is shown meeting with his troops in the traditional performance of an *adlocutio* (speech). Along with the motto (SALUS REIPUBLICAE, "Safety of the State" or, maybe better, "National Security"), this scene conveys the close tie between emperor and army and suggests that the coin was probably minted to pay his troops.

Given the proximity in time between Lactantius's description and the appearance of this emblem on Constantine's coin, it seems reasonable to conclude that this monogram is what Lactantius was trying to describe. The problem is that, unlike the other versions, this one was more of a novelty. Such Christograms are attested in earlier Christian usage, but they are rare, making its use by Constantine something of a novelty. At the time, it would have been easy for non-Christians to take it more as a symbol for Constantine and his dynasty than as a marker for Christ.[9] To complicate the issue even more, there is simply no way to squeeze a chi-rho out of Lactantius's phrase without positing that something has dropped out of the text. That is precisely what the Belgian scholar Henri Grégoire proposed in 1930. He argued that *trans-versa* should be translated as "intersected" and the letter *iota* added to the text, so as to read *transversa X littera <I>, summo capite cir-cumflexo*.[10] The emendation is modest enough, amounting to a single letter, but the change is enormous, since the phrase would now read, "The letter X intersected by an I turned at its top," producing the chi-rho.

Most scholars now reject Grégoire's emendation. The main thing the idea has going for it is that it produces a symbol that became closely associated with Constantine. But if this is what Lactantius meant, why did he use such circumspect language, "the letter X turned at the top," when he could have just said "intersected by a *rho*"? And how does any reading of Lactantius coincide with the symbol Eusebius tells us the emperor saw in the sky?

It is no idle question. For a population that was largely illiterate, the images on a coin would be studied more closely than the script, so putting that emblem on the emperor's helmet had to be by design. Non-Christians might not have known what to make of it, but because it was on his helmet rather than, say, his breastplate or shield, it took on special significance. The location said it was something that was, literally, on the emperor's mind, which is where Romans thought not just the intellect but also the higher emotions resided. Whatever this talisman meant, Constantine was saying it was important.

WHEN DID HE SEE IT?

As if figuring out what Constantine saw and how he saw it were not problem enough, there is also the issue of when and where it happened. Lactantius's story comes with a specific time and place—it was the night before a battle for which we have a precise date

(October 28, 312) and place (the outskirts of Rome). But Eusebius is much more vague about the circumstances of his story. All he says is that the emperor was campaigning "somewhere," which may be all that Constantine told him, since a decade or two after the event the vision story would not have needed the kind of details about time and place that modern historians crave. But Eusebius embedded the story in the same circumstances as Lactantius. While still in Gaul, which he had been ruling since 305, Eusebius wrote, Constantine looked with dismay on the misery of the city of Rome, mistress of the empire but herself under the thumb of a tyrant and usurper (who was also Constantine's brother-in-law).

After reaching the conclusion that none of the other emperors was up to the job, Constantine realized it was left to him to right this wrong (*Life* 1.26). The problem was that the "tyrant," Maxentius, had the dark arts at his disposal. So as he prepared for war, Constantine also cast around for a deity who would protect him from such devices, one that would be "irresistible and invincible." In this frame of mind, the bishop continued,

> a clear impression came to him, that of the many who had in the past aspired to government, those who had attached their personal hopes to many gods . . . met an unwelcome end, nor did any god stand at their side to protect them from divinely directed disaster; only his own father had taken the opposite course to theirs by condemning their error, while he himself had throughout his life honoured the God who transcends the universe, and had found him a saviour and guardian of his Empire and a provider of everything good. (*Life* 1.27)

This is the god the emperor was trying desperately to identify when he experienced the vision that gave him the answer—or at least most of it.

But Eusebius also knew about a dream experience. After witnessing the cross in the sky and while he was pondering what it might have meant, the bishop tells us, Christ himself came to Constantine in a dream and gave him the sign he should use as protection.

> It was constructed in the following design. A tall pole plated with gold had a transverse bar forming the shape of a cross. Up at the extreme top a wreath woven of precious stones and gold had been fastened. On it two letters, intimating by its first characters the name "Christ," formed the monogram of the Saviour's title, rho being intersected in the middle by chi. These letters the Emperor also used to wear upon his helmet in later times. (*Life* 1.28–31)

So here we have what seems a resolution: a vision followed by a dream that resulted in a standard incorporating both the cross and the emblem that is still visible on Constantine's helmet in the Ticinum coin from 315.

CONSTANTINE'S "PAGAN VISION"

With all this overlap, it is not surprising that historians have long thought that Eusebius and Lactantius were describing what was, basically, the same event. Accordingly, the traditional date for Constantine's conversion to Christianity is the year 312. But theirs is not the only evidence for a vision experience.

In 310,[11] Constantine listened to a panegyric that survives as part of a collection put together later that century in Gaul, which has been titled *XII Panegyrici Latini* (*PL*).[12] Eleven of these panegyrics were delivered to various emperors by Gallic orators (the first, an oration to Trajan by Pliny the Younger from the early second century, was presumably included as a model of the genre). Panegyrics were not, like coins, issued by the government. Usually, they were delivered by local orators to celebrate a specific occasion—an imperial visit or anniversary, for instance. They were set pieces for a culture that liked to hear as much as to read (Augustine a century later recorded his surprise at seeing Ambrose reading silently, instead of sounding the words out loud[13]), and every town worthy of the name had at least one classically trained orator to perform the task. For those that did not, handbooks—a sort of ancient Toastmaster's Guide—could be consulted for advice on what to say and how to say it.[14]

Even though theirs were not official pronouncements, the orators who delivered these speeches would naturally have taken pains not to say anything that would be taken amiss by their imperial auditors, both for the sake of protocol and even more because such speeches frequently came with a request for imperial benefactions. To get a good hearing for such a request, it was advisable that the emperor be in a good mood. It is clear that this set of speeches was not collected for historical interest (they are, for one thing, not in chronological order). That makes them even more valuable in a way, because they were presumably selected as successful examples of the genre, and not carefully edited with an eye to posterity, as, say, Ambrose did with his letters. Given the controversy that surrounded Constantine from the start, the fact that these speeches were not collected for a tendentious purpose is what makes them so useful, once we learn how to read them.

They are not histories, and like coins a lot of their content consists of platitudes and stock praises. But to contemporary elites looking for hints to what an emperor was like and what would best please him, the particular platitudes selected could mean a great deal. Silence could mean even more. If, for instance, a panegyric praised the emperor's military bearing and the way he kept the armies in top shape while saying next to nothing about his interest in philosophy, an elite listener would know that this was not the time to propose a Roman endowment for the humanities.

The 310 oration stands out because it came at a critical time for Constantine. He had just put down an attempt by his father-in-law, the retired emperor Maximian, to stage a coup. Maximian paid for his treachery with his life, and that was what made the subject so sensitive. To this point, Constantine had relied heavily on his marital ties to legitimize power that had originally been conferred on him by his late father's troops. Such military actions had been the pattern in the chaotic third century, until Diocletian stabilized the situation by creating the Tetrarchy (see chapter 1). Constantine's elevation in 305 had been a throwback to the bad old days, and his wedding alliance with Maximian (along with grudging recognition from the eastern emperor Galerius) had sealed the breach. Putting Maximian to death definitely compromised Constantine, especially with troops who remained loyal to Diocletian's former colleague.

This was the situation when the orator spoke in 310. We do not have to assume he checked in advance with the court before raising so sensitive an issue, because he tells us as much: "I am still very hesitant as to how I am to speak about this man," he states, "and I am awaiting for your divinity [i.e., Constantine] to advise me with a nod."[15] Evidently, he got the nod.

Earlier in the oration, the speaker had already distanced Constantine from the Tetrarchy by claiming that Constantine "deserved this ruling power from birth,"[16] because he was descended not only from a father, Constantius I, who had been an Augustus but also through Constantius to the third-century emperor Claudius II (268–270), a fact that the orator admits few people knew until that very moment (2.1).

This strong reassertion of a dynastic principle to rule was a direct challenge to the process Diocletian instituted. But the orator had something even more astonishing to reveal. After putting down Maximian, he relates, Constantine was on his way to the front when he learned that the barbarian incursion he was racing to confront had been taken care of, and he turned aside "to the most beautiful temple in the whole world" to offer thanks. There, he had a vision:

> You saw, I believe, Constantine, your Apollo accompanied by Victory offering you laurel wreaths, each of which bear the token of thirty years .... (5) And—but why do I say "I believe"?—you saw and you recognized yourself in the form of that one to whom the divine songs of the poets have prophesied the kingdoms of the world are owed. And I believe that this has now finally come to pass, since you are, like him, young and joyful and health-bringing and very beautiful, emperor.[17]

Among scholars, this incident is known as Constantine's "pagan vision," and it has been the center of no little controversy. On one side are those scholars who argue that this was Constantine's only vision, later appropriated by Christians. In support, they cite the appearance of the sun god, Sol Invictus, on Constantine's coins from this time and, especially, a gold medallion minted early in 313 for a meeting Constantine had in Milan with his eastern ally, Licinius, only months after the battle of Rome and his supposed conversion to Christianity. The obverse of this coin shows Constantine in twin profile with the god Apollo/Sol, reflecting in a strikingly visual way the claim of the 310 orator that Constantine saw himself in the face of the god who promised him victory and a long rule (Figure 3.4).

Figure 3.4. Gold coin of Constantine, minted at Ticinum for his meeting with the eastern emperor Licinius in Milan early in 313, thus only months after his victory at the Milvian Bridge. The obverse shows the diademed emperor (right) in a striking twin profile with the god Apollo in his guise as the sun god (as indicated by the solar helmet that he wears, with points that symbolize the sun's rays). The image recalls the scene recounted by an orator in 310. The inscription reads, INVICTUS CONSTANTINUS MAX AUG ("Unconquered Constantine the Great Augustus"). Photo by Jastrow 2006, Wikimedia Commons.

This argument has been given new life by associating the 310 vision with an atmospheric event known as a "halo phenomenon," in which ice crystals in the upper atmosphere are reflected by sunlight to form either pillars of light or mirror suns ("sun dogs"). Sometimes a combination of these can create the impression of a cross beaming out of the sun (Figure 3.5).[18] The effect can be stunning, since the image appears seemingly out of nowhere and can last for minutes or hours before disappearing just as quickly.

Figure 3.5. Ice-crystals create a "halo phenomenon." The image can crystalize in seconds and last for hours or dissipate in minutes. This one appeared in south-eastern France on January 23, 2015. Photo by Gabor Szilasi, Wikimedia Commons.

This would be the vision Eusebius narrates, according to this interpretation, with the dream that both he and Lactantius recounted occurring not immediately afterward but some time later. As further proof, supporters propose that the phrase in Lactantius usually translated as "heavenly sign of God" (*caeleste signum dei*) should be translated more literally as "the sign of God in the heavens."

Fascination with the phenomenon and the way it seems to track with the panegyric of 310 encourages a kind of reductionism, implying that the momentous changes associated with Constantine's reign all depended on this one moment. Intriguing as the problem of locating Constantine's vision is, however, far more serious questions surround his conversion.

WHAT DOES IT MEAN?

Our age is infatuated with scientific explanations for supernatural phenomena, and this one is so compelling that it is doubly important to keep in mind that what Constantine made of his experience is at least as important as whatever it was he saw or when he saw it.[19] Halo phenomena are relatively rare, but they were not unknown before Constantine's time. Among classical witnesses, they were taken as signs of regime change: impending civil war or the death of an incumbent ruler. A particularly significant parallel is provided by the first emperor, Augustus, whose arrival in Rome appears to have coincided with a halo phenomenon.[20] Like Constantine, Augustus particularly favored the god Apollo, and his reign—as long as half a century, depending on when you start the clock—coincides with the long reign promised by that god in Constantine's pagan vision.

Miracles are not self-explanatory events. A pagan, for instance, would not have considered the cruciform shape of a halo phenomenon significant, if that was indeed what Constantine witnessed. It took a Christian, with the particular sensibilities of that faith to the shape of a cross, to assign so much meaning to—or even to notice—that aspect of the phenomenon. And only a Christian would have thought this form had anything to do with a divine sign. For others, if they even noticed it, the cross would have called to mind a form of execution that was still inflicted on low-status members of society.

So the most important aspect of this story is its emphasis on the shape of the cross. That it plays such a central role tends to confirm that the story we know came from Constantine himself, as does Eusebius's report that Constantine told him about this experience "a long time afterwards" (*Life* 1.28.1). Scholars have usually applied to Constantine the literary idea of conversion as a single, sublime moment, a 180-degree turn from one set of beliefs to another.[21] The classic example is St. Augustine's description of his own conversion in his *Confessions* (8.12). By this standard, the continued use of pagan gods on Constantine's coins after 312 (as on the Constantine-Apollo coin) looks decidedly fishy. Even more important, indications that Constantine was interested in Christianity prior to 312 wind up being either completely ignored or blown out of proportion.[22]

In real life, conversion is a more gradual process, usually preceded by a long period of inquiry and followed by an even longer period in which the convert is socialized into the customs and values of his or her new community. At the end of this long process, the convert may well look back on the moment at which the balance tipped and ascribe to it more theological and emotive significance than it had at the time.[23] In other words, the long period converts spend learning the customs, beliefs, and habits of their new faith is much more important than the moment they made the decision to convert.

For this reason, the length of time between the event—whatever it was—and Constantine's report to Eusebius adds to, rather than subtracts from, the bishop's testimony. The obvious explanation for all of the discrepancies in the various accounts of Constantine's miracle is that his own understanding changed over the years.[24] During this time, a set of experiences that may have begun in 310 or even earlier, perhaps only coming together during the stress of his Italian campaign, became combined in the emperor's own memory into a single, dramatic event. In light of this alternative model for conversion, it might avoid misunderstanding to talk about an emperor who "adopted" Christianity in 312, rather than one who was "converted" in that year.

But any understanding of Constantine's miracle must also take into account a statement by Eusebius later in the *Life*. Describing the pious way in which Constantine conducted his military campaigns, the bishop indicates that Constantine's visions did not end in 312. Prior to every campaign, Eusebius writes, Constantine would retire to a special tabernacle, within which he would pray for divine guidance. He continues:

> While taking his time in making supplications to his God he would sooner or later receive a manifestation of God, and then as if moved by a divine inspiration he would rush suddenly from the tent, immediately rouse his troops, and urge them not to delay, but to draw their swords at once.[25]

Eusebius makes similar assertions elsewhere.[26] Given what we already know of Constantine, there is no reason to dismiss these as literary fictions. It is conceivable that the emperor was a particularly vision-prone individual, especially in stressful situations, especially given the ancient understanding that dreams were where the divine made contact with mortals.[27] Even if so, however, for a full understanding of Constantine's vision we need to broaden the horizon to take into account trends that were not related to Christianity except to the extent that Christians, like everyone else, were influenced by them.

IMPERIAL IDEOLOGY

It is unfortunate that Constantine's reign is universally regarded as a turning point in Western history, for what that means is that in the chronic battle historians fight between "change" and "continuity" in historical eras, "change" wins easily for this one.

Accordingly, Constantine starts a fresh page in historical study ("change"), with too little attention paid to the influence of the past ("continuity") on the thinking of contemporaries. The miracle story only compounds the problem. Thanks to the artificial divide we have created between Christians and everyone else, a Christian emperor must be diametrically opposite in every respect from a pagan one.[28]

Identities are not shed that easily. The chief reason Constantine's adoption of Christianity seems so miraculous is that it came in the context of Diocletian's systematic effort to stamp out that faith once and for all, in what is now known as the Great Persecution. The contrast is stark, especially since the document traditionally known as the Edict of Milan enunciates a new policy in no uncertain terms. As we have it, this document is a letter to the governor of the province of Bithynia reporting on deliberations between Constantine and his eastern colleague Licinius just a few months after Constantine's victory over Maxentius. (This meeting, in Milan, is the event for which Constantine's Apollo coin, Figure 3.4, was minted.[29)]) In a report that appears in the pages of both Lactantius and Eusebius, Licinius writes that he and Constantine had decided to grant

> both to Christians and to all men freedom to follow whatever religion each one wished, in order that whatever divinity there is in the seat of heaven may be appeased and made propitious towards us and towards all who have been set under our power.[30]

The document usually is remembered as a grant of freedom of worship to Christians, but as this sentence shows its reach was far greater. Ancient states did not practice, or even understand, our distinction between church and state. They were first and foremost religious institutions, and the chief responsibility of their rulers was to ensure that the gods would be favorably disposed to their decisions (hence the concern in this sentence to appease divinity). But unlike Diocletian, who decided that Christians were damaging those relations by refusing to recognize Rome's traditional gods,[31] this document adopts a refreshing neutrality, referring only to "whatever divinity there is in the seat of heaven." Its grant of freedom of worship not just to Christians but to all Romans constitutes a milestone in Western history.

Like Diocletian, Constantine and Licinius in this document emphasize the importance of divine support, one of the distinguishing characteristics of late antiquity. During the tumultuous third century, when Rome faced predators on every border and a breakdown in the senatorial system for selecting new emperors, a marked change occurred in the way emperors justified their rule. Since the armies had made it perfectly clear that they were no longer awed by senatorial endorsement, emperors started to emphasize their divine support, particularly by singling out a particular deity with whom they shared a special relationship—a divine *comes* (friend or companion). Effectively, this made them charismatic rulers—rulers whose authority rested on ties to a supernatural power (Figure 3.6). The authority of the prophets of the Hebrew Bible was purely charismatic, for instance, for it depended on popular recognition that they spoke for God, despite their lack of power or status as defined in human terms.[32]

Hence, an important tenet of imperial ideology in this late Roman period was insistence that the emperor's special relationship with a deity had to be recognized by the consent of all if it was to be effective—one reason that Roman coins of this age frequently proclaim *consensus omnium* (everyone agrees). Diocletian had made Jupiter, the traditional head of the Roman pantheon, his *comes*,

Figure 3.6. In this gold medallion, probably minted in 333, Constantine (center) points to a crown being placed on his head directly by God. He is flanked by two of his sons, one being crowned by a soldier, the other by Victory. The inscription reads "Gaudium Romanorum" ("Joy of the Romans"). Reprinted by permission of the Kunsthistoriches Museum. Vienna.

assigning Hercules, Jupiter's strong right-hand man, to his colleague in the West. Driven by the imperatives of late Roman imperial ideology, and probably also by a cabal of pagan priests and philosophers, Diocletian gradually decided that Christians were preventing consensus, and thus interfering with the critical communication between emperor and deity; national security required him to compel Christians to recognize his gods. Once again, Christians, who had enjoyed legal privileges for the past forty years, found themselves subject to state persecution. The result was turmoil.

A MIDDLE GROUND

It did not take a particularly deep thinker, or a Christian convert, to figure out what the problem was. Christians could not honor Diocletian's gods without denying Christ; nor could they honor the emperor if that honor had to be expressed through the ritual act of sacrifice. Even if it was not the animal sacrifice they abhorred but simply burning a few grains of incense at an altar to the emperor's "genius," a sort of patron saint, it still amounted to worship of false gods.

In modern terms, it amounted to a question of citizenship: what were its basic duties, and how were these duties to be performed? By insisting on the performance of sacrifice to a specific deity, Diocletian had turned back the clock to the requirements that had sparked the first empire-wide persecutions in the middle of the chaotic third century (persecutions prior to that time had been localized, as much the result of popular pressure as government initiative).

The effort was a failure. Diocletian's loyal lieutenant, Galerius, admitted as much when he conceded in 311 that Christians could meet their obligations by praying to their own god for the emperor's safety. Galerius died shortly afterward, to the delight of Eusebius and Lactantius, but his edict opened the door to a rethinking of a citizen's duties, for by allowing Christians to pray to their own god, he effectively removed sacrifice as a criterion. Even earlier, Maxentius had worked cooperatively with Rome's Christian community (despite the persecutor he later became in Constantinian propaganda), and from the start Constantine's own father, Constantius I, had not bothered to do more than tear down a few prominent Christian structures in his territory. Constantine himself, in a speech he gave in later years, lamented the persecution as a "public disaster" and claimed that it lacked popular support.[33]

In that same speech, Constantine repeatedly emphasizes the tolerant and forgiving nature of the Christian God.[34] Given the close ties between Constantine and his patron deity, it is inconceivable that he would make such a claim if he did not intend to act the same way himself.

Equally important is the way Constantine went about making his case for Christianity in this speech: instead of exclusively biblical texts, he relied on classical sources as proofs of the Christian message. In one section he used a response attributed to one of the famous Sibylline oracles as testimony to Christ's divinity, and in another he put forward the first known Christian interpretation of Vergil's famous Fourth Eclogue, the poem in which Rome's premier bard forecast the birth of a child who would bring peace and prosperity.[35] By these constant references to classical sources, Constantine was communicating a simple but important message: classical education and Christianity were compatible.

In short, what Constantine seems to have realized was that a public religion that did not require the performance of sacrifice or move beyond such ambiguous language as Supreme Being or Divine Providence could bring an end to the divisions that prevented the divine *comes* from doing his job.

Galerius's 311 edict carved out an exemption for Christians, but the problem Constantine faced, once he accepted the Christian God as his own, was finding a way to achieve the coveted *consensus omnium* without either forcing Christians to abandon their religion or forcing everyone else to become Christians. Scholars have long accepted the premise that there was no way to effect this union, and they have had history on their side, for once in power Christians quickly became the oppressors themselves.

But we are more aware now of the way Cold War thinking influenced that model (see chapter 1), and now are increasingly intrigued by a trend toward recognition of an unnamed monotheistic deity, frequently called a *Summus Deus* (Highest God), *divina mens* (Divine Mind), or, in Greek, *Hypsistos* (the Highest). At least since the time of Plato, classical philosophy had posited the existence of such a Supreme Being, and a trend to roll all deities into one under the empire had spread the idea beyond the intelligentsia. At the same time, Christians had little trouble identifying such titles with their own deity.[36]

With its reference to "whatever deity there is in the seat of heaven," the document produced by Constantine and Licinius in Milan shows that precisely such a policy was under active discussion in the aftermath of Diocletian's persecution. To "conflict" scholars, the thought that Constantine himself could have agreed with such a policy is anathema. But this is not the only indication that he did so. After ridding himself of Licinius in 324, Constantine sent an edict to all of his new subjects in the East in which he made clear his own preference for the Christian God but made clear as well that his policy was for everyone to live in peace:

> Let no one use what he has received by inner conviction as a means to harm his neighbour. What each has seen and understood, he must use, if possible, to help the other; but if that is impossible, the matter should be dropped. It is one thing to take on willingly the contest for immortality, quite another to enforce it with sanctions.[37]

Such ambiguities suggest another way to read Lactantius's description of Constantine's sign. Although Lactantius is clear that the sign he described denoted Christ, his strange phrasing may suggest that, like Constantine's public statements, it was meant as a code— something that could be understood one way by insiders and another way by everyone else. In other words, the various ways this sign has been explained, both in antiquity and in the present, suggest that its key characteristic was its novelty—few if any signs of its use exist prior to Constantine. The novel use to which Constantine put it in turn suggests that its ambiguity was deliberate. It was a sign that could be read as Christian, but also as an emblem for Constantine's dynasty and his close relationship to a deity.[38] In other words, it was part of a policy to sponsor a public religion that would allow all his subjects to support and acknowledge his rule.

There has been no final agreement on the meaning of Constantine and his vision. In all likelihood, there never will be. But the parameters of a pathway seem a bit clearer. It would seem that Constantine was more interested in bringing everyone into the tent than he was in doctrinal purity. But if this was his intention, then what happened? There is a simple answer: Constantine's miracle, and with it his program, was hijacked. And it is pretty clear who the culprit was.

Chapter 4

Miracle Doctors

By the latter half of Constantine's reign it was pretty clear that, as far as Christian leadership was concerned, the emperor needed to be reined in. He had showered the bishops with unprecedented riches and power, and they loved the imperial goal of a unified state religion. But they were discovering that the emperor's priorities were not necessarily their own, and they were also discovering that, when push came to shove, the emperor had a lot of shove. Even more unsettling than his ideas about orthodoxy and community was his belief in his special standing with their God, which threatened their right to communicate directly with their own deity.[1]

His miracle was the place to start. Constantine's account of his Vision of the Cross virtually demanded comparison with the apostle Paul, who also had experienced a transformative vision on the road—in his case to Damascus instead of Rome. There are signs that this was intentional. One of Constantine's most discussed utterances is his claim, when sitting among a group of bishops, that just as they were bishops of "those inside" the church, he had been "appointed by God" to be bishop of "those outside" the church.[2] The remark has many meanings. It has been taken as definitive of the role the emperor played vis-à-vis the clergy, but it also calls to mind Paul, the "apostle to the gentiles," who took the new religion to those outside the Jewish faith. Constantine also echoed Paul in his

claim to have been "appointed by God," a claim that he repeated in
a surviving speech: "no human education ever gave me assistance,
but God is the source of whatever gifts of character or conduct are
of good report among people of understanding." What is especially
significant about this assertion of a direct tie to God without the
need of human intervention is that he made it not to a court audience but to one that was primarily, if not entirely, Christian.[3] In letters, he took to referring to himself as "the Man of God," a phrase
Christians reserved for their saints and holy men.[4] As if to underline the point, toward the end of his life Constantine arranged to
be buried amid memorials of the twelve apostles, a physical statement of the title by which he eventually became known, *Isapostolos*,
"Equal to the Apostles."[5]

It was a brilliant way to carve a space for himself in the Christian
hierarchy without surrendering the religious authority Roman
emperors had always held. Imperial ideology posited precisely this
kind of close, personal relationship between the ruler and a divine
comrade (*comes*) on whom he relied to protect the empire in war and
peace. As a pagan panegyrist in 313 succinctly put it, "You must share
some secret with that divine mind, Constantine, which has delegated
care of us to lesser gods and deigns to reveal itself to you alone."[6]

Just because he was now a Christian, Constantine had no reason to think this traditional relationship needed to be altered.
This attitude is what Christian thinkers found threatening. While
they were ready to recognize the emperor's special mission to create peace and unity in the church, they had to worry about any
enhancement to the powerful position he already held. It obviously
did not fit Ambrose of Milan's picture of an emperor who "is in,
not above" the church, and this might well be the reason Ambrose
showered attention on Constantine's mother, Helena, in his funeral
oration for Theodosius while giving only perfunctory attention to
the emperor himself (chapter 5).

When Ambrose spoke, more than half a century had passed since Constantine's death, giving him some freedom to take an axe to the emperor's miracle. Christian thinkers who wrote while Constantine was still alive had to operate more surgically, with a scalpel instead of a cleaver. Two of these, the "Christian Cicero" Lactantius and Eusebius, bishop of Caesarea, appeared in chapter 3 as two important sources of the miracle story. In this chapter, we will look at ways in which they shaped Constantine's experience to meet other needs.

The trick was going to be to corral his ambitions without dampening his enthusiasm or, worse, raising his hackles. The first of our two surgeons, Lactantius, had a broader agenda. But the other, Eusebius of Caesarea, proved to be just the one for the job.

LACTANTIUS (C. 250–325)

Lactantius is the author who in chapter 3 told us about Constantine's dream and the problematic emblem it inspired. The story appears in a pamphlet he wrote *On the Deaths of the Persecutors* (*De mortibus persecutorum, DMP*) discovered only toward the end of the seventeenth century; its authorship remained in doubt for another two centuries.[7] Lactantius had risen to prominence as a professor of rhetoric—a field that at that time was something of a cross between training in law and training in public relations. At some point prior to the outbreak of persecution in 303 he had been appointed to the chair of Latin rhetoric in Diocletian's capital of Nicomedia on the Asian side of the Hellespont (the modern Izmit in Turkey). Jerome's *De viris illustribus* tells us that in his old age Lactantius served as tutor to Constantine's son Crispus.[8]

The thesis of *On the Deaths of the Persecutors* is summed up by its title. In what one of the greatest of twentieth-century ancient historians, Arnaldo Momigliano, once described as a "voice shrill with implacable hatred," Lactantius set out to show how, from the beginning, the Christian God had brought down emperors who so much as thought of harming his people. When he came to the Great Persecution, Lactantius pulled out all the stops. Instead of depicting the emperor Galerius's 311 edict of toleration as a game-changing concession, for instance, he embedded it in an account of that emperor's miserable death—a prolonged agony caused by something that might have been cancer of the bowels. Lactantius describes the progress of the disease in loving detail, claims that it stank up the whole city, and so provides the edict as the equivalent of a deathbed confession. Instead of being a significant step toward redefining the criteria for participation in the *consensus omnium*, the edict serves merely as a belated recognition of the power of the Christian God.[9]

Momigliano had a point, but in the aftermath of the failure of the Great Persecution, Lactantius was doing more than simply crowing. Consciously or not, he wanted to show how his God measured up to the usual criteria for a potent deity. In traditional belief, the purpose of a deity was not so much to provide an afterlife as to protect his or her worshippers in this one. By that standard, for the previous three centuries the Christian God had failed miserably. In the second century, a philosopher named Celsus taunted Christians with just this gibe. "Do you not see," he wrote,

> that anyone who stands by your daemon and not only blasphemes him, but proclaims his banishment from every land and sea, and after binding you who have been dedicated to him like an image takes you away and crucifies you; but the daemon or, as you say, the son of God, takes no vengeance on him?[10]

In response, Christians could only point out that their kingdom, as Jesus had said, was "not of this world." Now, finally, with

Constantine's miraculous victory, they had an opportunity to answer pagans on their own terms, and Lactantius was not about to let it go to waste. He looked back at those centuries with revisionist eyes and pointed out the terrible end emperors who acted against the church suffered, beginning with Nero and continuing all the way to Diocletian (who was a tough case; the best Lactantius could do was claim that he died of a broken heart).

On the Deaths of the Persecutors is not the work that made Lactantius a Father of the Church. That would be his magnum opus, *The Divine Institutes* (*DI*), a work also prompted by the Great Persecution. Here, too, Lactantius aimed to present Christianity in terms that pagans could understand, but on a much more sophisticated level. When and where Lactantius wrote the *Divine Institutes* is debated, but a plausible case has been made that he was in Gaul, and that he originally delivered the work as lectures to Constantine and his court between 310 and 313.[11] Titled to echo the kinds of works (Institutes) written for the training of law students, the *Divine Institutes* aimed to prove to pagans that true justice could be achieved only in a Christian system. Significantly, Lactantius avoided the scriptural proofs that Christians usually put forward as evidence because, as he observed, pagans were only going to be convinced by the use of more elevated language. Accordingly, he had to put the message in the type of language that pagans, and even classically educated Christians, were trained to respect and, more important, use evidence from their own authorities.[12]

Lactantius accomplished this goal by citing beloved stories from Rome's past and then arguing that, by enduring persecution, Christians were living up to these models better than their pagan persecutors. For example, he cites women and children who endured the gruesome variety of tortures employed by the late Roman judiciary as proof of greater moral fiber than shown by two names from Rome's legendary past—Mucius Scaevola, who stuck his hand in a fire to demonstrate what Romans were willing to endure, and Marcus Atilius Regulus, who voluntarily returned to certain death in Carthage because he had given his word. Like these, Lactantius wrote, "look at our weaker sex, and look at our children in their weakness, enduring the torture of every limb and the torture of fire, not because they must—they could avoid it if they wished—but willingly, because they trust in God!"[13]

His argument is a sign of how much moral ground pagans had lost because of the Great Persecution. They lost something else as well. Earlier, Celsus had berated Christians for refusing to debate their articles of faith. Christians, he wrote,

> would never enter a gathering of intelligent men, nor would they dare to reveal their noble beliefs in their presence; but whenever they see adolescent boys and a crowd of slaves and a company of fools they push themselves in and show off. . . . And if just as they are speaking they see one of the school-teachers coming, or some intelligent person, or even the father himself, the more cautious of them flee in all directions.[14]

Now it was Lactantius's turn. Throwing the use of force in the face of the persecutors, Lactantius argued that coercion could never produce true belief. Rather, he wrote, it is

> something to be achieved by talk rather than blows, so that there is free will in it. They must unsheathe the sharpness of their wits: if the reasoning is sound, let them argue it. We are ready to listen if they would tell; if they keep silent, we simply cannot believe them, just as we do not yield when they use violence.

Reversing Celsus's argument, Lactantius issued a challenge:

> Let them come out into the open ... and let them invite us to
> a meeting and encourage us to adopt cults of gods; let them
> convince us that these gods by whose power and foresight in all
> things are many in number. ... Let them copy us, and so bring
> out the reason in it all; we use no guile ourselves, though they
> complain we do; instead, we teach, we show, we demonstrate.
> No one is detained by us against his will—anyone without
> devotion and faith is no use to God; but when truth detains,
> no one departs.[15]

In arguing that belief could not be forced, Lactantius was drawing
not on a classical argument but on a long-standing Christian one
that only was adopted by pagans later in the century, when they
faced state-sponsored coercion of their own.[16]

Lactantius's views clearly resonated with Constantine. A long
oration of Constantine's titled *The Oration to the Saints* (*Oratio
Constantini ad coetum sanctorum, OC*) shares a number of traits
with the *Divine Institutes*, and it remains an open question whether
Lactantius influenced or merely echoed the emperor's own thinking.[17] Either way, both shared the belief that there was nothing to
prevent a fusion of classical culture and Christian religion. It is a
belief that subverts the starkly polarized picture of reason versus superstition or the winner-take-all view favored by the conflict school. And it just might explain as well the ambiguous way
Lactantius presented Constantine's miracle. Dream or vision, chi-
rho or dynastic symbol—these elements were less important to
Lactantius than the opportunity Constantine's miracle provided to
demonstrate that the Christian God did indeed conform to standard views about the role of deities, and that classical learning did
not stand in the way of a relationship with this God.

Given these similarities, it is worth asking why Constantine's vision does not appear in *On the Deaths of the Persecutors*. Although there is good evidence for placing Lactantius at Constantine's court as early as 310, it is possible that he had returned to the East by the time he wrote this work, and so simply never heard about the vision. But it is just as possible that he, like so many modern scholars, saw a connection between this vision and the one described by Constantine's pagan orator in 310. His silence, in that case, would be telling: rather than baptize a pagan story, he preferred to present Constantine's claim to charismatic authority in the more traditional setting of a dream—the place where ancients believed divinity made contact with mortals.[18]

EUSEBIUS OF CAESAREA (C. 260–339)

Lactantius is considered a Church Father, but his primary aim was to make Christianity palatable to elite pagans. The other doctor of miracle, his contemporary Eusebius of Caesarea, was a Christian bishop, and his aim was more institutional: to harness Constantine's zeal for the use of the church. Much earlier in the century—before he had even met Constantine or been elevated to the bishopric—Eusebius started work on a trail-blazing *History of the Church* (*Historia Ecclesiastica, HE*) that for the first time organized and recorded events in Christianity's first three centuries. It is virtually impossible to overestimate the importance, and influence, of this work. Without it, as one scholar has observed, we would know less about the early centuries of Christianity than we do about Mithraism (and if you have to wonder what Mithraism is, you get the point).[19] In so doing, Eusebius joined such greats as Herodotus and Thucydides in being recognized as the founder of a new field, now known as church history. More important for present purposes, by setting up clear lines of division between orthodox Christianity and deviant versions ("heresies"), Eusebius locked in a model of a single, unchanging "true church" that dominated study of the early church until relatively recent times.[20]

Similarly, in a speech delivered during the closing ceremonies of Constantine's Thirtieth Jubilee celebration in 336, Eusebius stressed the opposition of "monotheism" and "polytheism," which scholars accustomed to the rigid thinking of Cold War binaries carelessly translated as "Christianity" and "paganism."[21] This is certainly what Eusebius intended, but as with his use of "orthodoxy," his sleight of hand in this case defines out of existence the large middle ground of pagan monotheists for whom Constantine's deliberately ambiguous state church was created.[22] Indeed, Eusebius may well be the first scholar we know of to mask an aggressive agenda behind bland polysyllables.

This degree of subtlety made Eusebius just the one to handcuff Constantine's pretensions. But it also requires some precise surgery of our own. Because he wrote the equally influential *Life of Constantine*, in which he insinuated an intimate relationship with the emperor, Eusebius long was treated as virtually Constantine's alter ego; scholars took whatever he said about the emperor's aims and intentions as tantamount to Constantine's own words. Few now hold that position, but the task of separating Constantine from Eusebius's own overlay is not an easy one.[23] His speech to Constantine gives us a means to do so. It is one of two of his own that Eusebius attached to his *Life of Constantine* (the other was delivered about nine months previously at a private gathering in Constantinople).[24] Although on the surface the speeches and the *Life* share a common theme of reverence for the first Christian emperor, there is one difference that is crucially important: Constantine died in 337, well before Eusebius finished his *Life*, but he was very much alive, and attentive, on the two occasions when Eusebius spoke in his presence. So in these speeches Eusebius had to tread more carefully, and this makes any differences between the Constantine of the speeches and the Constantine of the *Life* important indicators of the way Eusebius operated on Constantine's image.[25]

The difference shows most clearly in the different way Eusebius treated Constantine's claim to a direct relationship with God. In his speeches, Eusebius had no trouble agreeing with the emperor. "These revelations," the bishop said, referring to his discussion of Christian theology,

> are not intended to initiate you, who have been instructed by God, nor to lay bare secrets for you, to whom well before our account God Himself, "not by men nor through men" but by means of the Common Savior Himself and frequent enlightening visions of His Divinity revealed and uncovered the secrets of the holy rites.[26]

The quotation in this passage is from Paul's Epistle to the Galatians, which makes it doubly important, for it caters to Constantine's pretensions in a way that Eusebius does not do in the *Life*. In that work, Paul stands out in the same way as the "dog that did not bark" in a beloved Sherlock Holmes tale—his absence makes him noteworthy.[27] Instead of likening Constantine to the apostle, Eusebius returned to an analogy he had already tried out decades earlier in the *Ecclesiastical History* and compared the defeat of Constantine's opponent in 312, who drowned in the Tiber River, to the death of Pharaoh in the Red Sea. If that opponent, Maxentius, was Pharaoh, then Constantine had to be Moses. Eusebius made the connection explicitly when he compared Constantine's years in the entourage of the persecuting emperor

Diocletian with Moses's youth in the house of Pharaoh, but he carried it out implicitly in other ways.[28]

Given Moses's outsized presence in both Jewish and Christian history, comparing the emperor to the prophet instead of the apostle can easily seem a promotion. But there are significant differences between Paul and Moses. For one thing, Paul exercised an immediate authority over Christians through his missionary activity and his pastoral letters that Moses, for all the standing he owned in biblical history, could not match. For another, what made Moses so attractive to Eusebius was that he could serve as the model of the perfect king as well as the perfect bishop. And in the Hebrew Bible good kings submitted to the authority of priests.[29]

Eusebius was far less subtle when it came to Constantine's miracle. In his official speech, Eusebius alludes to the event in two places. Toward the beginning, the bishop describes how God armed Constantine with "standards from above" to defeat his enemies, and he later elaborates on this point by saying that God had revealed to Constantine "even His own Saving Sign," a "victorious trophy, apotropaic of demons," by means of which Constantine "has won victories over all his godless foes and barbarians, and now over the demons themselves, which are but another type of barbarian."[30]

Eusebius's account in the *Life*, discussed in chapter 3, was much longer, but there is a much more important difference between these two versions than length. In the speech, Eusebius was emphatic that God had favored Constantine with a unique gift, "alone of those who have yet been here since the start of time" (*LC* 6.21). This confirmation and his other indications of Constantine's direct and intimate relationship with God amounted to a Christian anointing of standard imperial ideology, as well as of Constantine's pretension to apostolic standing. But in the *Life*, the bishop did not stop where most accounts (including the one in chapter 3) do. Instead, he went on to say that even after both the vision and the dream, the emperor was not sure what these phenomena meant. Therefore,

> he summoned those expert in his [God's] words, and enquired who this god was, and what was the explanation of the vision which had appeared of the sign. They said that the god was the Onlybegotten Son of the one and only God, and that the sign which appeared was a token of immortality, and was an abiding trophy of the victory over death, which he had once won when he was present on earth. They began to teach him the reasons for his coming, explaining to him in detail the story of his self-accommodation to human conditions.

Once he was so informed, Eusebius continued, the emperor decided "personally to apply himself to the divinely inspired writing," taking "the priests of God as his advisers."[31]

This new information, so casually inserted, is a dazzling reversal of what Eusebius had said in Constantine's presence. There, Constantine's standard came directly from God, unmediated by clergy or anyone else.[32] By inserting clerical tutors into Constantine's miracle, Eusebius not only denied the special status that Constantine claimed but also set up boundaries to the exercise of his authority. Obviously, if the emperor needed to be schooled by religious specialists, he was in no position to usurp the authority of those specialists. With a few deft strokes of his pen, Eusebius had completely overwritten Constantine's pretensions.

Why would he do such a thing, especially to an emperor he admired almost to the point of adulation? Eusebius evidently had no difficulty perceiving Constantine as a fellow bishop, or even as a bishop with a special supervisory jurisdiction. In addition to recording Constantine's claim to be "bishop of those outside" in the *Life*, Eusebius made a similar claim in his own words at the start of that work, where he described Constantine as acting "like a universal bishop appointed by God."[33] But to Eusebius, a fellow bishop was one thing: it recognized the emperor's religious authority and enhanced the stature of bishops in the process. Apostolic status was something else entirely, especially when added to the emperor's more mundane but very considerable earthy powers.

In one passage of the *Life*, Eusebius voiced some gentle criticism of his imperial hero for failing to control "wicked, rapacious men" who were doing great damage to the state, as well as the "unspeakable deceit on the part of those who slipped into the Church and adopted the false façade of the Christian name." This critique is all the more surprising since, as the instance of Paul showed, the bishop preferred simply to tiptoe around matters on which he and Constantine did not agree. Eusebius tempered this criticism by attributing what he saw as Constantine's gullibility to "his kindness and generosity, . . . the straightforwardness of his faith, and the sincerity of his character," which "led him to trust the outward appearance of those reputed to be Christians, who with a faked attitude contrived to keep up the pretence of genuine loyalty to him."[34] Nevertheless, the mere presence of this critique is a strong indication of the reason Eusebius wanted to clip the wings of this high-flying emperor: Constantine was far more willing than Eusebius—and, presumably, other bishops as well—to accept lip service as the standard for Christian behavior. His elastic definition of the faith explains why Eusebius was leery of Constantine's apostolic pretensions, and why he made a point of the emperor's need for episcopal tutors.

A POSTHUMOUS STRUGGLE

Constantine died in 337, Eusebius no more than two years later, apparently before he was able to smooth all the wrinkles out of the

Life.[35] Before his death, Constantine had already made plans for his mortal remains. Instead of burial in Rome, where a magnificent porphyry sarcophagus awaited him, the emperor built a resting place in Constantinople's new Church of the Apostles, where he would lie in the center of a magnificent rotunda, surrounded by markers and relics of the twelve apostles. In placing himself in the center of these markers, Constantine created a physical space for himself in their number, which undoubtedly contributed to his posthumous epithet of *Isapostolos,* "Equal to the Apostles." More than one scholar has concluded that his ultimate aim was even more grandiose: he wanted to replace Christ with his own cult.[36]

It would seem that, by gaining the title Isapostolos, Constantine ultimately won the struggle to be equated with Paul. But there was a big difference between achieving such a position while alive and attaining it after death. As a leading scholar has observed, "Constantine was made a saint so as to avoid making him a model of kingship."[37] The difference is this: unlike "Augustus" or any of Constantine's other titles, Isapostolos was one that none of his successors inherited.

There are other reasons Eusebius should not be counted out of this posthumous contest too quickly. Just about everyone now agrees that, when Eusebius wrote the *Life,* he aimed not just to celebrate Constantine but also to provide the outline for a model Christian emperor. The same can be said for the state oration he delivered to the emperor in July of 336, although here, as we have seen, Eusebius had to choose his words carefully to be sure he did not articulate goals that veered too far from Constantine's own agenda.

That agenda, as presented in chapter 3, appears to have been to promote a state religion to which both Christians and pagans could subscribe. Christians, including Constantine, would be free to define this deity more specifically in their private gatherings, but to make that distinction in public would endanger the universal consensus that imperial ideology demanded. So Constantine wrote in a letter addressed to the antagonists in the dispute that led to the Council of Nicaea in 325:

> And this I say without in any way desiring to force you to entire unity of judgment in regard to this truly idle question, whatever its real nature may be. For the dignity of your synod may be preserved, and the communion of your whole body maintained unbroken, however wide a difference may exist among you as to unimportant matters. For we are not all of us like-minded on every subject, nor is there such a thing as one disposition and judgment common to all alike. As far, then, as regards the Divine Providence, let there be one faith, and one understanding among you, one united judgment in reference to God.[38]

Those "unimportant matters" were a dispute over the relationship of the Son to the Father in the Christian Trinity! Constantine's judgment usually is attributed to his theological naïveté, but it is better seen as evidence for his priorities: Constantine aimed to construct a public religion around worship of an imperial *comes* vaguely identified as the Supreme Being or Highest Power, and for this purpose questions about the relative divinity of Father and Son were indeed "unimportant matters."

The type of Christian Constantine envisioned was not implacably opposed to either imperial rule or classical culture; he would reason with nonbelievers and set an example for them of piety and compassion, but he would compel none. Eugenius, the usurper defeated by Theodosius at the Battle of the Frigidus River in chapter 2, is an example of just such a Christian. Lactantius and Eusebius had other plans, but at least on the surface Lactantius's

Divine Institutes would have assured Constantine that Christians agreed with his views on classical culture, while Eusebius's state oration demonstrated how easily Christians could adapt to classical political theology.

The strength of Constantine's policy was that this language was compatible with both Christian belief and the concept of a single greatest divinity that philosophers had taught at least since the time of Plato, meaning that it was acceptable to the educated classes on which emperors relied to govern.[39] That strength was also its weakness: for it to work, Constantine had to rely on vague, general terms for his public religion. It was a bit like French, which wags like to say is the perfect language for diplomacy not because it is so precise but because it is so imprecise that all parties can leave the table thinking their views have prevailed. So it was with Constantine's policy: as Eusebius showed, one could use the same words to mean completely different things. This studied lack of precision made Constantine's policy vulnerable to uses he never intended and his miracle subject to manipulation in ways he could never have imagined.

But Eusebius could. To a remarkable degree, he was a thinker who knew how to play the long game. An example is the way he deployed the word "piety." Over the centuries, classical theorists had created a vast literature on the topic of the "good king," in which they agreed that it was the duty of the earthly king to behave like the human counterpart of the divine king who ruled over the cosmic universe. In addition to this mimetic role, the good king also shouldered the task of teaching his subjects to acknowledge the cosmic order—to lead them to the truth. So long as the Roman emperor was a pagan, Christians could not accept such a role. But with the advent of a Christian emperor, a new path emerged, as Eusebius acknowledged in his opening remarks.[40] He went on to draw an elaborate comparison between the emperor and his divine "friend" (*philos*), in which he depicts an emperor who summons "the whole human race to knowledge of the Higher Power, calling in a great voice that all can hear and proclaiming for everyone on earth the laws of genuine piety" (*LC* 2.4).

"Friend" (*philos*) is a word Eusebius used for the prophets and others who came to their knowledge of God through instinct rather than training. But it is also a term that is close enough to the imperial *comes* (companion) to be readily understood by non-Christians. The kicker in this Christianized version of the good king is the word "piety." In traditional Roman usage, *pietas* (*eusebeia* in Greek) basically meant doing what was expected in relations with gods and men, doing one's duty. As such, it became one of the "cardinal virtues" of a good ruler, along with bravery, clemency, and justice.[41] So Eusebius's decision to emphasize this aspect of Constantine's rule is hardly surprising. But as this quotation suggests, Eusebius used the term differently, in a way more aligned with our modern meaning of "devotion to God."[42] By using "piety" in this sense, he brought the emperor into his own sphere of competence, for bishops were judges of the spiritual lives of their flocks.[43] It is a cord that, half a century later, Ambrose happily replaced with a chain.

Eusebius took the edge off of this control by casting the emperor as the earthly champion of a cosmic struggle, doing battle with the enemies of God on earth while the Logos warred with their demonic counterparts above. This cosmic link was typical of political thought in late antiquity,[44] and it helped Eusebius make a critical connection between the founding of the empire and the advent of Christ. In the second of his own speeches that he appended to the *Life*, Eusebius depicted empire and religion as both part of a divine plan:

But two great powers—the Roman Empire, which became a monarchy at that time, and the teaching of Christ—proceeding as if from a single starting point, at once tamed and reconciled all to friendship. Thus each blossomed at the same time and place as the other. For while the power of Our Savior destroyed the polyarchy and polytheism of the demons and heralded the one kingdom of God to Greeks and barbarians and all men to the farthest extent of the earth, the Roman Empire, now that the causes of the manifold governments had been abolished, subdued the visible governments, in order to merge the entire race into one unity and concord.[45]

Eusebius knew what he was doing. The measure of his success emerges from comparison of Constantine's miracle story with that of Theodosius, discussed in chapter 2. Even with Eusebius's modifications, Constantine's miracle still identified him as a divinely charged individual, a status carried over from traditional political thought, which granted the emperor special standing as the link between humans and the divine.[46] Constantine's miracle thus demonstrated to contemporaries the intimate tie that connected him to divinity. The same cannot be said of Theodosius. His miracle was a response to his piety, and the arbiter of that piety—the person who claimed that the emperor was "in, not above," the church—was his bishop, Ambrose.

What Eusebius implied in theory, Ambrose demonstrated repeatedly in practice: bishops would not surrender their own position as intermediaries between God and humans, even when that human was the emperor himself. Effectively, bishops became the arbiters of the image an emperor was going to leave for posterity. So it might fairly be said that, even if Eusebius lost the battle, he won the war.

On another front, however, Eusebius wound up being completely outflanked.

Chapter 5

The Miracle of the Cross

Constantine was hijacked once more, this time by his own mother. And once again it looks like a bishop—this time Ambrose of Milan—had a hand in it. His opportunity came in the same funeral oration that told us about Theodosius's miracle. Just when he appeared ready to bring his oration to a close, Ambrose suddenly reached back almost three quarters of a century to tell an amazing story about Constantine's mother, Helena. Shortly after Constantine had finally gained control of the entire empire in 324, Ambrose said, Helena traveled to Jerusalem, where she was led by the Holy Spirit to discover the wood on which Christ died, the Holy Cross. After making the discovery, he continued, Helena used the nails of the cross to make both a bridle and a crown for her son, the emperor. She did this so that "persecution should end and true religion take its place." He continued:

> Wisely did Helen act when she placed a cross on the head of kings, so that the cross of Christ might be adored among rulers. . . . A good nail, then, this nail of the Roman empire, which rules the entire globe, and adorns the forehead of princes so that men [emperors] who used to be persecutors might become preachers. . . . On the forehead a crown, in the hands a bridle: a crown made from the cross, so that faith spreads its light; reins

too from the cross so that power rules, but here is just government, not unjust enactment.[1]

The jury is still out on what prompted Ambrose to make what looks
like a last-minute digression on Helena,[2] but if length is any indication, the story was important to him. Where Theodosius's battlefield miracle needed only a couple of sentences, and Constantine's
none at all, Helena's adventure warranted eleven chapters
(40–51)—three pages of a text that is only nineteen pages long in a
printed edition.[3]

Ambrose gave Constantine himself only a supporting role in
this story—first, welcoming Theodosius into heaven, then as the
fortunate son of such a blessed mother. But Helena rises to the
point where she stands virtually equal with the Virgin Mary—a
spectacular promotion for a woman who, Ambrose admits, began
life as a *stabularia* (politely, a "stable maid," but in common parlance denoting a woman who took care of more than a traveler's
horses).[4]

Yet it was not Helena but Constantine who set in motion the
train of events leading to the most spectacular discovery of this century of miracles.

MAKING A LAND HOLY

In the aftermath of the epochal Council of Nicaea, called by
Constantine in 325 to settle a theological dispute over the nature
of Christ's relationship to God the Father, the emperor undertook
an ambitious building program in the province of Syria Palaestina,
which housed Jerusalem (then known as Aelia Capitolina) and the
biblical lands of Galilee and Samaria. In his *Life of Constantine*,
Eusebius tells us that churches were built at the site of Jesus's birth

in Bethlehem and Ascension on the Mount of Olives (*Life* 3.41), as well as at Mamre, a site southwest of Bethlehem where tradition-ally the patriarch Abraham had built an altar (*Life* 3.51–53). But the most sensational development occurred in Jerusalem where, "con-trary to all expectation," according to Eusebius, the tomb where the body of Jesus had been interred came to light, "resurrected like Christ himself" (*Life* 3.28).

As bishop of the provincial capital of Caesarea, Eusebius was well situated to report on these events, and his account of the dis-covery of the tomb and description of the buildings Constantine ordered constructed over the site constitutes a substantial portion of the third book of the *Life of Constantine* (*Life* 3.25–40). Moved by the Holy Spirit, Eusebius says, Constantine determined to undo the injustice committed by certain of his predecessors and estab-lish a memorial over the tomb in which Jesus's body had been laid (*Life* 3.25–26). These "godless and wicked people" (*Life* 3.26.2) had been driven by demons to obliterate the site; to add further humili-ation, after they had buried it under rubble, they built a temple to the shameful love goddess above it. Planning to build a memorial over the site, Constantine ordered all of this filth removed. Then, Eusebius continues, something miraculous occurred: "the revered and all-hallowed *martyrion* of the Saviour's resurrection was itself revealed," coming back to life just like the Saviour himself. (*Martyrion*, the Greek word for "testimony" or "proof," later in the fourth century came to mean a building that commemorated a mar-tyr; Eusebius's use can be taken either way.[5])

Stripped of Eusebius's theological overlay, a relatively straight-forward account can be teased out of his narrative. During the reign of the emperor Hadrian (117–138), the Jews in Palestine rose in revolt under a charismatic leader who went by the name of Simon Bar Kokhba. It took Hadrian two and a half years to put it down. When he finally did, in 135, he ordered Jerusalem refounded as a

Roman colony, bearing the name Aelia Capitolina. To signal its new Roman roots, Aelia needed a proper forum, and it was in the process of constructing this site that the backing and filling Eusebius laments occurred. Archaeology has since confirmed that the present church sits on the site of Hadrian's forum, where a temple to Jupiter and another to Venus were built.[6]

How likely is it that the site where Jesus's body was laid was recovered after being obscured for almost two centuries? Two considerations bolster the case for believing that the local community kept a memory of the site, if not of the tomb itself. The first is that Jerusalem's bishop, Macarius, identified a site that was inside the fourth-century city's walls, despite the testimony of the Letter to the Hebrews and the Gospel of John that Calvary and the tomb were outside the walls.[7] Without sure knowledge, Macarius would not have dared make a claim that could be refuted so easily, and archaeology has now confirmed that an extension of Jerusalem's wall in the decade following the Crucifixion brought this region inside the city.[8] The temple to Venus that drew Eusebius's ire is the second reason. In the Near East, Venus was correlated with the traditional fertility goddesses such as Astarte, whose temples were sites of ritual prostitution. Given Christian sensibilities, Hadrian could have provided no better marker of the site.

Eusebius's account includes a letter from Constantine to Macarius, the bishop of Jerusalem, in which the emperor marvels at the miracle that has brought to light "the evidence of his most sacred passion." Constantine commits himself to building "a basilica superior to those in all other places," such as would be fitting for "the world's most miraculous place," and itemizes the precious materials and skilled craftsmen that he will provide for this purpose.[9] Eusebius also provides a detailed description of the finished church, which was dedicated with a lavish, eight-day Encaenia ("Dedication") ceremony in 335, intended to rival the original

Encaenia at which Solomon's Temple had been dedicated. Eusebius makes much of the visible contrast between this new Christian edifice and the ruins of the Jewish temple visible from its gates (see Figure 5.1).[10]

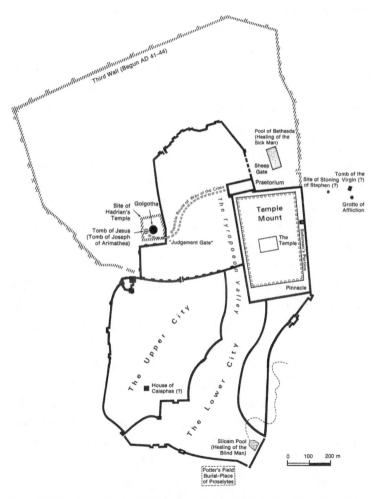

Figure 5.1. Map of Jerusalem in the first century, showing the location of Golgotha and the expanded wall of Herod Agrippa, built a decade after the Crucifixion, in upper left.

FINDING THE CROSS

It is noteworthy that the original plan was only to build a com-memoration over the site: after two centuries, not even the local Christians would have had any hope of finding the tomb itself. Eusebius's language still reflects the excitement generated when the excavators uncovered a rock-hewn tomb sealed by a round stone, just as scripture described.[11]

The present Church of the Holy Sepulchre invites skepticism. When Mark Twain visited it in 1867, he marveled at how "the place of the Crucifixion, and, in fact, every other place intimately connected with that tremendous event, are ingeniously massed together and covered by one roof."[12] The divine economy is truly remarkable. But as with the location of Christ's tomb, there is more to the story than met Twain's raised eyebrow. The Gospel of John (19:41), for instance, tells us that the garden tomb was in the same place as the hill of the crucifixion. In the present-day church, the two places are about seventy paces from each other, which is not an unrealistic distance.[13]

But where is the hill, Golgotha (also known as Calvary)?[14] More than the location of the tomb, it was the presence of this hill under the rubble of Hadrian's forum that gave testimony to the authen-ticity of the site. Here, cultural differences play a role. If such a site were uncovered today, our sensibilities would be to hallow it by pre-serving it as much as possible in its pristine state. But the ancient way of hallowing a site was to replace nature with the most elabo-rate adornment of which human art was capable. Accordingly, both hill and tomb were whittled down to a size that would be amenable to architectural enhancement, with Calvary in particular "cut back like a loaf of bread with parts sliced off on four sides" and standing about fourteen feet in height.[15]

Additionally, it is useful to bear in mind that the present structure is not the one Constantine built. Damaged by fire and earthquake over the centuries, Constantine's church was finally destroyed early in the eleventh century by the caliph al-Hakim. The fully enclosed building that replaced it, often called the "Crusader church," still showed the effects of a crippling 1827 fire when Twain visited it. The Constantinian structure, by comparison, was composed of several distinct buildings bound together by courtyards and an enveloping colonnade. For present purposes, the significant elements are the tomb and the basilica, indicated in Figure 5.2 as numbers 5 and 2, respectively.

Eusebius's description of this site in the *Life of Constantine* focuses attention on "the sacred cave" uncovered by the excavators, by which he meant the site of Jesus's burial. Starting at this innermost point, he takes the reader across a paved open space bounded by a colonnade that led to an immense "royal temple" (evidently the basilica ordered by Constantine in his letter), then across this space to a set of three access doors that opened onto a colonnaded courtyard and, finally, to gates set in a portico through which passersby could glimpse the interior.[16]

A sixth-century mosaic known as the Madaba Map, uncovered in the late nineteenth century on the site of the Byzantine church of St. George in Madaba, Jordan (Figure 5.3),[17] includes a detail of Jerusalem that shows Constantine's church opening, as Eusebius described, off the center of the colonnaded "Market Street" that ran from the Damascus Gate to the Zion Gate of the Byzantine city.

Even more significant, potentially, are the places indicated by numbers 3 and 4 on the plan of Constantine's church (Figure 5.2), for they lie at the heart of a perennial mystery. As scholars have not failed to note, neither in his account of the discoveries nor in his

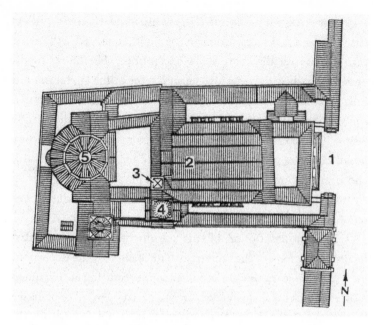

Figure 5.2. Plan of Constantine's Church of the Holy Sepulchre, showing the Basilica (2) and Anastasis Rotunda (5), which was not completed until later in the century. (3) indicates the remains of Golgotha, upon which a cross was set, and (4) the "hemisphairion." Constantine's church does not survive. The foundation of the present church dates to the eleventh century. After Coüasnon 1974, plate xv. Reprinted by the kind permission of the late Père Charles Coüasnon.

description of the building complex does Eusebius make any mention of the discovery of the cross. Given his reputation as a scholar and his proximity to these events, that silence has been sufficient to convince scholars that these accounts are the stuff of legend. One of Edward Gibbon's most delicious lines comes in chapter XXIII, where he discusses the discovery: "The silence of Eusebius," he wrote, "which satisfies those who think, perplexes those who believe."[18]

This skepticism may well be warranted. But elsewhere Gibbon exhibits a healthy distrust of Eusebius, and in fact the bishop's

Figure 5.3. Detail of Jerusalem in the Madaba map (sixth century), showing Constantine's Church of the Holy Sepulchre in the center, below the colonnaded Market Street. The three entry doors described by Eusebius are clearly visible. Photo by J. Housen, posted on Wikimedia, modified.

silence is not airtight. In Figure 5.2, number 4 stands for a curious structure that Eusebius refers to as the "hemisphairion," which he calls "the chief point of the whole."[19] It was lavishly ornamented, featuring twelve columns, "to match the number of the Apostles," each surmounted by a huge silver bowl given by the emperor himself. But what was it? Eusebius does not elaborate, and his presentation is muddled, the hemisphairion included almost as an afterthought. It evidently was built so that worshippers could look out from it to another place that Eusebius does not mention, the remnant of Golgotha left intact by the builders, upon which at some point a giant, jewelled cross was placed (number 3 in Figure 5.2).[20] So the hemisphairion appears to have been built to afford a view of Golgotha, the most certain marker of the tomb's whereabouts.[21]

The omission is significant because war and lack of agreement among the various religious denominations that now share ownership of the site long hampered systematic archaeological investigation, and even urgently needed repairs.[22] Consequently, Eusebius's account has exercised an outsized influence over efforts to create a plan for Constantine's structure, with most of them showing it built as Eusebius described, along a linear axis from tomb to street. But soundings in the late 1960s showed that the axis was actually "offset towards the south," evidently to take account of the hemisphairion and rock of Calvary.[23]

Compounding the mystery of Eusebius's silence is the testimony of Cyril of Jerusalem, who became bishop around the year 350. As a boy in Jerusalem, Cyril is likely to have watched the excavations that Eusebius described; in any case, in sermons to catechumens delivered in 347, when he was still a priest, Cyril was able to describe the tomb and hill of Golgotha as they looked prior to royal embellishment.[24] Cyril evidently delivered these sermons in the basilica, possibly in the hemisphairion itself, where he could point to Golgotha with one hand and to the empty tomb with the other. Together with the other visual effects he summoned, Cyril exploited the physical witness Jerusalem offered in a way that must have deeply impressed the initiates as they went through a grueling week of final instruction prior to baptism.[25]

Cyril's *pièce de résistance* was "the holy wood of the cross seen among us even to this day." More than once, Cyril claims that pieces of the cross had now spread throughout the world.[26] In 351, Cyril referred specifically to discovery of the cross in a letter to Constantine's son, Constantius II, that he wrote to report on another miracle—the appearance of a cross in the sky over Jerusalem that, he wrote, stretched from Golgotha to the Mount of Olives and lasted for several hours: "For if in the days of your Imperial Father,

Constantine of blessed memory, the saving wood of the Cross was found in Jerusalem ... now, Sire, in the reign of your most godly Majesty, as if to mark how far your zeal excels your forebear's piety, not from the earth but from the skies marvels appear."[27]

Was any wood discovered? As Eusebius indicated, Constantine's church was built over a previous construction site, so it is not unlikely that suitably sized beams were buried in the rubble, and given the excitement generated by discovery of a tomb on the site, it would not have taken much for such debris to be identified as the holy wood. In a way, it would have been more surprising had it not.

So why did Eusebius say nothing about such a find? One currently popular idea is that it was spite: he did not want to do anything that would add to the prestige of the bishop of Jerusalem, Macarius, who was technically his subordinate but busily lobbying for independence.[28] But Eusebius was positively rhapsodic about the Holy Sepulchre, which was also in Jerusalem, so political rivalry could not have been the only reason. More charitably, in 1956, Kenneth Conant thought the bishop's silence was due to nothing more than the unfinished state of the rock, as opposed to "the magnificence of the ensemble." Theology has also been proposed: Eusebius in general focused more on the Resurrection than the Crucifixion, so it was natural for him to say nothing about the discovery of the cross.[29]

There might be an even simpler reason: Eusebius could tell the difference between scrap timber and wood that would have been used in a crucifixion. In general, bishops were always on the alert to keep true miracles from being equated with the parlor tricks performed by street magicians, and Eusebius might well have worried that such wood, if identified as the cross, could easily be turned into a magician's wand by zealous entrepreneurs. It had already become perilously close to such usage in Constantine's hands, forming the basis for the famous *labarum* carried into battle by the emperor's armies.[30] It did not, in fact, take long for stories of the wood's power to cure illnesses and ward off demons to spread along with pieces of the wood across the Mediterranean. Eventually, the popularity of this instrument would be such that, a millennium later, it would lead to Jean Calvin's unfair but wickedly funny claim that there were enough pieces floating around in his day to fill a cargo ship.[31] To Eusebius, the tomb had significance as a physical proof of the Resurrection, but the cross had only symbolic importance—it was, as he frequently called it, the "symbol of salvation."[32] Actual wood added nothing to its meaning, and had tremendous potential for misuse. So he dealt with this in his preferred manner, by keeping his mouth shut.

But if so, this was a battle Eusebius was destined to lose. In fact, despite his reticence, Eusebius unwittingly facilitated stories of the cross's miraculous discovery. His account in the *Life of Constantine* makes discovery of the tomb a marvelous event, something that had occurred "contrary to all expectation" (*Life* 3.28). In fact, to magnify Constantine's role, Eusebius then recast the event as something that the emperor had foreseen all along, as if he "had looked into the future with superior foreknowledge" (*Life* 3.29). In that case, there would have been no need for a miracle to reveal the tomb. Rather than waste a good miracle, storytellers inserted the cross in its place. The switch was facilitated by Constantine's letter to Bishop Macarius, since here the emperor makes no specific reference to the tomb but instead uses other language—such as "the evidence of his most sacred passion" and "the pledge of the Saviour's passion"—that could easily make a reader think he was referring to the cross. Given his own attachment to that symbol, such a possibility should not be ruled out.[33]

ENTER HELENA

Helena sidled into the legend of the discovery of the cross as the result of a grisly family tragedy. In 326, Constantine executed Crispus, his adult son by an earlier marriage, and then his wife, Fausta. Nobody knows why, but the ancients could not help but connect it with Euripides's famous play, *Hippolytus*. This is the story of another king, Athens' legendary founder Theseus, whose son Hippolytus spurned sexual advances by his stepmother, Phaedra. The jilted queen took revenge by accusing Hippolytus of raping her. Enraged, Theseus immediately put his son to death, after which Phaedra herself committed suicide. The similarity of plot points virtually screamed for use in the Crispus and Fausta tragedy. In their case, moderns have spun a less romantic tale involving a power play by an impatient heir. But the truth is, the cause of this tragedy is entirely unknown.[34]

In its aftermath, Helena travelled to the Holy Land. Traditionally, her travel was understood as a pilgrimage to atone for her son's sins, as well as her own (supposedly, she had demanded Fausta's death to compensate for the execution of her favorite grandson). Once again, moderns suspect a more mundane motive: it was a goodwill tour, undertaken to reassure nervous elites that the emperor had not gone off the deep end. For the bulk of the empire's inhabitants, news of these deaths, if it ever even reached them, would have been met with indifference. But it had a different impact on the elites in the cities, on whom every emperor had to depend to administer his unwieldy empire. These elites worried about two things: stability and patronage (not necessarily in that order). An emperor who acted arbitrarily and erratically, who appeared to rule by rage rather than reason, unhinged the delicate mechanism whereby the reality of absolute power submitted to the restraints of traditional privilege. Hence the importance of Theodosius's willingness to do penance for the massacre at Thessalonica, discussed in chapter 2.[35] Whatever other motives she might have had, Helena made use of her progress through the eastern provinces to reassure elites in the many cities through which she passed that they could continue to count on imperial largesse. As an Augusta, a position to which her son had elevated her in 325, Helena had the imperial treasury at her disposal, and she dipped into it liberally, with both hands.

Eusebius devoted a long section of the *Life* (3.41–47) to Helena, beginning immediately after his description of Constantine's church. The bishop describes the piety and munificence with which she travelled through the provinces, and even takes note of her authority as an Augusta to mint coins with her own portrait and draw on the imperial treasury (see Figure 5.4).[36] In Palestine, he credits her with establishing churches in Bethlehem and on the Mount of Olives to commemorate Christ's birth and ascension into

Figure 5.4. Gold coin of Constantine's mother, Helena, identifying her as an Augusta—a position that gave her authority to mint coins in her own name. On the reverse, she is depicted holding a lowered branch with the motto "Securitas Reipublicae" ("National Security"). © Trustees of the British Museum.

heaven (*Life* 3.43), but he says nothing about any connection she might have had with the Holy Sepulchre.

How Helena worked her way into the cross legend remains something of a mystery. Ambrose's account is the first mention we have of her in this connection, and coming nearly three-quarters of a century after the fact it has naturally not been taken very seriously. About a decade after Ambrose's funeral oration, Rufinus of Aquileia published a Latin translation of Eusebius's *Church History* to which he added two books to bring the story up to his own day, ending with the death of Theodosius I. In the first of these, Book 10, he included the story of Helena and the cross. Rufinus added some crowd-pleasing details to Ambrose's account. According to Ambrose, to identify the True Cross from the other two with which it was found, Helena consulted the Gospels and there discovered that the real one would have a title plate, added by Pilate to identify Jesus as the "King of the Jews." In Rufinus, she is inspired by Bishop Macarius to touch a dying woman with each of the crosses in turn. When touched by the True Cross, the woman is instantly healed.[37] Except among curmudgeonly academics, Rufinus's version has won the day.

Rufinus had lived as a monk in Egypt and Jerusalem for more than two decades prior to his return to Italy in 397, and so he had ample access to written and oral sources for events in that region. For this part of his *Church History*, he has long been thought to have drawn on a now-lost church history written by Gelasius of Caesarea, the nephew of Cyril of Jerusalem. But that work now seems actually to have been cobbled together a century later, and thus no longer plausible as a source for Rufinus.[38]

Can a source be found that puts Helena closer to the excavation that Eusebius described? A century ago, Anton Baumstark suggested that a mosaic of Constantine and Helena with the cross—such as started being used on coins and icons no more than a century later (Figure 5.5)—had been put in the section Eusebius referred to as the hemisphairion. Such a depiction in a Christian church at that time would have been unprecedented, but Constantine's buildings were unprecedented in so many other ways that one more innovation cannot be completely ruled out. Indeed, if imperial images had been placed in the hemisphairion, Eusebius might well have kept silent simply because he was scandalized by such a breach of convention.[39]

Others, however, would have been less reluctant. Assuming that there were locals in Jerusalem eager to serve as tour guides,

Figure 5.5. Sixteenth-century Icon of Helena and Constantine with the Cross in the Museum of Byzantine Culture in Thessaloniki, Greece. Such icons proliferated throughout the eastern Mediterranean, and may originally have been based on an image in Constantine's Church of the Holy Sepulchre. Wikimedia Commons.

a mosaic of this sort would be all the explanation needed, since if there is one constant in human history, it is surely that tour guides, like nature, abhor a vacuum. A single question from a tourist about this representation, wherever it was placed, would have been the Big Bang of the Helena legend.[40]

If not earlier, a likely occasion for such a story to circulate was the week-long festivity in September of 335 to dedicate Constantine's buildings. Eusebius, who was present, tells us that the lavish ceremony drew a vast throng from everywhere in the East, and that the numerous prelates present offered prayers and sermons, some of which "recounted in detail the magnificent work connected with the *martyrion*."[41] Focus on this part of the complex was inevitable, since work on the Anastasis rotunda that eventually was built over the tomb would at most only have been started.[42] A sermon on Golgotha and the significance of the cross placed there alone would have provided a suitable opening.

Except for a direct connection between the empress and the discovery, Eusebius himself provided all the elements that the Helena legend would need. Not only did he write of her piety and her zeal for the holy places, but also he located her in Jerusalem at the time excavation for Constantine's church was underway.[43] It would indeed be strange if, while she was herself commemorating the site of Jesus's Ascension on the Mount of Olives, Helena had not once visited the site of the Holy Sepulchre, and it is not difficult to imagine a visit that coincided with, or was prompted by, discovery of beams that, in that electric atmosphere, would have been taken for the cross. But it is much more difficult to imagine what kind of source might yet turn up to make such a scenario anything more than imaginative.

In Rome, Constantine had given Helena the Sessorian Palace, an imperial residence built in the third century, where she dwelt after returning from the Holy Land. It was turned into a church in the last decade of Constantine's rule, and at some point it received the name by which it continues to be known—Santa Croce in Gerusalemme (Holy Cross of Jerusalem). The name comes from the deposit of a piece of the holy wood, but the earliest stories give the credit for this gift to Constantine, not Helena.[44] It would be consistent with the reverence he showed his mother for the emperor to have commemorated her death, around the year 330, in this way— just as he had earlier made a gift of Fausta's Lateran Palace to the bishop of Rome (Figure 5.6). All signs, therefore, point to a story that was still fairly new when Ambrose decided to incorporate it into his funeral oration for Theodosius.

Though Ambrose's funeral oration is the first surviving literary testimony to a role for Helena in the discovery, Cyril of Jerusalem's

Figure 5.6. Helena finds the Cross. Detail from a fresco of the Legend of the Cross attributed to the fifteenth-century artist Antoniazzo Romano, in the apse of Santa Croce in Gerusalemme, Rome. The scene depicts the moment Helena identifies the True Cross when it brings a deceased man (sitting on the ground) back to life. The bearded man in the center would be Jerusalem's bishop, Macarius. To the right, the Cardinal who commissioned the fresco is shown kneeling before the Cross. Photo by H. Drake.

claim in 347 that the wood of the cross itself had spread throughout the empire indicates how the cult of the cross grew rapidly during the course of the fourth century. In 1889, an inscription discovered in Algeria (ancient Mauretania) dated to 359 provided mute testimony to Cyril's claim. The stone commemorated the deposit of relics of North African martyrs and Sts. Peter and Paul, soil from Bethlehem, and wood of the cross. Louis Duchesne, who reported the discovery, noted that it constituted the earliest witness to any of the relics mentioned (though he subsequently also pointed out that the inscription could not be taken as confirmation of any role played in the discovery by Helena).[45]

Christians had of course used the cross as a symbol of their faith from the start, and Cyril himself testifies to the healing power of the sign in his own time. "To this day," he told candidates for baptism in 347, "the Cross heals diseases, puts devils to flight, and overcomes the deceptions of philters and incantations."[46] But the continuing shame of crucifixion as a form of punishment reserved for the meanest and most low-born criminals served as a retarding factor until that bar was removed, first by Constantine, who reportedly abolished the practice,[47] and then by the sensational news that the actual cross had been discovered. It is easy to underestimate the speed and extent of this story's spread. It affected theological debate, which previously had centered on the Incarnation rather than the Crucifixion, and from this time became "the most common form" for marking Christian allegiance.[48]

The rapid growth of the cult of the cross over the course of this century also coincides with the hardening of boundaries between orthodox Christianity and other forms of religious activity. As John Carroll wrote in his heartfelt study of Christian anti-Semitism, "Politics and theology were fluid until then [Constantine's conversion], but boundaries were suddenly defined around the grid of the True Cross."[49]

THE LEGEND OF THE CROSS

Over time, the story of Helena and the cross became more and more elaborate, eventually going all the way back to the beginning of biblical history, where a dying Adam sends his son Seth back to the Garden of Eden to ask for the oil of mercy. The archangel Michael refuses, but does provide three seeds from the Tree of Life, which he instructs Seth to place under Adam's tongue when he is buried. The act foreshadows the use to which the wood from these seeds eventually will be put, for a late Jewish–early Christian legend held that Golgotha ("Skull Hill"), where Jesus was crucified, was so named because it was Adam's burial site.[50]

Before thus coming full circle, the wood wends its way through every major event in biblical history, becoming the rods used by Moses to perform his miracles, the tree under which David composed his psalms, and a beam intended for Solomon's Temple before being rejected by the builders. When the Queen of Sheba discerns its holy nature and prophesies that in time it will replace God's covenant with the Jews, Solomon orders this beam to be buried at a site that he then flooded to create the lake of Bethesda. Miraculously, the wood rises from the depths at the time of Jesus's trial, at which point it fulfills its destiny by becoming the cross on which he is crucified.[51] Helena's discovery of the True Cross follows, and the legend closes with an account of the emperor Heraclius's war with Persia early in the seventh century to return the pilfered cross to Jerusalem.

A technical point: in modern English, a "legend" is a myth or folk tale. The account that comes down to us as the Legend of the Cross derives from the Latin *legenda*, meaning a story, or account. It is sometimes known instead as the Invention of the Cross, in this case meaning not a fictitious or made up account but based on another Latin word, *inventio*, meaning "discovery." So, even though we find elements of the story fantastic, it would be a mistake to conclude from the title that its authors were intentionally crafting a "legend" in the modern sense of the word. To the contrary, there is every indication that the story took its cue from a theological account of the discovery of the cross by Alexander Monachos that may date to the sixth century. Alexander concentrated on the symbolic importance of the cross, an approach that led him to start his story with the Garden of Eden and show how the wood affected every generation from Adam to Christ.[52]

Far more important than its pedigree, however, is the glimpse that the Legend of the Cross allows into doubts and anxieties that the process of Christianization created at the popular level. It addresses two immediate questions: Where has the cross been all this time? And how do we know it is the True Cross? Ambrose's fairly austere answer to the second question in the funeral oration may have satisfied elites, but the legend does a far better job, not only settling the question of authenticity in a dramatic and miraculous way but also allaying any doubts about the Crucifixion itself by showing that the event had been predetermined from the beginning of human history: it was not an accident or a mistake, but part of a divine plan. For this reason, for understanding the change from a pagan Roman Empire to a Christian Roman Empire, miracle stories are just as important as the theological debates that enthrall scholars. Although bishops like Ambrose and Eusebius held tremendous sway over the creation and distribution of such stories, the Legend of the Cross serves as a reminder that their influence extended only so far.

And the Legend of the Cross continued to grow, introducing a new character who will become pivotal to the story.

Chapter 6

Jews in Miracles

His name was Judas, and he did not much care to be involved in a miracle. But the miracle in question was Helena's discovery of the True Cross, and Judas was destined to play a major role in the story. He does not appear in Ambrose's account, but that account in general was thin on detail—the bishop's purpose was not to tell a story but to bind the empire to the cross. Ambrose did address one question that was sure to occur to his hearers: how do we know this was the True Cross? But his answer (Helena does some research), while satisfying to intellectuals like himself, did little to slake popular thirst. Within a few years, the cure (or sometimes resurrection) of a conveniently passing invalid/corpse provided a much more satisfying explanation.[1]

Ambrose was similarly vague about another likely set of questions: where exactly had the cross been for three centuries, and how exactly did Helena find it? For Ambrose, it was sufficient to say the Holy Spirit had led her to the site, but this, too, left a gap. Within a couple of decades, others had dragged in Judas to fill in the blanks.[2] In this version of the story, the Holy Spirit still sends Helena to Jerusalem, but once there she exercises the autocratic power of a Roman Augusta. Rounding up all the leading Jews, she demands that they tell her the location of the cross. They are mystified by this demand, except for one among them, Judas, who admits to the others that he is the one she is after. His family, he tells them, has kept the location of the cross secret. He then reveals something even more astonishing:

> My grandfather Zacchaeus warned my father Simon and he on his deathbed told me, "Watch out, my son, if ever you are asked about the cross of Christ, reveal it before you suffer any torture, even though from that time the Jewish people will no longer rule but those who worship the crucified, because he was indeed the Son of God." Then I said to him, "My father, if our forefathers truly knew Jesus Christ was the Son of God, why did they nail him to the cross?" He replied, "God knows that he [Zacchaeus] never participated in that decision but opposed it. The Pharisees crucified Him, because He exposed their vices. But He truly rose on the third day and entered heaven before the eyes of His disciples. My brother Stephen believed in Him, and for that the enraged Jews stoned him. So see to it, my son, that you never dare to blaspheme Him or His disciples."[3]

The others marveled at this revelation, but still they kept Judas's secret, until Helena threatened to burn them alive, at which point they gave him up. Initially, Judas dissembled. "How am I supposed to know?" he exclaims. "That happened two hundred years ago and I was not even born."[4] But Helena was not deceived. In true Roman imperial fashion, she sent Judas to ponder his answer at the bottom of a dry well (Figure 6.1). Judas held out for a week but finally gave in. Leading her to the site, he offered up a prayer, at which point the thirteenth-century archbishop Jacobus de Voragine tells us in his popular *Legenda Aurea*, "the ground parted and he smelled a marvelous scent of spices, such that Judas was amazed. Praying with both hands, he said, 'Truly, Christ, you are the Savior of the

Figure 6.1. Helena throws Judas into a well. 15th-century woodcut, reprinted in Ashton 1887, plate 41.

World!' "[5] Judas converts, takes the surname Kyriakos ("the Lord's Man"), and ends his days as bishop of Jerusalem.

The introduction of Judas was an enormous success. Once he appeared, he quickly shoved all other contenders aside.[6] At first glance, Judas's popularity is not easy to understand. He gets the chronology wrong by a century and, even at two (instead of three) hundred years, his father and grandfather would have to have lived lives of patriarchal longevity. His account even gave Jacobus pause.[7]

Even with its irregular chronology, the Judas story put to rest questions about the missing centuries between the Crucifixion and discovery, and other parts were even more satisfying. Judas, for instance, has an excellent pedigree. His grandfather, Zacchaeus, calls to mind the tax collector of Luke 19, whose good deeds led Jesus to call his house blessed, and his uncle was none other than the protomartyr stoned to death in Acts 6. And it was not just the location that Judas's family kept secret; it was the truth of the Christian message itself.

All of this raises an obvious question: where did such a story come from?

THE MEDICINE CHEST (PANARION)

Constantine's Church of the Holy Sepulchre, discussed in chapter 5, was the historical foundation of the Helena legend, but the story of Judas might trace to another source, one of the most curious works to survive from this period. About half a century after the discoveries reported by Eusebius in the *Life of Constantine*, Epiphanius (c. 310–403), who became bishop of Salamis on Cyprus around 365, published a book designed to help Christians identify and refute heretical beliefs. Entitled *Panarion* (usually translated as "Medicine Chest," but perhaps better thought of as "The Book of Antidotes" or, perhaps better, "Cure-All"[8]), it traces all deviant belief back to four original sources, labeled Barbarism, Scythism, Hellenism, and Judaism. From these derive the four Greek "heresies" of Pythagoreanism, Platonism, Stoicism, and Epicureanism, as well as a variety of Jewish sects. Before he was through, Epiphanius catalogued a total of eighty heresies, likening most of them to a particular vermin or viper and prescribing a way to combat the poison in each of them—a new low in the practice of heresiological discourse.[9]

To a modern reader, it seems perverse to brand as heresies not just a religion like Judaism but even philosophies and ways of life that existed well before Jesus, but it is less so if we take the term in its original sense. In Greek, *hairesis* simply means a choice. It came to be used in the specific sense of choosing a philosophy, so to know to which school of thought a person subscribed you would ask, "What is your heresy?"[10]—the same way you might ask a student now, "What is your major?" In Christian use, the word took on the sense of a *bad* choice and was applied to teachings about Christian faith that deviated from orthodox belief. In *Panarion*, Epiphanius used the term in both its original and later sense to classify the many ways that Christian belief in a God who was both 100 percent man and 100 percent deity, and at the same time part of an indivisible Trinity, could be misunderstood. His book became wildly popular.[11]

Among the Jewish sects, Epiphanius identified the "Ebionites," Jews who believed in Christ but taught that the Holy Spirit was something separate from the man Jesus, although it had settled on him. Like Judas's family, the Ebionites have Hebrew translations of Christian scripture that they keep hidden (*Panarion* 30.3.8), and Epiphanius claims that their patriarch, whose name he thought was Hillel and came from the line of "that Gamaliel who lived at the time of the Savior" (*Panarion* 30.4.2), secretly asked for baptism on his deathbed. All this Epiphanius claims to have heard from the mouth of one of the patriarch's agents, a man named Joseph, who converted to Christianity during the reign of Constantine and was raised to the rank of *comes* (count) by that emperor.[12]

Now in his seventies, Joseph proceeded to tell Epiphanius such stories as to make the one told by the fictional Judas tame by comparison. Joseph told Epiphanius about a secret, off-limits treasure house in which he had found Hebrew translations of New Testament books and also how, when he had become seriously ill, he had been visited by Jesus three times as he slept. Each time, Jesus cured him on condition that he convert, but Joseph still refused to believe. After one relapse, Epiphanius writes,

> When his [Joseph's] fellow Jews supposed that he was going to die, he was taught by them what they always do as a sacred rite. One of those learned in the law, an elder, came and spoke in his ear, saying, "Believe <in> Jesus, who was crucified in the time of the governor Pontius Pilate, who preexisted as Son of God and later was born of Mary, who is God's Messiah and rose from the dead, and who will come to judge the living and the dead." This is what Joseph himself told me in his narrative, as I affirm.

Still Joseph did not believe. On his third visit, Epiphanius continues, an exasperated Jesus told the invalid, "So that you may be fully convinced, if you wish any sign from God to be worked in my name, call upon me and I will do it." Joseph accordingly used the name of Jesus to deal with a madman in his village. It worked. But despite all these signs, Joseph refused to believe until he received copies of the Gospels from a bishop he had befriended. Alienated from his fellow Jews, Joseph made his way to Constantine's court and told the emperor about the visions that had led to his conversion. With resources from the emperor, he built churches in his home town of Tiberias in Galilee and elsewhere, and he ended his days in the city of Scythopolis at the northern end of the Jordan River Valley (now Beit She'an in Israel).[13]

The supernatural elements in Joseph's account are significant because of the striking number of parallels between the fictional Judas and Epiphanius's Joseph. Like Judas, Joseph has excellent credentials and ties to Jews who lived at the time of Jesus. Like Judas, he knows of a secret storehouse that contains important evidence of Christian origins, and like him he has learned from Jewish elders that Jesus really is the Son of God. Finally, like Judas, Joseph converts after witnessing a miracle.

These coincidences are not sufficient to prove that Epiphanius's *Panarion* inspired the story of Judas. But given the book's popularity, and the fact that Epiphanius himself hailed from Palestine, it is safe to say that the *Panarion* indicates that Joseph's stories were in circulation in this region at the time the Judas legend got its start. If nothing else, it suggests, as one critic has put it, "Whatever our opinions about the veracity of some of his [Joseph's] stories may be, he was clearly a good *raconteur*."[14]

ANTI-JUDAISM, ANTI-SEMITISM

Joseph's story, as reported by Epiphanius, included other bizarre circumstances: secret rites in which leading Jews practiced magic, cast spells to seduce chaste women, and used both violence and spells to thwart Christian progress. It is difficult for a modern reader, conscious of the baleful effect such stories were to have in later ages and the unspeakable horrors of the Holocaust, to react in any way other than shame and disgust at the casual way in which such libels were broadcast in the accounts of Joseph and Judas.[15]

One distinction, however, needs to be made. Throughout antiquity, Jews were not the ghettoized, stigmatized minority that they became during the later Middle Ages. Indeed, in the great city of Alexandria, Jews, along with pagans and Christians, constituted one of the major power blocs.[16] Nor were Jews identified only by their religion. They were, rather, a "people" (*ethnos*), one of many who made up the Roman world. Like other ethnicities, Jews had their own customs, dress, and deity. What marked Jews out as odd was the fact that their God refused to recognize the divinities that presided over other ethnicities, a trait that certainly set Jews apart, and often struck other peoples as odd or perverse. But Jews mingled freely with other ethnicities in the cities of the empire and, especially after the emperor Caracalla made virtually all inhabitants of the empire citizens in 212, enjoyed all the rights of Roman citizenship.

Throughout this period, Jews engaged in a spirited give and take—with Greeks, Romans, and, increasingly, Christians—and this is where we need to be cautious, for a modern reader is all too likely to read such attacks as evidence of "anti-Semitism." In the generic sense of a label for hostility against Jews, the phrase works, but it is a modern term, only coined in the nineteenth century, and like "pagan" it carries a lot of baggage that imposes constraints on its application to antiquity.[17] Although the relationship between Christians and Jews was frequently adversarial, it was just as often collegial. To capture this difference, scholars have coined the phrase *Adversus Judaeos* ("against Judaeans") to use instead of "anti-Semitism" when discussing polemics directed at Jews in this period.[18]

Another caution: it is equally important to draw a distinction between the relative power and importance of Christians and Jews before and after this century of miracles. Nobody knows exactly how many Jews there were in the Roman Empire, although the claim that Jews made up as much as 20 percent of the population has been pretty much discredited.[19] But whatever the number, it was much greater than that of the fledgling communities of early Christians. Moreover, Jews had credibility and standing in these communities, and exemptions from the duties and obligations of their polytheist neighbors guaranteed by the emperors themselves, who were mindful of the antiquity and demands of the Jews' ancestral religion. One way to read the hostility toward Jews in the books that became part of the New Testament canon is to see it as a reflection of the frustration that a powerless minority feels in the face of a much more powerful competitor.[20]

A LINGUA FRANCA

This shared living environment explains what was once a startling archaeological discovery. In the 1960s, a team of archaeologists from the Israeli Exploration Society led by Moshe Dothan, digging in Hammat Tiberias, a spa on the Sea of Galilee, uncovered a richly decorated mosaic floor in a synagogue that Dothan dated on the basis of iconographic parallels to the late third/early fourth centuries.[21] An inscription by one Severus, "the pupil of the most illustrious patriarchs," helped confirm the dating, since the Jewish high court, the Sanhedrin, sat in this town from 270 to 358. As the seat of the Sanhedrin, Tiberias was one of the most important Jewish centers in Palestine, home to more than a dozen synagogues. Pride of place in the Hammat Tiberias synagogue went to a large central panel, about 3.3 meters square, featuring figures from the zodiac (Figure 6.2). In the center, the sun god (Sol/Helios)—in his specific guise as Sol Invictus (the Unconquered Sun)— is depicted driving his four-horse chariot across the sky.[22] The scene was, and is, highly controversial, since it depicts not only pagan deities but also naked human forms in the Greek heroic tradition. There have been efforts to deny the structure's identity as a synagogue, despite a Torah ark flanked by two seven-branched candlesticks in a panel just above the zodiac, as well as the Severus inscription with its reference to the Sanhedrin.[23]

The mosaic testifies to a concept of Jewish identity that embraced a much broader spectrum of practices than the teachings of the rabbis would lead us to believe.[24] The rabbinical instructions became normative, and the issue is still touchy enough that in 2012 the mosaic was vandalized, allegedly by ultra-orthodox Jews offended by its depiction of human images, even if 1,700 years old. Though controversial now, the image of Sol is part of what has been called a "religious *koinē*" of the day, a common ground that Jews

Figure 6.2. Floor mosaic of fourth-century synagogue, Hammat Tiberias, Israel. The god Sol/Helios—easily identified by his upraised right hand and the rays beaming from his head—sits in the middle of a wheel showing the signs of the zodiac. Photo by Praisethelorne, Wikimedia Commons.

"shared with the other communities throughout the Mediterranean and the Near East."[25]

The Hammat Tiberias mosaic reflects one aspect of this religious sharing, an understanding of the Sun God as a symbol for monotheistic belief. The connection is a very old one, for obvious reasons. It explains how a single God can be everywhere simultaneously, and also answers the philosophical objection that a Perfect Being would soil itself by coming into contact with imperfect mortals. Look at the sun, a monotheist could say: it goes everywhere, bringing the goodness of light and warmth through its rays, without suffering any diminution of its perfection.

Jewish texts readily lent themselves to such depictions. The prophet Malachi speaks of the "Sun of Righteousness" (*Sol Iustitiae*) at 4:2, and Psalm 27 "the Lord is my light and my salvation," gives rise to the concept of God as the "Sun of Salvation" (*Sol Salutis*). Indeed, Christians long ago appropriated these texts in their efforts to explain the nature of their God to pagans.[26] It should be no occasion for surprise to find Jews themselves making use of the same symbolism.

But the mosaic at Hammat Tiberias has more to tell us, for it is not the only zodiac motif uncovered in Roman synagogues. Their number once was an occasion of great surprise, with one scholar calling the "sheer quantity" of such mosaics "startling," and another describing them as "By far the most stunning Hellenistic-Roman depiction to appear in Jewish art of Late Antiquity."[27] Two other synagogues with Helios/Sol representations, at Sepphoris and Beit (or Bet) Alpha, have been dated to the fifth and sixth centuries, respectively, and comparison with them isolates the unique features of the fourth-century mosaic at Hammat Tiberias. The fifth-century Sepphoris mosaic replaces the anthropomorphic Sol Invictus figure in the Hammat Tiberias chariot with an abstract image of the sun and its rays, and the one at Beit Alpha uses cartoonish figures for both Sol and his horses.[28] The differences freeze Hammat Tiberias at a specific point in time, a period when Constantine promoted solar symbolism as a generic monotheism that he thought could provide the religious unity required by imperial ideology.

To say this is not to say that Constantine was not himself a Christian, or that there is a simple equation to be made between Jewish, Christian, and pagan uses of solar imagery. What the Hammat Tiberias mosaic testifies to is the ubiquity of such imagery, and the ease with which various groups could adapt it to their own uses. We can think of solar imagery in this period as a *lingua franca*, a common tongue, uniting Christians, pagans, and Jews in a shared allegiance to the empire. Ultimately, what the Hammat Tiberias mosaic shows us is the extent to which Constantine's emphasis on a Highest God (*Summus Deus*) and use of solar imagery was designed to tap into this unifying imagery.

SETTING BOUNDARIES

In addition to being the seat of the Sanhedrin, Tiberias in the fourth century had another distinction. It was the hometown of the count Joseph who may have been the inspiration behind the figure of Judas Kyriakos in the Legend of the Cross. Epiphanius tells us in his *Panarion* that Joseph founded several churches in Tiberias and its environs after his conversion, but we would never learn from him that such foundations were part of a vibrant lifestyle in the region, with the kind of fluid religious and cultural exchange reflected in the Hammat Tiberias mosaic. What is it that led Epiphanius to ignore all these signs of shared identity and replace them with his bizarre tales of forbidden lust, magic incantations, and Gothic intrigue?[29]

Part of the answer lies with Epiphanius himself. The general view among scholars is that the bishop of Salamis represents a new and narrower version of Christian belief.[30] His practice of likening heretics to specific kinds of vermin not only had the effect of dehumanizing them but also eliminated any need for reasonable discussion of their teaching.[31]

The ardor with which Epiphanius snooped out dissenters and heretics puts him in a class by himself, but the attention he paid to identifying and classifying heresies was also a sign of the times.[32] Whereas the huge doctrinal controversies of this century, dealing with the precise relationship between Father and Son in the Christian Trinity, grab the lion's share of scholarly attention, Epiphanius's lists of evildoers reflect a more widespread phenomenon, the spread of simple guidebooks—a sort of late antique Cliff's

Notes—that ordinary Christians could use to quickly identify dissidents without the trouble of a long and intricate interrogation that would in all likelihood simply confuse them.[33]

If Epiphanius's obsessive cataloguing makes him seem a bit paranoid, he was not alone. Bishops much higher in intellect displayed the same symptoms. As we saw in chapter 2, Ambrose of Milan constantly pestered Theodosius to protect a church that he saw as surrounded by enemies of all sorts, but especially Jews. In his ultimately successful effort to make Theodosius disavow any effort to punish the bishop of Callinicum for destruction of that town's synagogue or to force him to make restitution, Ambrose launched into a furious attack against the Jews. They are not simply "unbelievers" but "perfidious" "treacherous," "slanderers"; their synagogue was "a site of perfidy, a house of impiety, a refuge of madness, which God himself has condemned."[34]

Ominously, Ambrose insisted that Theodosius had to choose between the two religions, polarizing the issue to the extent that this "loss" for the church would constitute a "victory" for the Jews:

> Will you give the Jews this triumph over the Church of God? This trophy at the expense of the community of Christ? This rejoicing, emperor, to the faithless? This celebration to the synagogue? This grief to the Church? The Jewish people will enter this feastday into their calendar, and will assuredly rank it with the days on which they triumphed over the Amorites, or over the Canaanites, or over Pharaoh, the king of Egypt, or that on which they succeeded in freeing themselves from the hand of Nebuchadnezzar, king of Babylon. They will now add this festival, signifying that they have celebrated a triumph over the people of Christ.[35]

But Ambrose's efforts are nothing compared to those of his younger contemporary, John Chrysostom (c. 349–407), the future bishop of

Constantinople. In 386, a young Chrysostom was starting to make his mark in his native Antioch as a priest of unusual passion and eloquence. Over the course of the next twelve months, he preached a series of blistering sermons "Against the Jews" that dramatically escalated anti-Judaic rhetoric. Jews were not only a "disease" and "enemies of the truth" but also "beasts," unfit for work but "fit for killing" and, quite literally, demonized. "They live for their bellies, they gape for the things of this world, their condition is no better than that of pigs or goats because of their wanton ways and excessive gluttony," he says at one point, and at another, "Do you [not] see that demons dwell in their souls and that these demons are more dangerous than the ones of old?" The synagogue itself is "a table of demons because they slew God."[36] John's language was a sign of the times. In the course of this century, Christians started to take the phrase "Christ-killers" out of its specific historical context of those Jews who opted for Jesus's death and started to apply it to all Jews everywhere.[37]

Just reading these sermons now is a painful experience. But to gauge their full impact, we need to imagine them delivered with the same intensity that, today, we associate with tent revivalists in the mold of, say, Burt Lancaster in "Elmer Gantry."[38]

What accounts for this outpouring of venom? With the serenity that a millennium and a half of distance can bring, it is relatively easy to see that much of this rhetoric was prompted by the fluid state of religious identity captured by the Hammat Tiberias mosaic. Closer inspection, for instance, shows that the real object of Chrysostom's diatribes was not so much Jews themselves as Christians who participated in Jewish festivals and ceremonies, and who went to the synagogue to swear oaths and seek cures for physical ailments out of a belief that God's power was stronger in that setting. One indication that Judaizing Christians rather than the Jews themselves were Chrysostom's target is the fact that his argument was aimed at Greek, rather than Jewish, criticisms of the faith. Indeed, the evidence is so compelling that a modern translation of Chrysostom's sermons changed their title from the traditional "Against the Jews" to "Against Judaizing Christians."[39]

Ambrose's attacks on Jews fall under a different category of boundary maintenance. Hate and fear are strong emotions, and his constant warnings of a church encircled by enemies helped Ambrose galvanize his flock behind his stalwart leadership.[40] But whether it was a matter of attacking the Jews like Chrysostom, labeling any variance from orthodox belief a heresy like Epiphanius, or denying legal rights to any groups deemed to be enemies like Ambrose, Christian leaders sought to define these fuzzy, gray areas out of existence.

Inevitably, in the course of defining an unacceptable "other," leaders like Ambrose and Chrysostom also sharpened and narrowed the boundaries of "true" Christianity. They did so in what now would be recognized as a classic effort at polarization: defining out of existence the middle ground to limit the choice to one or the other of the extremes. As Chrysostom put it in his first sermon against the Judaizers, "If the Jewish rites are holy and venerable, our way of life must be false."[41]

Attention to such matters has led to a new understanding of the famous "parting of the ways"—the development of a clearly defined Christianity separate from and hostile to its Jewish roots. At one time, the anti-Jewish rhetoric of the New Testament led scholars to conclude that this split had occurred no later than the early second century. Discoveries such as the Hammat Tiberias mosaic, revealing a much broader spectrum of both Christian and Jewish identities, and signs of continued dialogue between the two sides at a much later time, have led to an alternative picture. Instead of a decisive split that was early recognized and understood by all, it is possible now to see a longer and more gradual process during which a range of hybrids existed between the two choices of rabbinic Judaism on the one end and what became Orthodox or Catholic Christianity on the other.[42]

At the same time that Christian leaders were insisting on a more rigidly defined normative Christianity, religious specialists on the Jewish side were taking steps to corral the various forms of Judaism into a more rigidly defined norm. The Jerusalem Talmud, a massive compilation of rabbinic teaching stretching back over centuries, was completed during this period, and long was accepted as the hallmark of Jewish orthodoxy, just as the Church Fathers were for Christianity. Now scholars are not so sure that anybody other than the rabbis themselves was listening to their regulations. But it does seem likely that Jews in general more and more came to define themselves as primarily a religion, in tandem with (if not in response to) the redefinition of Christian identity that was taking place.[43]

WORDS THAT KILL

Context mitigates much of the vehement language employed by speakers like Ambrose and Chrysostom. The classical curriculum laid heavy emphasis on training for public speaking, and in the oral culture of antiquity audiences were as well versed in its principles as the speakers themselves. Philosophers in the rival schools of antiquity had set the pace with their over-the-top attacks on each other, all consumed in joyful dollops by ancient audiences. So it should be no occasion for surprise to see effective speakers like Ambrose and Chrysostom celebrated like rock stars or to find them employing the same tools in their sermons.

Chrysostom favored one in particular, hyperbole (overstatement for rhetorical effect), and—according to this thesis—his hearers would have immediately recognized it, and simultaneously appreciated and discounted it, as such.[44] Confirmation of sorts comes from a young Augustine, who tells us in his *Confessions* that as a young teacher of rhetoric in Milan he went to Ambrose's sermons primarily because of the bishop's fame as a speaker. He paid little attention to their content, his sole interest being to study the bishop's style and delivery.[45]

There is yet another way to account for this language. For most of their history, Christians had been the underdogs in their conflicts with the large and well-established Jewish communities of the Mediterranean, and their anti-Jewish language, which begins as early as the New Testament, reflects the frustration they felt when Jews refuted truth claims that were in large part based on Jewish scripture. As one scholar has observed, "Abuse tends to gain in volume when it is powerless."[46]

But it is equally common for reality to outpace rhetoric. A true appreciation of what happened to Christianity in the fourth century can be achieved only by realizing the continued hold on the Christian imagination of an outlook formed during those powerless centuries, despite the radically changed circumstances in the aftermath of Constantine's miracle. John Chrysostom provides a clear example when dealing with another formerly powerful group, the pagans. In the 370s, when antipagan legislation had been on the books for decades, Chrysostom still taunted pagans with the claim that "no emperor of Christian persuasion enacted against you legislation such as was contrived against us by those who served demons."[47]

What changed the balance to the Christian side was the vastly increased powers that their leaders now exercised. It is perhaps understandable that, after centuries of being the underdog in contests with the well-established Hellenistic Jewish communities of the Mediterranean, Christians like Chrysostom and Ambrose did not fully grasp that the relationship had become so fundamentally altered that Jews were now the vulnerable party, since it often takes a period of time before reality catches up with long-established perceptions.

All these observations are important and need to be made. But so does another: words have consequences. The way this anti-Judaism morphed into something else, the religious hatred of anti-Semitism, is a sobering reminder of the unintended consequences to which hate language can be put. Later ages in Christian Europe could not imagine the spirited give and take in which these tracts were written, nor were people in these later ages in a position to appreciate the crowd-pleasing rhetoric of a bygone day. The Jews they knew were a hated and isolated minority, and they took these works to be reasoned arguments by Church Fathers of unimpeachable authority that told them it was permitted to attack these enemies of the church with impunity.[48]

JUDAS REDEEMED

By comparison with the strong language used by Ambrose and Chrysostom, the Judas in the Legend of the Cross comes off fairly well. He is allowed some heroic characteristics, keeping the faith even after he is betrayed and yielding to Helena's demands only after spending seven days without food or water. And of course he seals the deal with his conversion. It all makes for a satisfying tale of redemption, yet since it is a story, it is possible to conceive of other endings. One suspects that if Chrysostom had had his way, Judas would have been incinerated by a lightning bolt after giving up his secret, and Ambrose probably would have had him lynched by an angry mob. So it is worth giving some thought to the reason this popular tale took a more generous path.

Judas's name is the giveaway. It was obviously intended to call to mind that other Judas, who betrayed Christ for a handful of coins (Matt. 26:14). By converting, our Judas redeems his namesake, but he does much more. For just as the legend resolved doubts and anxieties about the pedigree of the True Cross, so here through Judas it was able to deal with the most deep-seated of Christian anxieties, one that went to the very core of their identity: if Christian truth claims depend so heavily on Jewish texts, why do Jews themselves not accept them?[49] All of the varied responses seen in this chapter trace back to that one existential question. One response was to appropriate those texts, not just by relabeling them as the "Old" Testament that had been supplanted by the "New" one, but also to act like Ambrose and confidently change "their" stories to "our" stories, "their" heroes to "our" heroes.[50] Chrysostom represents a more sinister tack, even if only taken for rhetorical purposes. "They" are now lesser beings, no more worthy than dogs or draft animals. Worse, "they" are demons, "Christ-killers."

Closer to the popular level, Epiphanius took a third approach: Jews know the truth and have always known the truth. They refuse to confess it simply because they want to hang on to power. Judas, in the legend, completes this storyline, and in so doing he fulfills the most deeply held of Christian wishes. However reluctantly, then, Judas has led to a useful insight: at the very moment when their leaders were doing everything they could to cement the parting of the ways, storytellers continued to hope that, by some miracle, the two might yet be joined.

Chapter 7

Miracle in the Desert

It was once said of the modern state of Israel that it "made the desert bloom." A similar phenomenon in Egypt in the fourth century led Athanasius, bishop of Alexandria from 328 to 373, to speak of the desert becoming "a city."[1] In both cases, the image is a strong one—that of reclaiming what was wasteland, taming it, and making it productive. In both cases also, the phrase was intended to call attention to an important achievement, one that promised a qualitative change in the lives of contemporaries. But here the similarity ends. Whereas the Israeli miracle was achieved by scientists and farmers, Athanasius's reclamation project relied on a new phenomenon—men and women who abandoned the comforts of city life to achieve spiritual perfection through fasting and prayer in the great wastelands of Egypt and the Middle East.

There is another revealing difference. Athanasius's choice of the city, rather than the farm, to illustrate the new productivity was rooted in a strong identification ancients made between the city and civilization.[2] In effect, by using it, he was saying that these solitaries, or monks (from the Greek *monachos*, a loner), were pioneers, pointing the way to a better life for the rest of us. His image was so powerful that 1,500 years later Derwas Chitty chose it as the title of his standard study of monasticism.[3]

The way to achieve that better life is of significance here, for these fourth-century innovators tamed not the desert but the demons that dwelled therein, and their product was not food for the stomach but food for the soul. Everyone knew that this world was plagued by demons, ever-ready to pounce; like dogs, they could smell fear and were attracted to it, as well as to every other strong emotion. But the ascetics (from the Greek *askēsis*, "training") conquered their fears and appetites and thereby became impervious to the powers of these invisible enemies. By denying their physical needs, these spiritual entrepreneurs allowed room for their souls to grow; some became so adept that they were able to work miracles. With the fame from this skill, the desert saints came to populate the late antique imagination as firmly as they began to populate the desert landscape.

This use of the same imagery for two very different purposes can help us navigate what might otherwise be treacherous waters. Whereas our age is willing to place infinite faith in scientific agriculture, the type of spiritual investment praised by Athanasius does not resonate as strongly. In fact, the monastic movement that drew Athanasius's admiration is today more likely than not to be cited as a reason for the fall of Rome: a harebrained scheme that deprived the empire of manpower vitally needed for more productive uses.[4] Yet any hope of understanding this century of miracles must be grounded in an appreciation of that world as it looked to the people who lived in it.

Today, talk about saints inevitably focuses on the miracles they performed. But for these desert saints, miracles (if they occurred at all) were simply by-products of a program designed to train the individual to be indifferent to the troubles of this world and thereby to become worthy of life in the next. To them, the struggle with demons was of paramount importance.

Nevertheless, their impact on this century of miracles was profound. Desert saints like Antony have a specific role to play in the reordering of knowledge that took place in this century, because public fascination with the kind of supernatural support they channeled soon influenced the tenor of public debate.[5]

THE LIFE OF ANTONY

The work in which Athanasius described this transformation is one of the most influential ever written. The *Life of Antony* celebrated the career of the man who came to be known as Antony (or Anthony) the Great. The passage of time has made a different saint from this era more familiar to us. Today, the most popular—and probably also the best known—of fourth-century saints is undoubtedly Nicholas (270–343), bishop of Myra (now Demre on the coast of southwestern Turkey), the historical figure behind the modern Santa Claus. Nicholas became famous not just for working miracles, but even more for his self-effacing generosity: he would sneak up to needy households in the middle of the night and toss gifts of money and trinkets for worthy children through open windows (or sometimes down chimneys). The story of Nicholas's transformation—which weaves from Myra to Italy to New Amsterdam, and from the imaginations of Washington Irving and Clement Moore to the department store wars between Macy's and Gimbel's—is a case study of the way events in late antiquity made their way into the modern world. "Claus" is a shortened form of Nicholas, and "Santa," usually the title of a female saint, is actually a corruption of the Dutch "Sint Niklaas" ("Saint Nicholas")—an echo of which survives in those parts of New York where his name is still pronounced "Sinter" Claus. The date for Santa's annual visit was not firmly set until the "Christmas shopping season" was introduced in the 1930s, and then firmly fixed by the classic 1947 film, "Miracle on 34th Street."[6]

At the time, however, Nicholas and any other saint in the making from that era lived in Antony's shadow. This pioneering ascetic, who lived more than a century, from 251 to 356, became the founder of Christian monasticism, a movement that began in earnest during this century. Born in the delta region of Lower Egypt, Antony was moved by the Gospel account of Jesus's advice to a young man who sought eternal life: "Jesus said to him, 'If you would be perfect, go, sell what you possess and give to the poor, and you will have treasure in heaven; and come, follow me'" (Matt. 19:21). After disposing of his inheritance in this way, Antony apprenticed himself to a local hermit, with whom he spent fifteen years before striking out on his own. During this time he wrestled with some very human frailties—including boredom, laziness, and his libido—all of which he saw as temptations sent by the devil (Figure 7.1).

The Devil whispered foul thoughts, but Antony rebuffed them with his prayers; the Devil titillated him, but Antony, as though he were blushing, fortified his body through faith and

Figure 7.1. Saint Antony Beaten by the Devils. Painting by Stefano di Giovanni (1392–1450) now in the Siena Pinacoteca. Wikimedia Commons.

fasting. But the Devil stood his ground, the wretch, and now dared to take on the form of a woman at night and imitated all of a woman's ways, solely for the purpose of deceiving Antony.[7]

To strengthen his resolve, Antony enclosed himself in an ancient tomb, such places being notorious for the terrors they held within. This was the experience that transformed him from a follower into a pioneer. As Athanasius reports, it was here that the saint received divine confirmation that he had passed a test:

> The Lord did not forget Antony's struggle at that time, but came to help. Looking up, Antony saw the roof appear to open and a beam of light descend on him. Suddenly the demons vanished and the pain in his body immediately ceased and his dwelling was once again whole. Antony perceived the Lord's help, and when he took a deep breath and realized that he had been relieved of his suffering, he entreated the vision that had appeared to him: "Where are you? Why did you not appear at the beginning so you could stop my sufferings?" And a voice came to him: "Antony, I was here, but I wanted to see your struggle. And now, since you persevered and were not defeated, I will be a helper to you always and I will make you famous everywhere." When Antony heard these things he stood and prayed, and he became so strong that he felt in his body more strength than he had had before.[8]

Antony did not invent the solitary life. There had always been individuals, and even groups (like the Essenes who surfaced with the Dead Sea Scrolls), who renounced settled life for one reason or another. Other Christians, like the hermit who was Antony's first teacher, had already sought to live a more spiritual life in this way. But this hermit, with whom Antony stayed for so many years, continued to live near settlements where pious followers could always check up on him. Now Antony struck off on his own, moving away from the vicinity of villages to find seclusion deeper in the desert. Making a cell for himself in an abandoned Roman fort, he wrestled with demons in the shape of vipers and wild animals for the next twenty years. With this experience, Antony grew stronger in mind and body, "being neither fat from lack of exercise nor weakened from fasting and fighting with demons" (*Life of Antony* 14.3), and his fame began to attract disciples and pilgrims.

Diocletian's persecution was now underway, and Antony went to Alexandria to strengthen the resolve of Christians in the Egyptian capital. Afterward, seeking a more isolated site, he was led by nomadic traders to a high mountain that was a three-day walk from Alexandria, between the Nile and the Red Sea. It had a cave to which he could retire to maintain his ascetic regimen and an oasis nearby that provided an abundant supply of fresh water. Here is where Antony spent the remaining half century of his life, counseling his disciples, providing miraculous cures, and adjudicating disputes for the steady stream of visitors to the site. The monastery he founded still exists in Egypt's eastern desert, about 171 miles from Cairo on the modern highway.[9]

The growing number of Antony's disciples is the phenomenon that prompted Athanasius's pregnant line: "And so monastic dwellings [*monastêria*] came into being in the mountains and the desert was made a city by monks."[10] The *Life of Antony* in which this sentence occurs was written within a few years of the saint's death in 356. It was a biography of a new sort, now called hagiography, or "saint's life." Not overly long ago, this body of literature was barely tolerated by historians, and then only for the occasional factual "kernel" it contained. Scholars now routinely find these works to be gold mines of social and cultural information.[11] Because the authors of such lives always proclaimed themselves not up to the task and called on the saints who were their subjects for help, hagiographies themselves became a miracle of sorts. As one learned observer has put it, "A hagiographer who protests his inability to do justice to the saint's accomplishments in his writing and prays to the saint to inspire him and to guide his pen, effectively presents his own text as a miracle brought forth through the intercession of the saint."[12]

Saints' lives are written with the intentional design of holding up the saint as a model.[13] In Antony's case, it is clear that Bishop Athanasius (who also became a saint), used the *Life* as well to put forward his own agenda, portraying his ideal monk as someone who was unfailingly orthodox, properly respectful of bishops, and functionally illiterate—positions that have all been undermined by other evidence.[14] But his primary aim was to spread the word about this new form of Christian devotion, and in this he succeeded in ways unimaginable before the printing press and mass circulation.

The *Life of Antony* hit the Mediterranean world like a tsunami. St. Augustine has left a vivid account of the way he learned of Antony's exploits while he was teaching rhetoric in Milan, between 384 and 386, a time when he was wrestling with his own decision to convert. While he stood "amazed" and "in awe," his friend, the courtier Ponticianus, told of two friends who found the book in a communal dwelling in the far northern capital of Trier, and how, as they "began to read, wonder at it, and to be inflamed with it," both immediately decided to abandon their imperial careers and remain with that small band of monks. Filled with self-loathing, Augustine wrote, "the more ardently I loved those two whose wholesome purposes I heard tell of . . . so much the more detestably did I hate myself in comparison of them."[15]

What accounts for this extraordinary popularity and influence? To Athanasius, Antony's fame was proof of God's love for his servant. More prosaically, it can also be seen as the result of two strong currents that converged in a uniquely powerful way in the fourth century.

MARTYRS AND THINKERS

It did not take long for Christian authors to connect the monastic movement with a uniquely Christian figure. From the beginning of their religion—as Christians told their history to themselves—they were called upon to demonstrate their commitment by standing fast in the face of scorn and hatred. Jesus himself had warned his disciples that they would face persecution (e.g., Luke 21:12), and over the next several centuries those who did not flinch in the face of local populations or government officials who demanded that they renounce their belief came to hold a hallowed position in the Christian imagination.

These were the martyrs, a word derived from the Greek legal tradition in which a *martūs* was a witness. By their willingness to accept torture and death rather than abandon their faith, Christian martyrs testified to their belief in the truth of Jesus's own death and resurrection. Martyrs (Figure 7.2) were the exemplary Christians. A lot of the stories about them were heavily embroidered, and others completely fabricated. But some were not, and in any case their impact on the Christian imagination, and Christian sense of identity, cannot be overestimated.[16]

In the centuries prior to Constantine, Christians had been taught to revere the memory of brethren who chose to suffer torture and death at the hands of Roman authorities rather than deny their faith. The ordeal of these witnesses, or *martyrs*, came to be recounted annually on their feast days, and their remains were venerated for the contact they provided to divine energy.

Martyrs and, even more, accounts of their endurance served as proof for more everyday Christians that God would support and protect them. In this sense, martyr stories inverted the pagan narrative, which depicted the suffering and death of these individuals as crushing defeats and proof that their god was useless.

Figure 7.2. Santa Julitta, believed to have been martyred in Diocletian's Great Persecution, was hammered with nails, tossed into a cauldron of burning pitch, and finally dismembered and decapitated. She is said especially to hear prayers from students during final examinations. Detail of twelfth-century fresco in the National Art Museum, Catalonia. Wikimedia Commons.

This is exactly what the philosopher Celsus said in the second century in his attempt to convince Christians of the error of their ways (see chapter 4). Instead, their resistance to the point of death came to be depicted as the ultimate sacrifice; the "loser" became the winner who thwarted the "victor's" plan to make him or her recant.[17]

Martyr tales—especially the more lurid ones that started to be told during this century—had an unintended consequence as well: they maintained a Christian "persecution complex" long after the physical realities that might have justified such feelings ceased to exist. The persistence of this sense of persecution by pagans (persecution by other Christians is another matter) is a prime reason that some modern authors have been eager to discount martyr tales, even to the point of questioning whether any actually occurred. The martyr tradition encouraged Christians from the fourth century onward to see themselves as victims, and as the stories got ever more fanciful, they became a means to justify Christian mistreatment of others.

It used to be commonplace to connect the rise of monasticism with a decline in opportunities for martyrdom following Constantine's conversion. Other factors, ranging from a reaction against prevailing social norms to a desire for spiritual growth and a wish to inoculate oneself against demons, now seem far more important. But the appeal of ascetics like Antony was also rooted in an age-old distinction ancient philosophy made between the physical and spiritual components of human nature, especially in the version of this philosophy that began to flourish in late antiquity.

That is the second development that helps us understand the impact of Athanasius's *Life of Antony*. Plato, in his *Republic*, had created the ideal of the "philosopher-king," a person who was indifferent to the appeal of material comforts and who instead focused on those abstract principles that constituted the only true reality.[18] There were obvious parallels between this figure and Antony: both had learned through a long and arduous training to be indifferent to physical needs and material comforts, and both focused on eternal priorities. So in this sense it comes as no surprise that Christians revered Antony for the mastery he had achieved over the needs of his body, for this allowed him to concentrate on the eternal truths of the Christian message.

There was, of course, one important difference. Plato's philosopher-kings found their way to truth through the exercise of reason, whereas ascetics like Antony gained strength and knowledge by following truth that had already been revealed in scripture and need not—indeed, dare not—be questioned. But by late antiquity this difference had narrowed considerably. Even philosophers now sought a goal of mystical union with the One and saw the body as an impediment to that goal. In the third century, the philosopher Plotinus (204–270) reoriented Platonic philosophy to focus on this spiritual union, a change that is now labeled Neoplatonism.

Plotinus's priorities were summed up by his famous refusal to sit for a portrait because it would only capture the least significant part of him. As his student Porphyry put it, Plotinus "seemed ashamed of being in the body."[19] Other philosophers who sought mystical union with the divine began to stress ritual actions and the use of secret labels. Both Christian and pagan thinkers gave pride of place to those who came to wisdom through a natural understanding rather than book learning.[20]

In the light of this shift in classical philosophy, Antony's teaching no longer sounds so strange. Although the monastic movement is often characterized as an effort to deny all physical needs, its aim actually was to free the soul by limiting, not denying, the needs of the body. According to Athanasius, "Antony used to say, 'The mind of the soul is strong when the pleasures of the body are weak,'" and also taught that

> it is necessary to give all one's time to the soul rather than to the body, but to concede a little time to the body for its necessities; all the rest of the time, however, one ought to devote to the soul and to what is profitable for it, so it will not be dragged down by bodily pleasures but so the body will instead be made a servant by the soul.[21]

Antony's teaching shows that Christian ascetics, like the philosophers, taught that the body had a role to play, but it needed to be trained to obey rather than to rule.

Christian ascetics and Neoplatonic philosophers shared one trait in particular that distinguished them from their classical predecessors. In the *Republic*, Plato's philosopher-king did not become a "holy man," a *theios anēr*. But in late antiquity pagan philosophers and Christian ascetics like Antony who had achieved complete control over their physical needs were perceived as having achieved a spiritual and an intellectual mastery that at times allowed them to perform miracles. The type of miracle differed: where Christian holy men performed miraculous cures and drove out demons, their pagan counterparts asserted a control over natural phenomena, averting floods and earthquakes through prayer or prescience. And an even more important difference: whereas Christian holy men performed their miracles in public, often before large crowds, pagan holy men preferred to demonstrate their powers behind closed doors.[22] And, unlike their pagan counterparts, Christian holy men were careful not to take personal credit for the miracles they performed. "It is not right for someone to boast that he casts out demons or to be proud about effecting healings," Antony warned. "For the doing of miracles is not our work but the Lord's."[23]

But the greatest difference of all is that Christian holy men were not dependent solely on the abstract principles of classical philosophy. Through self-mortification, the desert saint achieved the spiritual power of the martyr, and his unfettered soul in turn gave him the power to intercede with God for present human concerns. This is what attracted record numbers to the holy man's dwelling, for in him they found cures for physical and mental ailments.

Still, what gave ascetics like Antony such appeal is not just that they showed the endurance of martyrs but that—at least in the literary record created on their behalf—they fused both traditions. The combination helps explain why this new genre—hagiography, or the recording of saints' lives—had such an explosive impact. These two strands came together in Athanasius's *Life of Antony*.[24] By concentrating on the training by which the saint conditioned his body to be subject to his spiritual being, the *Life* provided a do-it-yourself manual for spiritual self-fashioning that quickly spread to the farthest reaches of empire.

The emergence of Christian holy men in this century was as novel a phenomenon as a Christian emperor, but in their personal charisma and in their renunciation of wealth and status they symbolized a far more revolutionary force. In Eusebius of Caesarea's depiction, as we saw in chapter 3, Constantine held a privileged position in the cosmic struggle between the forces of good and evil: he was the earthly counterpart of the Common Universal Savior, warring against the mortal allies of the demons. But in the *Life*, Antony develops far greater powers that allowed him to fight the demons himself, something no emperor was ever able to do.[25]

No one brought out the revolutionary implications of the monk's social agenda more clearly or forcefully than John Chrysostom, the fiery preacher who later became bishop of Constantinople. Around the same time that Augustine was first learning about the monastic movement, Chrysostom, then still a priest in Antioch, penned one of the most subversive texts of the century. His *Comparison Between a King and a Monk* completely inverted standard thinking about monarchy. Where centuries of predecessors had defined and refined the virtues of the "good king," Chrysostom depicted the monarch as someone who was inherently corrupt and, even if a philosopher, still bound to commit injustice. Instead, Chrysostom blithely transferred the king's traditional virtues to the lowly monk: "the king and the monk rule in ways such that it is fairer to call the monk a king than the one who wears a shining, purple robe and crown and sits upon a gold throne."[26]

The growth of this alternative authority is an important part of the story of Christian success.

THE SPREAD OF MONASTICISM

The monastic tradition may have spread from Egypt, as Athanasius claimed, but it took on distinct regional differences. In Egypt itself, a communal form of monasticism developed by Antony's younger contemporary, Pachomius (c. 292–348), soon overtook Antony's more individualistic system and became the model for others, both East and West.[27]

Jerusalem, as might be expected, became a magnet for pilgrims and aspiring monastics from all over the empire, including some of the Roman nobility's most prestigious (and wealthiest) members. Melania the Elder (325–410), who hailed from a consular family, led a wave of what one scholar has called "ascetic tourism," visiting the famous Egyptian monks before founding her own convent in Jerusalem and a monastery on the Mount of Olives. Despite her own devotion to ascetic withdrawal, she knew how to pull rank when necessary. The monk Palladius (c. 363–c. 425), who later became bishop of Helenopolis (the former Drepanum in Asia Minor, possibly Saint Helena's birthplace), tells us of Melania's reaction when an unscrupulous governor threw her in jail and tried to blackmail her:

> "I am the daughter of So-and-so and the wife of So-and-so," she said to him, "but I am also the servant of Christ. Do not despise me for my lowly appearance for I am able to make myself look grand, if I wish. For this reason you cannot frighten me or take anything away from me. I made this declaration to you, in order that you might not incur charges as the result of your ignorance; for one must display a hawk-like pride in the presence of dull-witted people."

The governor, Palladius reports, "then grasped the situation and apologized."[28]

Melania's equally famous granddaughter, Melania the Younger (383–439), also adopted the monastic life in Jerusalem, but remained on a first-name basis with the imperial family in Constantinople. Both Melanias, and the scholars they supported (including St. Jerome and Rufinus of Aquileia), lent to the monastics in the

Holy Land an air of fashionable cosmopolitanism very different from the isolation that characterized Egyptian monasticism.[29]

In the wastelands of Roman Syria, the phenomenon took a more flamboyant turn, generating a breed of ascetic superstars known as "pillar saints" for their determination to live out their lives on a small platform atop columns that could reach fifty feet and more into the sky. This particular form of ascetic behavior may have its roots in a reverence for heights that seems to have been traditional in the region, but an account of the first and greatest of these pillar saints, Simeon Stylites (c. 388–459), attributes it to Simeon's need to put some distance between himself and the increasingly large crowds drawn to him by his reputation for asceticism: as Antony had his hilltop cave, so Simeon had his pillar, which thereafter served to distinguish him and others who followed his example, by adding the designation "Stylites" ("pillar dweller") to his name.[30]

In the late Roman Empire their actions were considered spectacular feats of renunciation that in turn empowered the more famous of them to work miracles. The result was large followings and vast influence. Standing above their supplicants, visibly removed from the cares of this world, pillar saints seemed both physically and spiritually to be mediators between this world and the heavenly realm.[31] But they are even more difficult for us to understand than Egypt's holy men. How are we to make sense of such behavior?

DEMON ECONOMICS

Monks were not universally admired. The great fourth-century orator Libanius dismissed them as "a black-robed tribe" who "eat more than elephants" and were distinguished only "by the quantities of drink they consume." The pagan historian Eunapius went even further, calling them "men in appearance" who "led the lives of swine." During Theodosius's reign, "every man who wore a black robe and consented to behave in unseemly fashion in public, possessed the power of a tyrant." He was echoed by the poet Rutilius Namantianus, who asked,

Who to shirk pain would choose a life of pain?
What madness of a brain diseased so fond
As, fearing evil, to refuse all good.[32]

These contemporary attacks long set the tone for modern scholars, especially classicists (medievalists have tended to be more charitable), to whom monks, especially the pillar saints, have long been an object of derision, going all the way back to Edward Gibbon's magisterial *Decline and Fall of the Roman Empire*, the first volume of which appeared in 1776. Some of the funniest footnotes in that work play on the commitment of Christian men and women to sexual abstinence. One must suffice: "Jerome, in his Legend of Paul the Hermit, tells a strange story of a young man who was chained naked on a bed of flowers, and assaulted by a beautiful and wanton courtezan. He quelled the rising temptation by biting off his tongue."[33]

Mocking these Christian preoccupations has been a popular scholarly sport for so long that it is easy to misjudge the significance of the ascetic movement. Of all people, economists have shown how to avoid this mistake. That might seem odd, since one of the most powerful arguments for the negative effect of the monastic movement is an economic one: it drained the empire of much-needed wealth and manpower at a time when both were in critically short supply.[34] But other economic concepts have proved more fruitful. The concept of the market, for instance, with its attention to supply and demand, has revolutionized the study of early Christianity, leading scholars to see it as one of many forces competing in a religious marketplace, rather than as the sole vehicle for change.[35]

Even more has been accomplished by the relatively young field of "religious economics," which applies economic analysis to the field of religion. The language can be odd, and even a little off-putting (the "product" Christians produce is "afterlife consumption"), but it has the great advantage of dispensing with all of the baggage that comes with the more normal use of theological language and categories. It is a way to avoid the anachronistic application of modern thinking about resources to the situation in late antiquity.[36] Instead of dismissing the behavior of Christian holy men as weird or irrational, for instance, religious economists would ask what product these individuals offered and what kind of market they supplied.

The answer is fairly obvious. In the religious economy of the day, demons were very real, a far greater menace than ordinary enemies. Antony characterized them as "terrible and cunning."[37] In this environment, asceticism had both a practical and a moral dimension. "Without a doubt," Antony taught, "demons are afraid of ascetic practices."[38] Holy men who had shed those physical desires that kept humans enslaved to these invisible enemies thus met a real need. One aim of the *Life of Antony* was to demonstrate to contemporaries the immense power that could be channeled through a person who denied the grip of material possessions. In this economy, the power over demons that holy men offered was indeed a precious commodity.[39]

MIRACLE DISCOURSE

It was not long before lives of saints focused more on miracle than on training. In the western empire the *Life of St. Martin* soon supplemented the *Life of Antony*. Martin was the soldier-saint famous for earning a vision of Christ by sharing his only cloak with a beggar, in conformity with Jesus's admonition, "As you did to one of the least of these, you did to me" (Matt. 25:40). Written after the saint's death in 397 by his disciple Sulpicius Severus (c. 363–c. 425), the *Life*, as well as a *Dialogue* on Martin's virtues that he wrote somewhat later, focuses almost entirely on the saint's miracles (he seems to have had a particular gift for bringing the dead back to life and immobilizing opponents).[40] Only one chapter of the *Life* is given over to anything resembling instruction (chapter 22, a sermon on repentance).

The contrast with the *Life of Antony* could not be more pronounced. Athanasius has much to say about the saint's powers of discernment and combat with demons, but surprisingly little space is given to examples of the kind of miraculous cures that brought crowds of suppliants to his doorstep. Two instances stand out. In one, Antony was beset by a military officer whose daughter "was troubled by a demon." Unwilling to come out of his refuge, Antony replied,

> "Man, why do you cry out to me? I am a man, just like you. If you believe in Christ, whom I serve, go and pray to God, according to your faith, and what you seek will come to be." Immediately the man believed and called on Christ and went away, and his daughter was cleansed of her demon. (*Life of Antony* 48)

Demon expulsion was the trademark of a holy man, but it usually required some sort of personal contact between the saint and the demon. In this case, Athanasius implied that Antony's powers were so great that, like Jesus when he cured a centurion's servant (Matt. 8:5-13, Luke 7:1-10), Antony could perform miracles at a distance. At the same time, the anecdote showed his hero's humility.

The second example involved a far less ordinary kind of miracle. It occurred while Antony was travelling with some monks through an arid and scorching desert and the group ran out of water:

> They were all in danger of dying, for they had gone around the whole area without finding any water. Finally, unable to walk, they lay prostrate on the ground. . . . But when the old man saw that all of them were in danger of dying, he became very sad and groaned aloud; going off a little way from them, he knelt down, raised his hands, and prayed. Immediately the Lord caused water to bubble out from the spot where he had stopped to pray. So all of them had a drink and their spirits were restored.

This was no run-of-the-mill miracle. It was one that illustrated the ease with which the saint was able to unleash supernatural support, and that unavoidably called to mind a similar miracle Moses was able to perform for the Israelites.[41]

Far more of the *Life of Antony* is given over to discourse. About a fourth of the work—twenty-seven of its ninety-four chapters (*Life of Antony* 16–43)—is taken up by a long discourse in which Antony advises his disciples on the ascetic life. Part pep talk and part user's manual, the bulk of this sermon-lecture is given over to the effort to conquer these "terrible and cunning enemies." There is "a great crowd of them in the air around us" (21.4); they can pass through closed doors (22.28), deceive people with false omens (31), and appear to prophesy when they are simply using their flying speed to bring word of what has already happened (31–33). The world Antony describes is very different from the theological pursuits that preoccupied Christian thinkers during this century.[42]

Antony provides a vivid description of the ways demons behave, including some that hardly seem so terrifying. For instance, they "talk and create uproars and play-act and stir up trouble ... [and] make obnoxious noises and clap their hands and laugh maniacally" (*Life of Antony* 26.6). Antony at this point seems to be describing behavior at the theater, a genuine school for scandal as far as the most outspoken Christian leaders, such as John Chrysostom, were concerned.[43] His point is that demons act in this way out of jealousy: they want to lead Christians astray and hinder the ascent of their souls to heaven, since this is a goal they themselves can never reach (*Life of Antony* 22).

This is the reason that ascetic discipline is so important, Antony explains. For him, as for St. Augustine in later years, the paradigmatic example is Job of the Hebrew Bible, who refuses to abandon his faith in God despite losing all his earthly possessions and suffering every imaginable illness. In the received version of the story, Job suffered so that God could prove to the Devil that there was no connection between Job's piety and his material possessions. Therefore, to Antony, the lesson to draw from Job's suffering is not that the Devil is so powerful but that even the Prince of Evil could not have done anything to Job without God's consent. "We ought to fear God alone," he concludes, "and hold the demons in contempt." He then offers a catalogue of ascetic virtues:

> For a great weapon against them is an upright life and faith in God. Without a doubt, demons are afraid of ascetic practices: fasting, keeping vigils, prayers, gentleness, tranquility, poverty, moderation, humility, love of the poor, almsgiving, the absence of anger and, above all, devotion to Christ.[44]

These virtues, especially tranquility and moderation, correspond to those traditionally taught by the philosophers, but the way they are mingled with goals of poverty and almsgiving reflect a new Christian emphasis on charity. Monasteries as a result served as hospices for travelers and centers of care for the poor.[45]

Another long section of the *Life* illustrates the impact of this desert miracle on the discourse of the age. In chapters 72 through 79, Antony engages in debate with philosophers and other pagan intellectuals who, it seems, came to test their wits against the desert sage. Antony, of course, always wins these confrontations, but the arguments he used point to a distinct shift in the type of evidence being offered—and (seemingly) accepted. In one encounter, Antony contrasts the revealed knowledge on which Christian truth was based with the logic-chopping methods of the Greeks:

> And that our faith works, look now: we depend on our faith in Christ while you wage war with sophistries; and while your idols and delusionary practices have got you nowhere, our faith is spreading everywhere. You people, with all your syllogisms and sophistries, are not persuading us to convert from Christianity to paganism; we, on the other hand, teaching faith in Christ, are stripping you of your superstitions, with everyone recognizing that Christ is God and the Son of God. . . . Wherever one sees the sign of the cross, magic loses its power and sorcery has no effect. . . . What is more, your religion, celebrated and protected on all sides, is falling into ruin, whereas the faith and teaching of Christ, ridiculed by you and often persecuted by emperors, has filled the whole world![46]

Shamed, the philosophers retreat with their tails between their legs. After confessing that they found the illiterate Antony to be "very wise," Athanasius writes, "They were amazed and went away, for they saw that even demons were afraid of Antony."[47]

It is important to bear in mind that this exchange occurs in a very partisan tract, written by a Christian with a specific message to deliver. So we cannot be sure that the philosophers in question traveled to Antony for any other reason than to satisfy their own curiosity, or that, satisfied with what they found, they concluded the meeting with a polite expression of respect that Antony's followers understood as an admission of defeat. But the intrusion of demons into the argument highlights the way the emergence of the Christian holy man fostered the spread of the language of miracles. Augustine's vivid picture of the way he learned of Antony as he wrestled with making his own commitment to Christianity is larded with this vocabulary. "We were amazed" (*stupebamus*) to learn of Antony's deeds, he recalls; "we marveled" (*mirabamur*) at them. When Ponticianus's companion read the *Life* it filled him with "wonder and a burning desire" (*et mirari et accendi*).[48]

This vocabulary reflects a change that was taking place in elite discourse, one that gave pride of place to miracles. Increasingly, the potency of one's argument depended on the potency of one's deity. Like the language of "postmodernism" today, in the fourth century the language of miracles began to bleed over into other forms of discourse.

Chapter 8

Miracles on Trial

As the fourth century drew to a close, Ambrose of Milan was not the only one spinning stories about Constantine's mother, Helena. She is also featured in the *Acts of Pope St. Silvester* that started to take shape around this time.[1] But here she plays a very different role. Instead of discovering the True Cross, she discovers Judaism. And she wants her son, the emperor, to convert with her. Constantine, on the other hand, has grown rather fond of the bishop of Rome, Pope Silvester (bp. 314–335), who cured him of leprosy. So he decides to settle the issue in the way Greeks and Romans loved best, with a debate. In what might well be the original "a priest and a rabbi" story, Silvester and the rabbis brought by Helena engage in a spirited but inconclusive debate over the meaning of passages in the Hebrew Bible. Finally, the chief rabbi orders a bull to be led into the assembly and then kills it simply by whispering in its ear the secret name of Jehovah. Convinced of the Jewish God's power, everyone is on the verge of converting until Pope Silvester, in turn, resurrects the bull in the name of Christ (Figure 8.1).[2]

The most intriguing aspect of this story is that the question was settled not by sober argument or oratorical mastery, but by a miracle. Skill at debate was the centerpiece of an elite Roman's education, and the ultimate display of this skill was putting forth

Figure 8.1. Silvester and the Rabbis. A scene from the thirteenth-century frescos of the legend of S. Silvester, in the Chapel of St. Silvester in the Church of the Quattro Coronati, Rome. The panel is damaged, but the chief rabbi can be seen on the right, killing a bull with the secret name of Jehovah. Helena, identifiable by her imperial regalia, stands behind him, while Constantine sits in the center with one of his judges. To the far left, just enough of the panel remains to make out Silvester's hand as he resurrects the bull in the name of Christ. Photo by Nelson Richards.

a brilliant case in just such a situation. Plato set a standard of sorts with the moving and insightful speech he put in Socrates's mouth after the philosopher's conviction on charges of impiety in 399 BCE, and a sample of dazzling footwork from the empire survives in a speech that the second-century author Apuleius gave in response to charges that he practiced sorcery.[3] One reason elites had such trouble accepting Christianity in its early years was precisely that Jesus stood, in their eyes, tongue-tied when brought before the Sanhedrin after his arrest. Two hundred years later, Origen of Alexandria (c. 184–c. 254), the most finely tuned mind of Christianity's early centuries, began his response to an attack by the philosopher Celsus with an explanation of why Jesus held his tongue at that moment (because actions speak louder than words).[4]

Silvester's use of a miracle to prove his case was not entirely new: Christian stories had long relied on miracles as proof, and Silvester's miracle shows the particular influence of the apocryphal *Acts of Peter*, which probably date to the late second century.[5] Nor does Silvester's story mean that traditional methods of debate were dead. On the contrary, the theology wars in this century—even though they are being ignored in this book—sharpened the thinking, as well as the rhetoric, of all sides in the debate.[6] What is more novel is the way the *Acts of Silvester* began with a traditional debate before resorting to a miracle as the clincher. Where debate (if that is the right word) between Simon and Peter barely lasts a paragraph in the *Acts of Peter*, the debate between Silvester and the rabbis here extends for some forty pages, making the need for a miracle to resolve the issue all the more striking.

The Silvester story is fiction. If nothing else, it serves as a reminder of the outsized role Jews continued to play in the Christian imagination. But it also serves as a marker for an important change taking place in the nature of public discourse. We have already seen in chapter 2 how the promise of divine intervention had entered debate at the highest levels in the promises (and threats) of Ambrose of Milan. This chapter and the next will explore the way proof of divine support became a key test of the superiority of one religious argument over another.

Christian assaults on the bastions of traditional religion triggered much of this debate. In the aftermath of an unprecedented rampage of temple destruction (including the famous Temple of Zeus at Apamea in Syria) in 385 led by one of Theodosius's lieutenants, the famous pagan orator Libanius of Antioch composed a speech "In Defense of the Temples" (*pro templis*) in which he excoriated Christian use of brute force. "Why these frantic attacks on the temples?" he asked the emperor,

> what advantage have they [Christians] won when adherence to their doctrine is a matter of words and the reality is absent? Persuasion is required in such matters, not constraint. If persuasion fails and constraint is employed, nothing has been accomplished, though you think it has.[7]

Similarly, as part of a religious dispute that will get more attention later in this chapter, the pagan senator Symmachus in the West invoked the goddess Roma to support his plea for toleration with a phrase that has become a watchword for the defense of religious diversity: "Not by one path alone can so great a mystery [as the nature of God] be approached" (*Uno itinere non potest perveniri ad tam grande secretum*).[8] Earlier, the philosopher-politician Themistius declared that to compel belief "is to deprive man of a power which has been granted to him by God." This is so, he said, because God himself "has made it a common attribute of the nature of men that they should be duly disposed to piety, but has made the mode of their worship depend on the will of each."[9]

These, and other like phrases, traditionally have served as proof of paganism's inherent tolerance, as opposed to the intolerant superstition that Christianity was now bringing into the world. The irony in this case is that these pagan speakers were parroting positions that had earlier been put forward by Christians themselves. Libanius, for one, was quite open about the source of his argument: "It is said that in their [the Christians'] very own rules it does not appear, but that persuasion meets with approval and compulsion is deplored. Then why these frantic attacks on the temples, if you cannot persuade and must needs resort to force? In this way you would obviously be breaking your own rules."[10]

In basing his plea for tolerance on Christian sources, Libanius was not trying to curry favor with Theodosius. To the contrary, he was employing a time-honored tactic of seeking to gain an advantage by throwing Theodosius's own principles in his face, in effect telling him he was being un-Christian. For good measure, Libanius threw in some common elite values as well—the importance of knowing one's place and acting at all times with measured reason. "And if they [Christians] prate to me of the teachings of the scriptures that they profess to obey," he thundered, "I will counter them with the despicable acts they have committed. . . . In estate after estate shrine after shrine has been wiped out by their insolence, violence, greed and deliberate lack of self-control."[11]

There is a further irony. The assertive attitude of Libanius, Themistius, Symmachus, and others once was taken as proof of a "pagan revival." More recent scholarship has put a damper on such thinking, but to the extent that it occurred, this newly assertive posture was prompted by one of the most unlikely figures ever to wear the imperial purple.[12]

JULIAN "THE APOSTATE"

In November of 361, Constantine's nephew Julian (Figure 8.2) began a brief but dramatic reign that has mesmerized scholars ever since. Raised as a Christian, Julian, once he became emperor upon the death of his cousin, Constantius II in 361, publicly renounced his faith (he said he had done so privately much earlier) and devoted himself to reviving the old gods. There is no sure reason why Julian turned away from Christianity, but it is a fair bet that the slaughter of his family in the aftermath of Constantine's death in 337, a bloodbath from which only he and his older half-brother, Gallus, escaped,

Figure 8.2. Electrotype of a coin the emperor Julian, made from a wax impression. The reverse shows a Roman soldier holding a victory trophy and taking a warrior captive, with the legend VIRTUS EXERCITUS ("Strength of the Army"). Wikimedia Commons.

had something to do with it. Julian blamed Constantius for the tragedy, but there appears to be plenty of blame to go around.[13] On the plus side of the ledger, it was Constantius who spirited Julian and his brother out of the capital, kept them safely away from court intrigues, and in 355 raised Julian to the purple, making him Caesar (the title of a junior emperor). Prior to this time, Julian had devoted himself to his studies; he was what one younger scholar has described as "a likeable but socially awkward genius with a tin ear for the niceties."[14] If fate had not intervened, he might well have become an enthusiastic, if sometimes waspish, professor in a provincial university.

But fate, and the iron law of ruling the late Roman Empire, did intervene. By late antiquity, it had become clear that the size of the empire required at least two people wearing the purple—one in each half of the empire—if for no other reason than to hold potential usurpers in check. Constantius II's two brothers initially ruled in the West, but by 350 they were both dead. Forced westward to deal with the crisis in those parts, Constantius made Julian's brother Caesar and sent him to the eastern capital of Antioch. But Gallus was both incompetent and insubordinate, a fatal combination; in 354, Constantius had him put to death. Now it was the East that demanded Constantius's attention, and that is what led to Julian's elevation in 355.

Prior to that year, Julian's chief distinction was his devotion to academic studies, which he pursued in Constantinople, Nicomedia, Pergamum, and, for a few weeks before his summons to the purple, Athens. Constantius's likely impression of his cousin at that time was of an overeducated and somewhat arty dilettante. But he needed someone safe to wear the purple in the West, so he sent Julian to Gaul, no doubt simply to show the colors while others did the heavy lifting. But Julian's studies had included Caesar's Commentaries, and he evidently learned from them—like Caesar in Gaul, Julian slept on the same hard ground as his troops, ate the same food, and won battles. In 357, he overrode the objections of the minders Constantius had sent with him and at Argentoratum (the modern Strasbourg) led an attack against a substantially larger army of Alamanni, a Germanic tribe that he mauled so thoroughly that he was able to successfully reassert Roman primacy in that region. As an administrator, Julian remitted taxes owed by the hard-pressed provincials, handled judicial cases even-handedly, and quarreled incessantly with Constantius's officials.

With the backing of an army thoroughly devoted to him, in 359, Julian asked Constantius to elevate him to the supreme rank of Augustus; when his cousin refused, he accepted the title from his soldiers in 360 and thereby threw the empire once more into chaos. With the bane of civil war looming, Constantius had the decency to name Julian as his legitimate successor before dying late in 361.

Even as emperor, Julian was eager to display his erudition. He has left behind more writing, in variety and sheer amount, than any other Roman emperor. In these works he is intensely self-reflective, if not self-absorbed. Consequently, he has left us a fairly good picture of his plans and intentions, sometimes revealing more than he might have intended.[15] His surviving writings include a satirical banquet in the great beyond, where each of his predecessors comes under the cynical gaze of the satyr Silenus—the god Dionysus's constantly drunk companion—who maintains a running commentary as each emperor is introduced. The only one to come off at all well is Marcus Aurelius, the philosopher-king of the second century after whom Julian patterned himself. Constantine comes in for withering scorn. When each emperor is allowed to choose a deity with whom to be associated, Constantine immediately runs to Luxury, who "received him tenderly and embraced him, then after dressing him in raiment of many colours and otherwise making him beautiful, she led him away to Prodigality."

But at this point, Julian was only getting started. Next, he reports, Constantine found yet another god,

> Jesus, who had taken up his abode with her and cried aloud to all comers: "He that is a seducer, he that is a murderer, he that is sacrilegious and infamous, let him approach without fear! For with this water will I wash him and will straightway make him clean. And though he should be guilty of those same sins a second time, let him but smite his breast and beat his head and I will make him clean again." To him Constantine came gladly, when he had conducted his sons forth from the assembly of the gods. But the avenging deities none the less punished both him and them for their impiety . . . until Zeus granted them a respite for the sake of [his ancestors] Claudius and Constantius.[16]

In a later work, *Against the Galilaeans*, Julian was even more bitter. His use of the term "Galilaeans" for Christians testifies to the depth of his scorn for his former religion, which he refused to dignify with the name of "Christian," presumably because that implied some divine nature was involved. By contrast, "Galilaeans" was a term that localized the religion, implicitly denying its claims to universal

MIRACLES ON TRIAL

truth. Like our "pagans," it was derogatory; in modern parlance it would translate to something like "Rednecks." (He also called them "atheists," because they denied the gods.)

Against the Galilaeans survives only in the extensive quotes used by Christians in later decades, but that is enough to show how Julian deployed his intimate knowledge of Christian teaching to devastating effect. He repeatedly cites chapter and verse of scripture to attack the credentials of the Mosaic God, while at the same time using those writings to undermine Christian claims that they confirm Jesus's divinity. "For if it is God's will that none other should be worshipped," he asks in a typical broadside, "why do you worship this spurious son of his whom he has never yet recognised or considered as his own?"[17] Julian particularly mocks the reverence Christians showed to martyrs (or, as he called them, "corpses newly dead"), building for them "tombs and sepulchres" despite Jesus's own admonitions:

> But you have gone so far in iniquity that you think you need not listen even to the words of Jesus of Nazareth on this matter. Listen then to what he says about sepulchres: "Woe unto you, scribes and Pharisees, hypocrites! for ye are like unto whited sepulchres; outward the tomb appears beautiful, but within it is full of dead men's bones, and of all uncleanness" [Matt 23:27]. If, then, Jesus said that sepulchres are full of uncleanness, how can you invoke God at them?[18]

Churches in Julian's time were still frequently known as *martyria* because of their connection to martyr sites and relics.[19] Considering the burst in church building during the reign of Constantine, which included the magnificent edifice over Christ's tomb that was completed little more than a decade earlier, Julian's words would have reverberated more strongly than they might seem today.

Such comments thrilled the *philosophes* of the eighteenth-century Enlightenment, who anointed Julian as one of their own in the contest of reason against superstition, a harbinger of their fight for intellectual freedom. His attacks on Christian belief, and his particularly biting taunts for the way Christians were now resorting to coercion and suppression (the only thing, he wrote, that Christians seem to have learned from Hebrew scripture),[20] are indeed modern sounding, but except for their detailed knowledge of scripture they only echo what philosophers—and in the case of coercion, other Christians—had been saying for the previous two centuries.

In other ways, Julian was very much a child of his age, preoccupied by the religious concerns of late Roman philosophy and so devoted to the revival of animal sacrifice that even the contemporary historian Ammianus Marcellinus, who made no effort to disguise his admiration for Julian, took exception to the way the emperor "drenched the altars with the blood of an excessive number of victims, sometimes offering up a hundred oxen at once, with countless flocks of various other animals," and encouraged all kinds of charlatans and hucksters "who professed a knowledge of divination."[21]

Moreover, when Julian was not writing polemics he could be keenly appreciative of the strengths of his former religion. "Why do we not observe," he asked a certain Arsacius, whom he had appointed a high priest of the revived state cult, "that it is their benevolence to strangers, their care for the graves of the dead and the pretended holiness of their lives that have done most to increase atheism?"[22]

Arsacius's position of "high priest" (*arch-hieros*) is another sign of Julian's continuing regard for Christian practice. There had been local officials with such a title, but Julian's high priests were to have much broader authority. In another letter, Julian placed one Theodorus in charge of "the government of all the temples in Asia, with power to appoint the priests in every city and to assign to each what is fitting."²³ The closest parallel to such authority was not in any pagan practice but in the Christian office of archbishop or metropolitan.

The parallel goes deeper than mere title. Priesthoods in the civic cults of the empire were prestige offices, held by the same people who served as town councilors and officials. The priests of these cults were not expected to alter their lifestyles in any substantive way. But Julian, like all Roman emperors before him, was also *pontifex maximus*, head of the Roman state religion, and as such he spelled out at length exactly how he wanted his priests to be selected and to behave.

Whereas social and political standing previously served as criteria for such appointments, Julian now made clear that he had a very different set of priorities in mind. His priests, he wrote to an unnamed one of their number, "ought to keep themselves pure not only from impure or shameful acts, but also from uttering words and hearing speeches of that character." They should never "be present at the licentious theatrical shows of the present day," even so much as enter a theater, or, gods forbid, "have an actor or a chariot-driver for his friends." His doors should be barred to dancers and mimes. Instead, "Even though he be poor and a man of the people, if he possess within himself these two things, love for God and love for his fellow men, let him be appointed priest."²⁴

In his letter to Arsacius, Julian showed his appreciation of another Christian practice, that of providing charity to strangers as well as its own members. "In every city," he wrote, "establish frequent hostels in order that strangers may profit by our benevolence," adding,

> I do not mean for our own people only, but for others also who are in need of money. I have but now made a plan by which you may be well provided for this; for I have given directions

that 30,000 modii of corn shall be assigned every year for the whole of Galatia, and 60,000 pints of wine. I order that one-fifth of this be used for the poor who serve the priests, and the remainder be distributed by us to strangers and beggars. For it is disgraceful that, when no Jew ever has to beg, and the impious Galilaeans support not only their own poor but ours as well, all men see that our people lack aid from us. Teach those of the Hellenic faith to contribute to public service of this sort, and the Hellenic villages to offer their first fruits to the gods; and accustom those who love the Hellenic religion to these good works by teaching them that this was our practice of old.[25]

The authenticity of this letter has been called into question, and Julian's praise does sound suspiciously like what Christians would have liked to hear him say.[26] But, as his program for a pagan priesthood has already shown, this is not the only place where Julian reflects the influence of his Christian upbringing. It just might be that the novelist John Steinbeck inadvertently did the best job of capturing Julian's agenda in one of his last works, *The Short Reign of Pippin IV*, a spoof on the postwar French Fourth Republic and its myriad political parties.[27] One of these was the Christian Atheists, whose platform was to get Christ out of Christianity. Julian might well have joined that party.

JULIAN'S SCHOOL LAW

There is no better proof of the way in which Julian's Christian upbringing continued to shape his outlook than in his attitude toward the texts that constituted the core of a classical education. In June of 362, Julian issued a seemingly innocuous edict in which he called on localities to emphasize character over eloquence when choosing teachers for their youth, and volunteered to approve these appointments himself, so as to increase the prestige of the profession.[28] In a letter that might have originally been a rescript (a legal response to an inquiry), Julian elaborated on his concerns,[29] putting it beyond doubt that his understanding of "character" was tied to belief in the old gods who inspired and populated the works studied in the classroom. "I think it is absurd," he wrote, "that men who expound the works of these writers [the classics] should dishonour the gods whom they used to honour." By doing so, such teachers showed that they were not interested in the moral formation of their students but only seeking financial gain.

Who were these despicable creatures? Why Christians, of course, whom Julian urged to "betake themselves to the churches of the Galilaeans to expound Matthew and Luke." This was a consistent position. As he wrote in *Against the Galilaens*, "If the reading of your own scriptures is sufficient for you, why do you nibble at the learning of the Hellenes?"[30]

Posterity may well have made more of Julian's letter than he intended[31]—the emperor rarely passed up an opportunity to poke his finger in Christian eyes, and a chance to point out that all the character-building lessons in the classics were inspired, and populated, by gods in whom they did not believe would indeed have been too delicious to resist. Still, there is a reason that, of all Julian's provocative acts, none touched so sensitive a nerve or had so lasting an effect as this one. This taunt for what he perceived to be Christian hypocrisy might seem frivolous today, but at the time it was a potentially ruinous blow, one that baldly revealed the fate he had in store for the faith in which he was raised. Homer and the poets were the core of the training a young man needed for a prestigious and lucrative career. Without access to this training, Christians also lost access to the best jobs.

There are reports of Christians who sought to make up for the loss of access to classical texts by setting the Gospels to heroic verse, but such efforts were premature. A day was coming when the important thing would be to recognize, and respond to, an allusion to scripture. But for now, a successful career depended not so much on one's ability to tell the difference between a dactylic hexameter and a trochaic tetrameter as to catch an adversary's allusion to, say, the *Argonautica* of Apollonius of Rhodes and respond with a witty rejoinder from Callimachus. Without having imbibed such texts since childhood, Christians might as well have been from another planet.[32]

Julian did not exclude Christian pupils; in fact, he explicitly ruled that they could continue their studies. But they should only be able to do so with teachers who believed in the gods that peopled ancient literature. If that did not suit, as Julian taunted, they could always simply obey their master, renounce earthly ambitions, and spend their lives eating nuts, grubs, and berries in the wastelands.

It was a shrewd move, on a number of levels.

For one thing, as Julian undoubtedly knew, there were Christians who agreed with him. In the late second century, for instance, the apologist and polemicist Tertullian railed against the same curriculum, identified philosophy as "the mother of all heresy," and pointedly asked, "What has Athens to do with Jerusalem?"[33] It is reasonable to assume Julian was familiar with this position, and therefore knew that one effect of his action would be to make elite Christians vulnerable to the kind of charge most famously recorded by the scholar-monk Jerome, who dreamt of being condemned as not a Christian but a Ciceronian because of his love of classical literature.[34] That is precisely the kind of polarization that Julian wanted to introduce. Like these Christian detractors, he wanted to use classical culture to draw a line between "ours" and "theirs."

One sign of how effective this strategy was survives in a work by Bishop Basil of Caesarea (c. 329–379), author of an influential code of monastic conduct who had also studied the classical curriculum with his close friend, Gregory of Nazianzus. In the aftermath of Julian, Basil wrote a work variously entitled *Advice to Young Men* and *On the Value of Greek Literature*, in which he defended the use of classical texts in Christian teaching. The gods that flit about in these texts are harmless, he wrote, and whatever is scandalous in them can simply be ignored. This literature remains worthy of study and emulation because it also provides examples of the deeds and sayings of good people. Near the end of this work, Basil drew an analogy between three diseases and their mental counterparts. The worst of these, which must be avoided at all cost because it is incurable, is that of people who are so sick that not only do they refuse to go to a doctor but also they will even refuse entry to one who comes to their sickbed. The analog to this disease, he explained archly, is found in those people who in his day refuse to learn from their betters. Basil minced no words about this group: such people were "incurable" (*anēkestos*) and "hopeless" (*melangcholias*). There is every reason to believe that Basil meant this group to stand for those Christians who rejected the classical education he had been advocating, without any idea of the benefits it could provide. His book, then, is one sign of the defensive position into which Julian's effort to sanctify these texts had forced elite Christians.[35]

Julian's action was polarizing in another sense as well. To this time, elites of all persuasions had considered the classical curriculum to be neutral territory, its stories about the exploits of gods and humans part of a common inheritance. Julian insisted that they were pagan scripture, and deserving of the same reverence Christians showed their holy books. Nothing betrayed the continued influence of Julian's Christian upbringing more than this action. In effect, he introduced theology into a curriculum that had become completely secularized. His action proved to be divisive in a way that even Julian's allies regretted. His friend and admirer, the historian Ammianus Marcellinus, subsequently characterized the school law as "harsh" (*inclemens*) and wished that it could be buried forever.[36]

Where Basil focused on the innate virtue of this literature, his close friend Gregory of Nazianzus took a different approach. In a pair of orations that dripped with invective, Gregory disputed Julian's claim to a monopoly on this literature, which Gregory defended as a shared inheritance. The bishop fused the classical heritage with Christian theology so effectively that later ages dubbed him "the Theologian." Far from proving a life-and-death struggle, the clash between Gregory and Julian (albeit posthumous in Julian's case) shows how much Christian and pagan elites in this century still shared a common grounding on matters ranging from philosophy and theology to politics and governance.[37]

Ironically, had Julian's law been in effect when he was growing up as a Christian, he never would have been able to study the classics that he loved so dearly.

THE ALTAR OF VICTORY

In the western empire, there was no Gregory to reconcile Christianity and the classics. There were intellectuals, notably Augustine and Jerome, who felt an abiding affection for these texts, but instead of reconciliation the record is filled with remorse and conflict—most notably Jerome's famous dream in which he was accused of being a Ciceronian instead of a Christian, and an equally famous clash between Ambrose of Milan and Symmachus, the eloquent leader of the Roman Senate, now known as the Altar of Victory controversy.[38]

The altar had deep roots in Roman history. It had been placed there almost five hundred years earlier by the first emperor, Augustus, in the aftermath of his decisive victory over Antony and Cleopatra at the Battle of Actium in 31 BCE (Figure 8.3). The golden statue of Victory that adorned it—of the type now best known by the Winged Victory that graces the Daru staircase in the Louvre—goes back even farther in the Roman past. It was captured early in the third century BCE, when Roman rule was pretty much limited to central Italy. Even leaving aside its religious significance, therefore, the altar stood in a unique way as a symbol of Rome's version of "manifest destiny"—a cultural as much as a religious symbol.[39]

Over the course of the fourth century the altar had become something of a political football. It was ordered removed by Julian's cousin, Constantius II, probably during his famous visit to the city in 357, then restored (probably by Julian) before being removed once more by Gratian in 382, leading to a petition from pagan

Figure 8.3. Reverse of a coin of Octavian (the future emperor Augustus) showing the golden statue of the goddess Victoria (Victory), bearing a laurel wreath. After his victory over Mark Antony and Cleopatra in 31 BCE, Octavian set up an altar with the statue in the Senate house. Photo of a coin in the Museo archeologico nazionale, Florence, by Sailko, Wikimedia Commons.

senators for its return. Prodded by Ambrose, Gratian on that occasion refused even to grant the senatorial delegation a hearing.

Two years later, in 384, the senators thought they had a stronger case, and they tried again. For one thing, Gratian was now dead and his thirteen-year-old brother, Valentinian II, was governed by his mother, Justina, no friend to Ambrose. For another, their leader and spokesman, Symmachus, not only was celebrated for his eloquence but also was now urban prefect, a position not to be trifled with. This was the occasion for Symmachus's eloquent plea for toleration, quoted at the start of this chapter. As this famous statement shows, diversity was a key part of Symmachus's argument. "Everyone has his own customs," he argued,

> his own religious practices; the divine mind has assigned to different cities different religions to be their guardians. Each man is given at birth a separate soul; in the same way each people is given its own special genius to take care of its destiny.[40]

But diversity was hardly the only arrow the Senate spokesman had in his quiver. He relied heavily on an appeal to custom and tradition— always a powerful argument in antiquity.[41] And, in keeping with the age's concern for supernatural support, he brought in the goddess Roma to remind the emperor of the victories Rome had won with the aid of the gods. Asking the emperor to "respect my length of years won for me by the dutiful observance of rite" and to "let me continue to practise my ancient ceremonies," Symmachus has Roma point out that "This worship of mine brought the whole world under the rule of my laws, these sacred rites drove back Hannibal from my walls and the Senones from the Capitol" (*Relatio* 3.9).

This reminder of the important role the gods had played in Rome's success was pertinent, because the previous year had seen not only Gratian's assassination but also a famine that hit the city of

Rome. Symmachus wisely left Gratian's untimely demise to speak for itself, content merely to observe that "We are not on such good terms with the barbarians that we can do without an Altar of Victory!" (*Relatio* 3.3). On the famine, however, he was much more blunt:

> The lands were not at fault: we should not blame the winds; rust did not spoil the crops, nor did weeds choke the standing corn. It was blasphemy that dried up the year's yield; and it was bound to follow that all would perish, for religion was being denied its proper support. If there is on record any other example of such a catastrophe, I would agree that we should blame the vicissitudes of the harvest-seasons; but it is a really serious case which brought about the kind of barrenness we have experienced. (*Relatio* 3.16)

This blunt assertion of consequences for displeasing the gods drew on traditional beliefs about the role of deities in human affairs, but its use also reflects the role miracle language played in decision making during this century.

Ambrose, as we saw in chapter 2, was more than up to this challenge. He pointed out that the current harvest was bountiful, and that even in the previous year the famine had not struck everywhere: other parts of the empire had experienced bumper crops (*Ep.* 73 (18).20–21). Ambrose also mocked the idea that Rome needed to be defended by gods who let Hannibal ravage Italy for years and who used cackling geese to defend the city from the Senones (*Ep.* 73 (18).3–5), alluding to a famous event early in Rome's past when the sacred geese of the goddess Juno alerted the city to a barbarian incursion. As a final insult, he put his own words in Roma's mouth:

> Why do you daily stain me with the useless blood of the harmless herd [sacrificial animals]? ... Why do you seek the voice

of God in dead animals? Come and learn on earth the heavenly warfare; we live here, but our warfare is there. Let God Himself, Who made me, teach me the mystery of heaven, not man, who knew not himself.

With a final slap in Symmachus's face, Roma asks, "Whom rather than God should I believe concerning God? How can I believe you, who confess that you know not what you worship?" (*Ep.* 73 (18).7)

MIRACLE TALK

This clash between Ambrose and Symmachus seems to fit the "either–or" categories of pagan–Christian relations encouraged by Cold War thinking (see chapter 1). Yet nowhere are the blinders of this approach more obvious than in the way it ignored the "business as usual" pattern that marked the overall relationship between these two antagonists. Both left behind an extensive selection of their letters—Symmachus's edited by his son, Ambrose's by himself. From these, one would scarcely discern a break in the manner whereby elites had conducted business with each other for centuries, especially when it came to maintaining their traditional patronage networks. In fact, it was Symmachus who called the young Augustine to Ambrose's attention when a chair as professor of rhetoric opened up in Milan.[42] It now seems likely that elite gentlemen of this age would have been horrified to think religious preference could disturb such carefully cultivated relationships.[43] Even with regard to this conflict over the Altar of Victory, recent scholarship has uncovered signs of a conflict that raged more among Christians themselves than between Christians and pagans.[44]

It is, therefore, less surprising than it once might have been to notice that, despite their opposing positions, both Ambrose and Symmachus shared an important premise about the nature and role of divinity: both took it for granted that a deity regularly intervened in human affairs, and that the support of that divinity was the most critical component of a successful agenda. They differed in the identity of this divine force and also, to a degree, on the evidence for its pleasure or displeasure, but neither challenged this basic assumption.[45] Thus, just as was the case in the dispute between Julian and Gregory, there is also an important underlying agreement between Symmachus and Ambrose.

This was the language of miracles.[46] Miracles at this level operated in different cadences. Symmachus and Ambrose were both products of classical education, and both could express themselves with unusual eloquence. Yet from the moment of his elevation when, we are told, God spoke through the voice of a small child, Ambrose became connected to miraculous events, and Symmachus belonged to a circle that prided itself on the number of cults into which they had been initiated. However much they conflicted about other things, a choice between classical reason and religious "superstition" was not one of them.

It was also the language of power. Even in this case, where the clash of religions is most obvious, the question was whose god was the more powerful. Nothing brings out the concern for power in this clash between two titans of classical eloquence so much as their use of the language of miracles, the promise to provide (or withhold) supernatural power. So Symmachus, after connecting the barbarian threat with the Altar of Victory, went on to claim,

> Your Eternities owe much to Victory and will owe more. Let those reject her powerful aid who have never received a benefit from it; do you refuse to abandon a patronage so ready to bring you triumphs? Everyone prays for power of that kind; no one should deny that such power is to be venerated if he admits that it is desirable.[47]

Never one to be outbid for divine support, Ambrose replied with ridicule for the weakness of the pagan gods. "Whom have the Roman temples sent out more prosperous than Cneius Pompeius?" he asked, linking Julius Caesar's opponent, Pompey the Great, with other worthies brought low: "Whom has the whole land of the East given to the world more noble than Cyrus, king of the Persians? . . . And whom do we find more devoted to sacrificing than Hamilcar, leader of the Carthaginians?" Yet each of these, he proclaimed, suffered an ignominious end.[48]

Because the antagonists in this exchange were operating in real time, so to speak, neither could settle this dispute as dramatically as had Bishop Silvester in his debate with the rabbis. But their shared belief in the regular intervention of deity in human affairs serves to underline the importance of miracle language at all levels of late Roman society. It is a language that helped Christians shape and understand the change in their fortunes taking place during this period.

JULIAN'S SHADOW

It is no wonder that Christians continued to hate and fear Julian long after his death. He was a prolific and skilled polemicist, and he had Christianity down cold: his years in the church had given him a depth of understanding that its opponents usually lacked.

For all that, Julian was more like his uncle Constantine than his disparaging comments in the *Caesars* and elsewhere would lead one to think. Like Constantine, Julian cast himself as a leader of religious change, and like him he insisted that his adversaries should be "persuaded and taught by reason" but not forced to convert or persecuted.[49] He was like his uncle also in that he wanted to have pagan and Christian intellectuals at his court,[50] and like him he grasped the importance of an alternative to the heavily entrenched elite system, one that would provide charity and justice for the poor. He was like him as well in his persistent overreach, and most of all in his sense of a divinely inspired mission.

The chief difference between them, as the next chapter will show, is that, like Silvester, Constantine had a miracle of his own to support his claims. Julian, unfortunately, did not.

Chapter 9

Failed Miracles

Can a miracle fail? Yes, if people have become so accustomed to tales of supernatural interventions that they start to predict them before they happen. And especially if the winners are the ones who tell the tale: then failed miracles become the lot of those who oppose God. In this way, premature predictions of success by Christian opponents became an important part of their own triumphal narrative in the fourth century. Stories of miraculous interventions at critical moments—from Constantine's Vision of the Cross in 312 to the windstorm Theodosius whistled up in 394—served to reassure Christians that their God was a powerful ally who was taking care of his chosen people. But equally important to this message were the stories about the failures of their enemies. In the religiously charged environment of the fourth century, miracle language readily colored the account of such events.

These failed miracles were the ones that Christian opponents conjured, solicited, or otherwise relied on for victory, and the fact that they did not work proved two things: first, that the old gods could not even protect themselves, much less their champions; second, that rulers who put their faith in these failed instruments had lousy judgment. The pattern was established early, with the failure of Diocletian's persecution, and had evolved into a robust scenario that virtually wrote itself by the time Theodosius faced off against the rebel emperor Eugenius. But the most spectacular examples were provided by the emperor who boasted of his ability to discern the will of the gods, Julian the Apostate.

It is important to remember that these stories were told by Christians and that they were crafted after the fact, when it is always easier to be confident about the outcome of an event.[1] Unless we take such basic biases into account, the stories can be terribly misleading. So in addition to illustrating the prominent role played by supernatural discourse, the stories in this chapter can also serve as a primer of sorts in the ancient and honorable art of defamation.

The death of the emperor Galerius in 311 is a fine example.

GALERIUS'S DEATH

As we saw in chapter 3, Diocletian's successor, Galerius, decided in 311 that it was no longer necessary for Christians to perform sacrifice to the old gods; all they had to do thenceforth was pray to their own God on the emperors' behalf. This was an important shift away from a criterion that had been used as a kind of loyalty test for centuries; in effect, it redefined the basis of citizenship. But the two Christian writers who provide us with the edict, Eusebius and Lactantius, were far more interested in conveying the reason for Galerius's change of heart, which they attributed to God's judgment on him: a wasting illness that made him cry out for mercy.

Initial efforts by Galerius's doctors were ineffective, Lactantius writes, and a remedy prescribed by the god Apollo made matters even worse. Then, he continues,

> his entrails putrefied from the outside, and his whole seat dissolved in decay. Yet the unfortunate doctors did not give up their ... treatment, even though there was no hope of

overcoming the ill. As the marrow was assailed, the infection was forced inwards, and got a hold on his internal organs; worms were born inside him. The smell pervaded not just the palace but the whole city; and this was not surprising, since the channels for his urine and his excrement were now confused with each other. He was consumed by worms, and his body dissolved and rotted amid insupportable pain.

This might have been a good place to end his account, but Lactantius was only getting started. "Cooked meats," he continues,

were placed near his dissolving buttocks so that the heat could draw out the worms; when these were broken up, countless numbers of these creatures swarmed around; the very disaster to his rotting flesh had proved fertile in generating an even greater quantity of them. Now that the evil had spread, the parts of his body had lost their form. The upper part of it down to the wound had dried up, and in its pitiable thinness the skin had turned sallow and sunk between his bones; the lower part had spread out like leather bags, and his feet had lost their shape. This had gone on continually for a year, when at last, subdued by his ills, he was compelled to confess God. In the intervals of the pain as it pressed on him afresh, he cried out that he would restore the temple of God and make satisfaction for his crime.

It is small wonder that, amid such graphic gloating, the reader has no inclination to credit Galerius for what was, effectively, an innovative and statesmanlike solution. Instead, his final actions and death merely served as proof of the avenging power of the Christian God.[2]

Christians did not need to develop the tools of this trade from scratch. For his picture of Galerius's death throes, for instance,

Lactantius drew heavily on scenes from the Hebrew Bible, especially the Book of Maccabees.[3] But where did he get these details about Galerius's illness? The fact is, he did not need a source. As a trained rhetorician, Lactantius had had the benefit of an education system that put enormous weight on the development of imagination and elaboration. With only one or two words—say, "cancer" and "tyrant"—graduates of this system knew how to talk about all the rest: often, it was just a matter of filling in the blanks. The great ones gave public displays of their skill by asking their audience to provide the words and then making up an elaborate speech on the spot.[4]

One favorite device was to depict the opposition as prematurely overconfident, which also meant they were foolish and had bad judgment. Five hundred years earlier, Julius Caesar employed it to memorable effect in his account of his civil war with Pompey, gleefully picturing his enemies squabbling over the division of his honors and properties before they were crushed in the decisive battle of Pharsalus in 48 BCE.[5] In Christian hands, persecutors showed overconfidence by hurling threats to destroy the faithful as soon as they won the battle that, by this point, we know they were destined to lose. We saw this process at work in the accounts of Theodosius's battle miracle in chapter 2. There, a prayer that started out as an illustration of the emperor's piety in Ambrose's funeral oration soon became in other hands a response to premature claims by his opponents—the usurper Eugenius and his barbarian general, Arbogastes—to restore the old gods. Buoyed by favorable omens, Arbogastes and the pagan senator Flavian also threatened that, on their victorious return to Milan, they would turn Ambrose's basilica into a stable and dragoon his clergy into the army.[6]

The schools had developed an especially rich body of images for dealing with tyrants. To Greeks, a tyrant was simply anyone who ruled unconstitutionally, by seizing power or otherwise acting without proper authority. Once Christians started using this word for persecutors, the keys to this storehouse of slander fell right into their laps.[7] Everyone knew that tyrants were illegitimate; accordingly, so were persecutors, no matter how they had come to power. Tyrant-persecutors were also lustful and cruel, vainglorious and prodigal. A good way to make sure modern students beginning their study of this era understand the role of rhetoric in the sources they will be reading would be to have them imagine how Constantine's history would have come down to us had he lost at the Milvian Bridge. Such an exercise is especially necessary because of one feature built into the narrative Christians had developed. Once Constantine emerged as God's hand-picked candidate, anyone who opposed him necessarily also opposed God. These opponents naturally became persecutors as well—even when their records were much more ambiguous.

Such was the case with the ruler of Rome against whom Constantine marched in 312 after his Vision of the Cross (chapter 3). At worst, Maxentius could be faulted for being even-handed in his treatment of Rome's Christian community during his six years of rule. Because Eusebius of Caesarea refers to him as someone who "at first feigned our faith," scholars have even toyed with the idea that, far from being a persecutor, Maxentius was himself a Christian.[8]

But once Maxentius was identified as an "enemy of God," tropes that Romans had used for centuries to defame "tyrants" fell readily into place. Maxentius's lust knew no bounds—not even senators' wives were safe. The more virtuous the woman, the more he craved her. A particular contrast that will show up time and again: whereas our hero (fill in the blank) trusted in God, the villain, craven and superstitious, resorted to magicians and sorcerers. True to form, Lactantius tells us that Maxentius was foolish enough to consult the ancient Sibylline books that the Romans had used in times of crisis since the very beginning of their republic. Here he learned that, if he went out to fight Constantine, "the enemy of the Romans would perish."⁹ If nothing else, the story shows that Christians loved tales about ambiguous oracles just as much as their pagan forebears did. (The classic example is the response of the oracle at Delphi to a question by Croesus of Lydia in 546 BCE, asking whether he should launch what turned out to be a losing attack on Cyrus of Persia. "If you attack," the oracle replied, "a mighty kingdom will fall." Too bad for Croesus, he forgot to ask which kingdom that would be.¹⁰)

But it seems that it was Eusebius, not Lactantius, who came up with a twist on the overconfidence motif that added an important new element to this narrative: reading the decisive battle as a deliberate clash of gods, provoked by the losers themselves. This is the way Eusebius dealt with the uncomfortable issue of Constantine's brother-in-law, the eastern emperor Licinius.

When we first meet Licinius in the pages of Lactantius and early versions of Eusebius's *Church History*, his piety rivals that of Constantine himself. As Constantine's ally, he battles an eastern rival, Maximin Daia, whose persecuting credentials were much more clear-cut than those of Maxentius in the West. Accordingly, just as Christ had visited Constantine in a dream, so an angel visits Licinius on the eve of his battle, dictating a prayer for his troops to recite beforehand. He, too, wins a smashing victory. But a decade later, Constantine decided to invade his erstwhile colleague's lands. To Eusebius, that meant Licinius had to have become a persecutor, and he adjusted his narrative in the *Life of Constantine* to fit the new circumstances.

Here is where Eusebius innovates. Instead of with angels, Licinius now aligns himself with demons. Taking his most trusted confidantes into a sacred grove filled with stone images "of those he thought were gods," Licinius, Eusebius tells us, threw down a gauntlet:

Now is the moment which will prove which one [of us] is mistaken in his belief: it will decide between the gods honoured by us and by the other party. Either it will declare us victors, and so quite rightly demonstrate that our gods are true saviours and helpers, or else, if this one god of Constantine's, whoever he is and wherever he sprang from, defeats our troops, who are very numerous and perhaps numerically superior, let no one hereafter be in doubt which god he ought to worship.[11]

Eusebius claims to have gotten this information from insiders who were present, but he could easily have taken it out of a rhetorical playbook. One telling question: would the emperor whose meeting with Constantine in 313 produced the document that legalized Christ (usually called the Edict of Milan) now, a decade later, wonder who that God was or where he came from? Other sentences are simply too good to be true. According to Eusebius, who of course knew the outcome of this battle when he wrote, an overconfident Licinius advised his followers that, if he should lose, "let no one hereafter be in doubt which god he ought to worship." Really? But the dullest of Eusebius's readers would have gotten the message, and that was the whole point.

By the end of Constantine's reign in 337, then, Christians had developed an all-purpose template for depicting their enemies. And then Julian came along.

KILLING WITH KINDNESS

Julian posed a challenge to this Christian narrative, because he preferred the carrot to the stick. Instead of trying to force Christians to abandon their God, he simply offered power and prestige to those who did. In later days, even ardent Christians had to admit that the tactic worked better than they would have liked. Bishop Gregory of Nazianzus, in the attack on Julian we looked at in chapter 8, lamented those Christians who had bought into Julian's program: "for the sake of temporary gain, or court favour, or brief power, these wretched fellows bartered away their own salvation!"[12]

This was a problem. Christians like Gregory knew what to do with opponents who engaged in persecution. But how were they supposed to handle opponents who did not persecute and create martyrs? Could they still be called "persecutors"? Gregory, whose eloquence earned him the sobriquet "the Theologian," tried his best. Julian, he claimed in his First Invective,

> begrudged the honour of martyrdom to our combatants, and for this reason he contrives now to use compulsion, and yet not seem to do so. That we might suffer, and yet not gain honour as though suffering for Christ's sake.

What was this fake compulsion that Julian was practicing? Unlike honest persecutors, who "thought it a fine thing to force impiety upon the nations of the world, and to tyrannize over a creed that had vanquished all other creeds," Julian chose to attack the faith "in a very rascally and ungenerous way, and introduces into his persecution the traps and snares concealed in *arguments*."[13] In other words, Julian had the nerve to do what Lactantius, in chapter 4, claimed persecutors were afraid of doing: he debated them.[14]

It took several generations, but eventually Christian thinkers were able to deal with this setback by redefining both persecution and martyrdom. So, as the fifth-century church historian Socrates explained, in his view anyone who upsets those who have placed their hope in Jesus Christ is effectively conducting a persecution. Problem solved. One scholar summed up this effort nicely: "If Julian could practice a different kind of persecution, the Christians would respond with a different kind of martyrdom."[15]

Storytellers did not have to fret over such niceties: they simply attributed martyrdoms to Julian anyway. Some of these stories might have been due to an inability or unwillingness to distinguish between prosecutions brought for civil crimes and punishments meted out for confessing Christ. Such was the case of Bishop Mark of Arethusa, who was ordered to pay compensation for columns he had taken from pagan temples to use in his church. Anticipating Ambrose of Milan's argument to Theodosius I over the synagogue in Callinicum (chapter 2), Mark refused to do so, even under torture, and even after the prosecution offered to release him for the symbolic payment of a single coin. Even though they gave up and released him anyway, Christians inflated Mark's ordeal into that of a confessor (a Christian who is tortured but not put to death), and some even made him a martyr anyway.[16]

On another front, Julian was far more vulnerable. As a criterion for rule in the late empire, all emperors were expected to demonstrate close ties with divinity; but Julian took his duties as chief priest very seriously: even his friends clucked their tongues over the number of animals slaughtered during his sacrifices. As one, the historian Ammianus, wrote, Julian "drenched the altars with the blood of an excessive number of victims," adding that "the ceremonial rites were excessively increased, with an expenditure of money hitherto unusual and burdensome."[17]

In the same passage, Ammianus called attention to the way Julian surrounded himself with diviners and soothsayers, with whom he interacted as an equal. But this activity in particular, as the monk Antony warned his followers, demanded the skill of discernment. The bulk of Antony's teaching about demons was devoted to the way these beings prey on human weaknesses by appearing in pleasing forms or whispering sweet nothings that they know humans want to hear. Devotion to ascetic practices, such as gentleness, tranquility, poverty, moderation, and humility, is what allows the spiritual warrior to tell the difference between a true and a false vision.[18]

Julian knew this danger as well. In a lengthy discussion of ruler-ship that was part of an earlier oration on his cousin, the emperor Constantius II, Julian warned how "evil changes its face and is apt to deceive, and that the cruellest thing that it does is that it often takes men in by putting on the garb of virtue, and hoodwinks those who are not keen sighted enough, or who in course of time grow weary of the length of the investigation."[19]

Yet in practice Julian found that advice easier to give than to take. Ammianus tells us that the night before Julian's troops pro-claimed him Augustus, the then-Caesar experienced a convenient vision in the form of "the guardian spirit of the state" who said she had been watching over him but now would leave if he turned down this opportunity. Later, Ammianus wrote, the emperor ignored signs warning him to go slow on his plans to invade Persia.[20]

So long as Julian experienced success after success, he could flaunt his skill in interpreting the divine will. But after becoming emperor the string of successes ended, and the Christian narrative got back on track.

JULIAN'S FAILURES

Christians had a limited vocabulary for dealing with opponents who did not persecute, but no trouble at all with opponents who suffered defeat. Julian suffered two signal defeats.

At some point before leaving Antioch in March of 363 to begin his long-awaited Persian campaign, Julian committed himself to rebuilding the Temple in Jerusalem, a potentially explosive act. The temple had played a central part in Jewish identity ever since King Solomon built the first one in the tenth century BCE as a perma-nent home to replace the tabernacle of Moses. Solomon's Temple was destroyed by the Neo-Babylonian King Nebuchadnezzar in the sixth century, the start of a half century of "Babylonian captivity." The Second Temple was built by those Jews who opted to return to Jerusalem, and rebuilt on a monumental scale by Herod the Great at the end of the first century BCE (Figure 9.1). This is the temple destroyed by the Romans at the end of the Jewish War of 66–70 CE.

Julian's decision to rebuild the temple could have been just one more sign of his quixotic temperament, but it was one with far-reaching consequences.[21] In ruins since the abortive Jewish uprising three centuries earlier, the shattered temple had served as another proof of Christian claims; when Constantine built his magnificent Church of the Holy Sepulchre within sight of the temple ruins, he provided a visual contrast between the fortunes of the two religions, as Eusebius of Caesarea did not hesitate to point out. In the *Life of Constantine* that he completed subsequent to that emperor's death in

Figure 9.1. Model of the Second Temple as restored by Herod the Great. Israel Museum. Photo by Ariely, Wikimedia Commons.

337, Eusebius heralded the Church of the Holy Sepulchre as the "new Jerusalem" and deliberately contrasted it with the still-visible ruins of Herod's Temple, destroyed two centuries earlier in the Jewish War:

> New Jerusalem was built at the very Testimony to the Saviour, facing the famous Jerusalem [Temple] of old, which after the bloody murder of the Lord had been overthrown in utter devastation, and paid the penalty of its wicked inhabitants. Opposite this then the Emperor erected the victory of the Saviour over death with rich and abundant munificence.[22]

Even more important than the visual contrast was Jesus's Gospel prediction that "not one stone will be left here upon another; all will be thrown down" (Matt. 24:1). In the fourth century, Christians generally understood this passage to be a prediction not only of the temple's destruction by the Romans but also that it would never be rebuilt.[23] A rebuilt temple, therefore, would expose Jesus as a false prophet.[24]

Is this what Julian was thinking? Given his familiarity with Christian writings, he certainly knew how Christians were exploiting this contrast between the "Old" and the "New" Jerusalem, and accordingly he must have known how damaging a new and better temple would have been to their cause. But this might not have been the most important thing on his mind. A major part of his religious program was the revival of blood sacrifices that had fallen out of use, partly due to Christian legislation, partly (perhaps even mostly) because cities had found cheaper and less divisive means to conduct public rituals.[25] Another important part was to restore pagan temples closed or pillaged under his Christian predecessors. Rebuilding the temple was an obvious way to implement both goals, especially since he knew that Jews could conduct sacrifices only in the temple and thus had not been able to offer any for three centuries.

Julian had plans for the Jewish God as part of his revamped pagan theology, although he did not lay these out with much consistency. At times he seems to have equated the Jewish God with the Creator god of his philosophy; at others, he seems to have thought of Jehovah as just one more regional or ethnic god and mocked Jewish pretensions to make him anything greater.[26] Either way, however, an act that would honor and boost the prestige of this deity would appeal to Julian, even if it had no implications for Christians. Ammianus Marcellinus framed Julian's intentions, in his one brief mention of the event, as part of the grand designs that are the hallmark of ambitious emperors:

> Turning his activity to every part, and eager to extend the memory of his reign by great works, he planned at vast cost to restore the once splendid temple at Jerusalem, which after many mortal combats during the siege by Vespasian and later by Titus, had with great difficulty been stormed. He had entrusted the speedy performance of this work to Alypius of Antioch, who had once been vice-prefect of Britain.[27]

Scholars now may be divided, but contemporary Christians had no doubt that Julian's plan to rebuild the temple had no other purpose than to harm their religion. To them, his plan (especially after it failed) was meant to put their God to the test.[28]

Whatever his reason for starting the project, Julian soon had to abandon it, and for no mundane reason. According to Ammianus, when workers began digging, "terrifying balls of flame kept bursting forth near the foundations of the temple, and made the place inaccessible to the workmen, some of whom were burned to death." As a result, Alypius was forced to abandon the project.[29] This was something Christians could run with: it was a sign that God had intervened to foreclose Julian's wicked scheme. They soon added an earthquake—the traditional sign of divine displeasure in antiquity—and a prediction by the bishop of Jerusalem that "the Jews would never be able to put a stone upon a stone there."[30] By the middle of the next century, the church historian Socrates had a fully developed story to tell. "Fire came down from heaven and consumed all the builders' tools," he wrote, adding:

> and the fire continued burning among these for a whole day. The Jews indeed were in the greatest possible alarm, and unwillingly confessed Christ, calling him God: yet they did not do his will, but influenced by inveterate prepossessions they still clung to Judaism. Even a third miracle which afterwards happened failed to lead them to a belief of the truth. For the next night luminous impressions of a cross appeared imprinted on their garments, which at daybreak they in vain attempted to rub or wash out. They were therefore "blinded" as the apostle says and cast away the good which they had in their hands: and thus was the temple, instead of being rebuilt, at that time wholly overthrown.[31]

Is this what "really" happened? It is entirely likely that an insurance adjuster today would conclude that the fireballs were created by pockets of methane gas that had built up in the rubble over the centuries. An earthquake might also have been a factor: one did strike the region in May of 363.[32] But the only thing that really matters is what Christians who controlled the story thought had happened, and what they believed was that God once again had demonstrated, in a singularly dramatic fashion, that Christ would protect himself and his flock.

Julian's second, and final, failure offered even better proof. On March 5, 363, the emperor set out from Antioch for his long-awaited invasion of Persia. Hopes were high. He commanded an army at

least sixty-five thousand strong—huge by late Roman standards—
and his reputation as a daring and effective leader was so strong
that the Persians thought it wise to make peace overtures (which he
rejected) before he embarked. In typical fashion, Christian writers
depict him muttering threats as he marched off and promising to
coat the old gods' altars with Christian blood when he returned.[33]

There is no way of knowing how much if any of this account is
true, because in fact Julian never came back. He achieved some initial successes, but once he reached the Persian capital of Ctesiphon,
the emperor realized he did not have the resources to mount a successful siege. It might be that he had counted all along on drawing
the Persians into the field to protect their capital. If so, he seriously
underestimated his adversary. The Romans had the best shock
troops in the world; against a massed enemy, they were virtually
unbeatable. In Gaul, Julian had been able to count on Germanic
barbarians always to rise to the bait, but the Persians were far more
sophisticated. Their strength lay in the mobility of their heavily
armed cavalry—the *cataphracti* who were the prototype for the
medieval "knight in shining armor"—and the vastness of their
land. Their time-tested strategy was to lure an invader inland and
practice a scorched earth policy to deny him the opportunity to live
off the land.

Julian played into Persian hands by burning the fleet that had
supplied his army while it marched down the Euphrates, thereby
closing off that secure avenue of retreat. He evidently believed that
such an action would make his army fight more fiercely: in an oration to Constantius composed while he was still a Caesar, Julian
had mocked the aged Nestor's advice to Agamemnon in the *Iliad* to
build a wall to protect the Greeks, calling it "a cowardly notion and
worthy indeed of an old man." Because of such defensive measures,
he claimed, the Greeks "grew careless and slackened their valour,
because they trusted to the fortification."[34] It might seem strange

to read comments on a story about the Trojan War as signs of Julian's strategy, but the ancients used such foundational poems to think about present concerns, none more so than this book-bound emperor. Indeed, this particular oration stands out in general for the musings it contains of Julian's thinking on a good king's duties.[35]

In any case, when Julian was forced to fall back overland, his army was subject to the constant hit-and-run tactics at which the Persians excelled. In one such night attack on June 26, Julian rushed from his tent to lead a counterattack without taking time to put on his defensive armor. He suffered a spear wound that did not respond to treatment, and three nights later he died. Christian authors immediately saw the death blow as divine retribution, exacted by an angel or saint; pagans suspected a Christian assassin. The controversy Julian provoked spilled over to accounts of his last moments. His friend the historian Ammianus painted the death scene in Platonic colors, with Julian spending his final hours in philosophic discourse with his friends; the church historian Theodoret thought it more appropriate for him to die with an admission of failure: "Galilaean, you have won!" Their differences point to a legacy of suspicion and recrimination.[36]

CLOSING BORDERS

Athanasius, the pugnacious bishop of Alexandria, is supposed to have viewed the threat Julian posed serenely, advising his companions that the apostate emperor was "but a small cloud that will soon pass."[37] By and large, modern scholars have shared the bishop's confidence, but hindsight has to be factored into the equation. Roman emperors had, if not a bully pulpit, something that was even better—a bag filled with highly coveted imperial appointments and privileges. Contemporary Christians had to admit, however grudgingly, that Julian's use of the carrot instead of the stick had been effective, despite the shortness of his regime, and the steps he had taken while alive were sufficiently threatening that Christians a quarter century later were still spooked by his name.[38]

A better gauge of the long-term prospects for his program might be Julian's experience in Antioch, where he spent nine months (July 18, 362, to March 5, 363) before embarking on his Persian adventure. Antioch was home to one of the earliest Christian communities. In fact, it was there that the term "Christian" was coined.[39] Over the centuries, the city's Christian, pagan, and Jewish communities seem to have worked out an amiable modus vivendi in which their shared identity as Antiochenes bound them together more tightly than the religious identities that separated them, and they had learned how to coexist in relative harmony.[40]

Instead of going along with Julian's divisive plans, the Antiochenes appear to have rejected his efforts to emphasize religious identity. His clashes with the Christian population of the city get the most attention, but equally important are signs that Antioch's pagan community did not share the emperor's zeal. On leaving the city, Julian posted a satire, Misopogon ("The Beard Hater"), a tract in which he took umbrage at the refusal of Antioch's pagans to follow his lead. It still survives, and despite the emperor's attempts at humor, it reveals not only the depth of his resentment but also, even more, how utterly clueless he was about sentiment in that city.[41] It is telling that even his admirer Ammianus, himself an Antiochene, reported that the populace considered the emperor's flamboyant sacrifices "excessive" and himself condemned Julian's law forbidding Christians to teach the classical curriculum (chapter 8) as "inhumane."[42]

Julian was not the only one irked by such indifference to religious identity. As we saw in chapter 6, John Chrysostom, while still a priest in this city, railed against the readiness of his congregation to participate in Jewish festivals and ceremonies, and he had equally stern words for Christians who enjoyed the theater and horse racing.[43] Chrysostom and Julian—strange bedfellows, indeed.

It is an unusual way to think about Julian, but his efforts to sharpen the divide between pagans and Christians align him with a growing trend on all sides to sharpen religious boundaries, to draw a bright line to separate communities on the basis of religious belief and practice. Julian might have thought that he was simply leveling the playing field by removing the incentives Constantine had put in place, but in his zeal to revive a paganism that scarcely existed anywhere except in his beloved books, he wound up abetting the efforts of others to polarize their communities. His chief legacy was to inject religious polemic into areas that previously had been seen, by elites at least, as neutral ground, and to rekindle Christian fears of renewed persecution. His incessant and flamboyant public displays combined with specific efforts to isolate Christians generated a fear that survived decades later.

One of the more ironic side effects of his regime was that he inadvertently strengthened the hand of Christian bishops, who responded to his assault by insisting on reining in the relative autonomy that emperors had traditionally enjoyed in religious matters. Henceforth, the suppression of idolatry and heresy would be a key marker of imperial "sincerity."[44]

Pagan voices survived Julian's death, but as the fourth century drew to a close, they did not have many Christian failures or successes of their own to point to. With the new century came new opportunity.

Chapter 10

Alaric, Augustine, and the End
of a Century of Miracles

The century of miracles ended on a summer day in the year 410. On August 24 of that year, after a lengthy siege, a barbarian army led by the Gothic king Alaric took control of the city of Rome. For the next three days, his troops brutally sacked the city, carrying away gold and jewels by the cartful and subjecting Rome's exhausted residents to "massacres, fires, looting, men murdered and tortured."[1]

Although not as destructive as the Vandal sack half a century later, Alaric's triumph was symbolically devastating for Romans: it was the first time the city had fallen to an invader since the Gallic sack of 387 BCE, some eight hundred years earlier. For that reason, 410 has taken on symbolic significance as the date for the fall of the empire as a whole: it symbolizes the end of the Pax Romana, the peace that Roman hegemony had brought to the Mediterranean for a longer period than it ever experienced before or has since.[2]

Since this is a book about the way miracle stories reassured Christians that their God wanted them to make Christianity the official religion of the empire, 410 is symbolic here for a somewhat different reason. Ever since Constantine's battlefield miracle in

312, Christians had pointed to the power of their God to help those who worshipped him with a pure faith, and only fifteen years earlier Theodosius I had demonstrated once again the awful power of that deity at the Frigidus River. Barely twenty years had passed since the same emperor had made Christ the official God of the Roman Empire. But this time no divinely appointed champion rode forth against Alaric, nor did some pious leader achieve a miracle that destroyed the enemy. If any celestial signs were seen or dramatic battlefield prayers uttered in the summer of 410, they went unrecorded, and evidently unheeded.

By the standards of the day, Alaric's victory amounted to a complete and utter failure of the Christian God to do his job. Yet Christianity survived this challenge, and others yet to come, with barely a scratch. A good deal of the credit for this strange outcome must go to something we have already witnessed in considering Ambrose's reaction to failure in chapter 2: the agility with which Christian thinkers reworked the rules. In this case, that credit goes to a brilliant response penned by the great Augustine of Hippo.

WHAT HAPPENED?

One thing is certain: the emperor Honorius did not emulate his father's example and enlist the aid of the Almighty on behalf of the Eternal City. When we met Honorius in chapter 2, he was a newly orphaned ten-year-old, standing at Ambrose's side during the funeral oration for Theodosius. It is fair to say that, after fifteen years of rule, Honorius had not lived up to whatever high expectations his father may have had for him. The closest he ever got to a battle was when he reviewed troops in his new capital of Ravenna, in northeast Italy just south of what is now Venice. Unlike Milan, which was too vulnerable in those unsettled times, Ravenna was protected from invaders by its mosquito-infested marshes. But that formidable barrier only served to reinforce the court's isolation. According to a widely circulated story, Honorius was so out of touch that, when he heard Rome had fallen, he initially thought the messenger was talking about his pet chicken, which he had named after the capital of his world (Figure 10.1).[3]

Equally certain: Alaric's sack was not the result of a sudden, irresistible flood of barbarians overwhelming a surprised and degenerate population. To the contrary, it is an event that, at least in retrospect, seems eminently avoidable, the result of a story that proceeds by fits and starts going all the way back to the beginning of Theodosius's reign in 379.

Figure 10.1. "The Favorites of the Emperor Honorius," by John William Waterhouse (1883), which now hangs in the Art Gallery of South Australia. By the time Alaric took Rome in 410, the emperor was so detached that, according to one story, he thought the news-bearers were talking about a favorite pet chicken that he had named "Roma." Waterhouse alludes to the story by showing the emperor feeding his fowl. For good measure, Waterhouse dresses the bearers of these tidings in Christian robes to reflect Gibbon's judgment on the role of religion in Rome's fall. Wikimedia Commons.

In that year, to make up for the fearsome losses at the Battle of Adrianople, Theodosius recruited large numbers of Germanic barbarians as allies. Results were mixed. These new forces helped stabilize the frontier, but they also went off on their own for long periods, in search of supplies and plunder. One of these groups, the Goths, was a major contingent in the army that fought for Theodosius at the Frigidus River in 394. They suffered horrendous losses after being placed in the forefront of the battle. The survivors, suspecting that they were deliberately exposed to reduce their numbers, withdrew and elected Alaric as their king. (A writer who will reappear in this chapter, the Spanish priest Orosius, was later indiscreet enough to support this suspicion by crowing that Theodosius had won two victories—one over Eugenius and another over the Goths.[4])

Theodosius died without resolving this problem. Instead, it was inherited by another soldier who rose rapidly in the aftermath of Adrianople, Flavius Stilicho. The son of a Vandal soldier and a Roman mother, Stilicho had risen in Theodosius's service to the position of supreme military commander. Theodosius married him to his niece Serena, making him part of the imperial family, and on his deathbed appointed Stilicho as Honorius's guardian.

Thus was set in motion the events that would lead, fifteen years later, to the sack of Rome, an event that was due as much to political as to military developments. As their new king, Alaric had to provide not only for his soldiers, who may have numbered as many as twenty thousand, but also for their families, which swelled their number fivefold. To pressure the court into giving him an official appointment, along with the resources that would come with it, Alaric twice invaded Italy. Twice Stilicho forced him to withdraw.

Then in 408, as the result of an ongoing power struggle at Honorius's court, Stilicho was put to death. Alaric quickly capitalized on the situation and laid siege to the city of Rome, the first of three he would stage over the next two years. To him, the city was no more than a bargaining chip. But Honorius refused to budge, and so in 410 Rome's eight-hundred-year-old record ended.

A MATTER OF IDENTITY

With the cool detachment that distance allows, it is easy to see that the Battle of Adrianople in 378 was a far greater disaster than the sack of Rome in 410, yet it occasioned none of the existential hand-wringing occasioned by the city's fall. One reason is that it posed far less of a threat to the triumphal narrative that Christians had put together over the course of that century. Valens, the emperor who died in that battle, was a Christian, but he had opted to support an unorthodox version of the religion and had come down hard on those who stuck to the Nicene Creed. Thus, as far as that group was concerned, he was a heretic who simply got what was coming to him. All his defeat meant was that God did not just want the empire to be Christian; he wanted it to be Nicene Christian.[5]

But a more serious question was bubbling under the surface. The defeat of Valens may have been good for Nicene Christianity, but it led to the collapse of the eastern front, to the use of barbarian armies, and ultimately to Alaric and the sack of Rome in 410. So what did this faith-based judgment about that disaster say about the ability of good Christians to be good Romans?

The sack of Rome brought that troubling question front and center. Pagans like Symmachus had warned that cutting off support for Rome's traditional deities would lead to just such a disaster (chapter 8), and they were not slow to point out the difference between the eight hundred years that the old gods had kept Rome safe and the twenty years that Christ had been in charge.

At heart, it was a question of Christian identity. That question had become acute in the middle of the third century, when emperors implicitly ruled that the act of sacrifice—not blood sacrifice of animals, but scattering incense on an altar to the emperor's *genius*—was the duty of a good Roman. But it seemed to be resolved in 311, when the emperor Galerius ruled that it was sufficient for Christians to pray to their own God, and it became a nonissue in 313, when Constantine himself converted to Christianity. With a Christian emperor, theorists like Eusebius of Caesarea readily aligned Christian thinking with a traditional political theology that viewed the emperor as a living reflection of the cosmic ruler (see chapter 4).

Julian, with his flamboyant revival of blood sacrifice, had reopened the question in a particularly ham-fisted way, but his spectacular failures merely served to confirm Christians in the belief that only they could win divine support for the empire. With the sack of Rome that proposition was now in doubt, and this doubt raised an entirely new question: how much should members of a religion focused on spiritual salvation care about what happens on this mortal coil?

In the aftermath of the sack, it became apparent that Christians cared a great deal. A famous case in point is St. Jerome, the Christian who worried that he was too Ciceronian (chapter 8). Writing from Bethlehem more than two years after the event, Jerome still felt the shock. "My voice sticks in my throat; and, as I dictate, sobs choke my utterance," he wrote. "The City which had taken the whole world was itself taken." Strikingly, to capture his feelings, Jerome turned not just to scripture but also to Rome's quintessential poet, Vergil:

> Who can set forth the carnage of that night?
> What tears are equal to its agony?
> Of ancient date a sovran city falls;
> And lifeless in its streets and houses lie
> Unnumbered bodies of its citizens.
> In many a ghastly shape doth death appear.[6]

Ordinary Christians were more moved by traditional thinking about the role of a deity than by Vergil's hexameters. In the Book of Genesis, God had promised Abraham he would spare even so wicked a city as Sodom if as few as ten innocent people could be found within its walls (Gen. 18:16–33); why, then, did he not spare Rome, a Christian city that was also home to precious and powerful shrines, including those to Sts. Peter and Paul? How had these not helped? Were the pagans right to point out that their gods had kept the Eternal City safe for eight hundred years, whereas Christ had blown it after a couple of decades?

We know about these concerns because of sermons preached by Augustine of Hippo (Figure 10.2) in the weeks and months following the sack.[7] In these, he chastised his congregation for harboring such thoughts and darkly suggested that such doubts smacked of pagan thinking; real Christians would not entertain them. Nevertheless, it appears that his own response (put simply, "It could have been worse") struck at least some members of his congregation as hard-hearted.[8]

Augustine's sermons were far from his last word on the disaster. In 413, he began work on an extended response that offered a definitive answer to the question of Christian loyalty and redirected the course of Western religion.

Figure 10.2. Fresco of St. Augustine (354–430) in the old Lateran library, Rome, c. 600 CE. This is believed to be the earliest known representation of the bishop of Hippo. From Wilpert 1924, tafel 140B.

THE CITY OF GOD

When we met Augustine in chapter 7, he was a young rhetorician electrified by the account of Antony the Great's spiritual journey in the deserts of Egypt, and about to be baptized by Ambrose of Milan. His baptism was the end of a long spiritual journey of his own that had taken him through Manichaeism (a religion that stressed the opposition of light and dark) and the late Roman version of Plato's philosophy that we now refer to as Neoplatonism.[9] He has given us his own account of his development in the *Confessions*, the first autobiography in Western history. It was written around the year 400, after his ordination as a priest in 391 and elevation to the bishopric of Hippo Regius in what is now Algeria in 395.

By 410, Augustine had established himself as a bishop of unusual eloquence, energy, and commitment. At the time Rome fell, he was lobbying Honorius's court to send officials with some backbone to deal with the "Donatists," a schismatic group whose roots went back a century at that point, all the way to Diocletian's persecution. He was probably also gearing up for a major conference between Catholic and Donatist bishops to be held in Carthage in 411.[10] This preoccupation might explain at least in part the sense one gets that he was on autopilot in his sermons on the sack of Rome.

The Donatist issue had finally been laid to rest by 413, and Augustine had yet to be fully immersed in his next great controversy, involving what became known as the Pelagian heresy. So in that year he finally felt able to grant the persistent request of Marcellinus, the imperial official who had been his ally against the Donatists, for a comprehensive work that would not only reply to pagan sniping about the sack of Rome but also explain the faith to intelligent and thoughtful pagans. The result was *The City of God* (*de civitate Dei*). It would take him more than a dozen years to complete it.[11]

He started on the offensive, claiming that the "worshippers of the many and false gods, whom we commonly call pagans"[12] should be ashamed of themselves. None of them complained when they found sanctuary in Christian churches. Even "those murderers [the Goths] who everywhere else showed themselves pitiless" curbed "their furious rage for slaughter . . . and their eagerness to take prisoners" out of respect for these holy places.[13]

Already at this early phase, Augustine began reorienting the argument and redefining the role of the Christian deity. When asked, "Where is thy God?" he wrote, Christians should reply that, unlike the pagan gods, "our God is everywhere present, ... and in return for our patient endurance of the sufferings of time, He reserves for us an everlasting reward" (*City of God* 1.29). Taking a page from the pagan justification of their persecution of Christians, Augustine argued that the Christian God should not be blamed for Rome's fall, but Christians themselves for allowing paganism to flourish in the capital city. That, and not the end of state support for the old rites, is what led God to chastise the Romans.

Augustine stayed on the offensive for the next nine books, mocking the notion that Rome had been better off under the old gods and scorning the premises of the philosophers. Most of his argument is standard fare, nothing that any rhetorician with half his training and skill could not have turned out, and distinguished mostly by the lengths to which he took his case.

A good sense of what this argument would look like in the hands of a lesser thinker survives in the *History Against the Pagans*, written (at Augustine's suggestion) by the Spanish priest Paulus Orosius. Orosius evidently understood his mission to be simply to invert the standard Roman account to show that the old gods were not any better at protecting the state than the Christian one. Not content with leaving the story there, Orosius insisted that Christ had actually done a better job. If for no other reason than this, his account of the sack of Rome is justly famous.

In his account of that event, Orosius tells us of a Goth who "chanced to find in a church building a virgin advanced in years." He continues:

> When he respectfully asked her for gold and silver, she declared with the firmness of her faith that she had a large

amount in her possession and that she would bring it forth at once. So she did. Observing that the barbarian was astonished at the size, weight, and beauty of the riches displayed, even though he did not know the nature of the vessels, the virgin of Christ then said to him: "These are the sacred plate of the Apostle Peter. Presume, if you dare! You will have to answer for the deed. As for me, since I cannot protect them, I dare not keep them." The barbarian, stirred to religious awe through the fear of God and by the virgin's faith, sent word of the incident to Alaric. He ordered that all the vessels, just as they were, should be brought back immediately to the basilica of the Apostle, and that the virgin also, together with all Christians who might join the procession, should be conducted thither under escort. . . . The pious procession was guarded by a double line of drawn swords; Romans and barbarians in concert raised a hymn to God in public. In the sacking of the City the trumpet of salvation sounded far and wide and smote the ears of all with its invitation, even those lying in hiding.

The "respectfully" (*honeste*) is a nice touch. So is the way Orosius slipped past the matter of the barbarian's own religion by claiming, "he did not know the nature of the vessels." In fact, Alaric's soldiers also were Christians, but they adhered to the same Arian understanding as the late, unlamented eastern emperor Valens. Did this mean God favored the heresy after all? Better just to elide the point. But Orosius's *pièce de résistance* was his picture of barbarians and victims joining in a celebration of their shared piety, assuredly a unique moment in the history of such catastrophes. The account inspired one historian (with, one suspects, tongue firmly planted in cheek) to describe the sack of Rome as "one of the most civilized sacks of a city ever witnessed."[14]

Orosius's approach might have served for the short term, but he was still playing by the old rules, according to which the deity who won battles was the strongest. For the long term, Augustine had something much more daring in mind: he intended to rewrite those rules. Even in his early books the bishop planted the seeds for what would now in the second half of the *City of God* grow into his answer to the identity questions raised by the sack of Rome: what is it that distinguishes the Christian religion from others, and how much should a true Christian care about what happens in this world?

THE TWO CITIES

Already by the fourth book of the *City of God* Augustine had begun to reconstruct the nature of the Christian relationship to the empire. His argument derived from the basic quandary of monotheism: if there is only one God, and if that God is both good and all-powerful, why do bad things happen to good people? The miracle stories in this book were not concerned with this question; instead, they focused on the victories that resulted from Christian piety and discipline. Such thinking was in line with the general attitude in late antiquity that deities intervened regularly, and decisively, in human affairs. But the question of evil was now front and center to Augustine.

To address it, the bishop laid out a line of argument that could be traced to Jesus's insistence in the Gospel of John that his kingdom was not of this world (*City of God* 18:36). For this reason, Augustine wrote, it is simply wrong to judge the power of a deity by how that deity's followers do in this world, or to assume that an all-powerful, monotheistic God plays favorites among earthly governments. Then he went one step further. Believers cannot judge divine action according to human notions. God "gives earthly kingdoms both to good and bad," he wrote, according to a plan "which is hidden from us, but thoroughly known to himself." For this reason, success or failure in earthly terms cannot be tied to a person's piety.

Instead, Augustine put forward a different concept of success, one based on his understanding of human nature. There are two cities, Augustine taught, like Athanasius (chapter 7) using a symbol that was uniquely appropriate to ancient thinking about the state.[15] The two cities have existed since the beginning of human history, the one composed of those who "wish to live after the flesh" and the other of those who "wish to live after the spirit." Those in the spiritual city are "predestined to reign eternally with God," while those in the other will "suffer eternal punishment with the devil." Rome typifies the earthly city, and whereas those who belong to the heavenly city can be grateful for the good things Rome did, which amounted primarily to creating conditions for the spread of the faith, they know better than to shed tears over its fate, for like all earthly things it is meant to perish. Only the City of God endures.[16]

As his use of the Gospel of John shows, Augustine's argument was grounded in scripture, and not just the New Testament. A favorite work, to which Augustine returned repeatedly in his writings, was the Hebrew Bible's Book of Job. Just as the monk Antony had used the story of Job's suffering as a paradigm for the ascetic life (chapter 7), Augustine now saw the example of a pious man who remains firm in his love of God despite being visited by the most horrible misfortunes as a way to break the connection ancients made between spiritual and material success. Also scriptural was the idea that Christians were a nation apart, a "third race" that was neither Greek nor Jew. In the second century, an anonymous letter writer described Christians as strangers in this world, destined for another realm. "They spend time on earth, but their citizenship is in heaven," this author wrote. "Simply put, what the soul is to the body, this is what Christians are to the world."[17]

But scripture was not the only source for Augustine's image of the two cities.

THE IDEAL CHRISTIAN

Were Augustine writing today, he very likely would talk about the two "natures" of mankind, instead of the two "cities." His use of the image of city directly reflects the central role this institution played in ancient thought. "City" (*civitas*) is the root of our word "citizen," as well as our word "civilization." It was the term ancients used to think about organized life. To them, the city was not simply an economic convenience; it served as a powerful symbol of human achievement, providing amenities that distinguished their way of life from what they considered the inferior living of farmers or nomads. Just one example: in the second century, when the orator Aelius Aristides reached for a way to characterize Rome's generosity in extending its citizenship to all parts of the empire, the image he came up with was that of the city. "What another city is to its own boundaries and territory," he exclaimed, "this city [Rome] is to the boundaries and territory of the entire civilized world."[18]

The city image points to another likely influence on Augustine's thought. A millennium earlier, during a period of similar unrest, the Athenian philosopher Plato pursued his concern about justice in a work that is also central to Western thought, one that we usually translate as *Republic* but whose Greek title was *Politeia*, meaning the government of a *polis*, or city. Augustine was a Platonist for a number of years before he accepted Christianity, so we can be relatively confident that he knew this work. Although he was critical of Plato in the *City of God*, he shared the Athenian philosopher's concern for justice. Indeed, one of the most frequently quoted lines in the *City of God* is Augustine's question, "Without justice, what are governments but robbery on a giant scale?"[19] Even though Augustine reached a distinctly different conclusion, some attention to Plato's purpose, and the way he went about achieving it, can help us understand what the bishop sought to accomplish in the *City of God*.

Plato's problem was twofold. First, Greeks had rarely taken time to consider the difference between "law" and "justice"—justice was simply the totality of the laws, which meant (at least theoretically) there was no way to distinguish a "bad" law from a "good" one. Second, the rise of sophism, with its careful attention to the use and meaning of words, had led to an alarming degree of relativism over what Plato considered moral imperatives. What the sophists taught would today be called legal, or forensic, reasoning. Even though their teaching often included a healthy dollop of philosophy, the primary aim with which they became associated was to teach students how to win a case, even if that meant manipulating evidence or obscuring truth. The catchword for the movement became "they make the worse appear the better reason," and that is what alarmed Plato. To him, the devastating Peloponnesian war between Athens and Sparta (431–404 BCE), which upended so much of what Greeks considered normal, was in large part due to the way demagogues had used sophistic training to manipulate the popular assemblies.

In the aftermath of the decision by one such assembly, a jury of 501 Athenians, to put his beloved teacher Socrates to death in 399 BCE, Plato undertook a systematic analysis of justice. The *Republic* was the result of that inquiry. Although this work is usually remembered for the ideal state it constructs, ruled by the philosopher-king (its famous line, which Plato put in Socrates's mouth, was that there will be no peace until "either philosophers become kings in our states or those whom we now call our kings and rulers take to the pursuit of philosophy"[20]), Plato's aim was to achieve what he considered a defensible definition of justice as an abstract principle. In the process of doing so, he laid out his famous theory of forms, or ideals.

For everything in this world, from law to kitchen utensils, there exists on another level—one that can be perceived only through the mind—a perfect version of that item. The mental exercise needed to perceive that perfect form was philosophy, and this is why Plato believed only philosophers should be rulers. In the just state that he created, humans were separated into three classes, each distinguished by a different racial component. The bottom class, "men of brass and iron," included not just laborers but everybody more concerned with wealth and creature comforts than ideal truths—bankers and corporate CEOs as much as the proletariat. The top class, the golden race, was made up not of all philosophers but only of those thinkers who showed an indifference to material goods, thereby assuring us that they would be guided only by principles. (The intermediate race, a silver class of guardians or warriors, does not concern us here.)

It is a good bet that Augustine's idea of the two cities was influenced by Plato's creation of these races. In effect, Plato's aim was to take justice out of the realm of shifting political fashions and expedients and put it in a place where it would be safe from the unstable and treacherous currents of the material world. Instead of being changed by circumstance, this ideal justice would now be a touchstone against which the laws shaped by passing fancies could be measured. In the remaining books of the *City of God*, Augustine undertook to do the same for the church. Just as Plato's philosopher-king would seek eternal truth, so the Christian in Augustine's spiritual city would seek eternal life, undeterred by the shifting fortunes of the earthly city.

In these books, Augustine reminds Christians that the heavenly kingdom is their only true destination; for that reason they must never think of themselves as anything other than wayfarers through this imperfect mortal life. States rise and states fall; some are better than others, but none can substitute for the eternal kingdom.

The message of the *City of God* is firmly grounded in scripture, both the Old and the New Testament. But Augustine's Platonic training allowed him to add a new layer of meaning to those texts. This is what turned the *City of God* into an enduring study of the Christian church and, as well, a cornerstone of Western civilization. With Plato's help, Augustine created the ideal Christian.

AUGUSTINE AND MIRACLE

One would assume that the lack of any miraculous intervention to save Christian Rome in 410 would have required some response from Augustine. Indirectly, of course, it did: his argument that Christians should be indifferent to matters of this world applied doubly to their God. To make the point, he took up the fate of Gratian, the very emperor on whom Ambrose punted in chapter 2. Instead of trying to rationalize Gratian's death, Augustine argues that God let Gratian die at the hands of a usurper so that ambitious men would not become Christian just to attain power. So, too, with the apostate Julian, whom God let rule for two years, while taking his Christian successor, Jovian, after only a few months: he did it to show that the only legitimate reason to convert was "for the sake of eternal life."[21]

In this same passage, Augustine made an exception for Constantine, but only to explain why God did show favor in this case. Even here, Augustine explained, God did not do so to favor Constantine but only to show that imperial rule did not depend on demons. Thus, to Augustine, Constantine was simply the exception that proved the rule, that rule being that "God, the author and giver of felicity, because He alone is the true God, Himself gives earthly kingdoms both to good and bad . . . lest His worshippers, still under the conduct of a very weak mind, should covet these gifts from Him as some great things."[22] In this way, Augustine blew a huge hole in the triumphalist narrative that Christians had put together over the course of the fourth century. As one author has observed, "These sentences in *The City of God* sound as if they were written expressly against Eusebius."[23] They might just as easily have been written against a closer target, Ambrose of Milan.

And yet, Augustine devoted a long chapter in the final book of the *City of God* to a catalog of miracles witnessed since the arrival of relics of St. Stephen, the first martyr, whose death by stoning is recorded in the Acts of the Apostles. Remains identified as those of the martyr had been discovered in Jerusalem in 415, and fragments arrived in Augustine's See of Hippo Regius the following year. His catalog of the healing miracles produced at the site has been seen as a precursor of the miracle books that flourished in the Middle Ages.[24]

This section of the *City of God* is a reminder that Augustine had a complicated relationship with the topic of miracles. Quite apart from the events at Rome, he felt a lifelong need to come to grips with the phenomenon, and over the years his position changed markedly. As a young man, he wondered why people obsessed about the absence of tiny miracles when evidence of the great miracle of Creation lay all around them. His view at that time was that the miracles in the New Testament were necessary to convince people that Jesus was truly the Son of God, but now Christians no longer needed this crutch.[25]

Why, then, did Augustine devote so much space to the miracles produced by St. Stephen's relics at the end of a work in which he had given so much thought and effort to showing that the absence of a miracle in 410 did not mean that God had failed his people?

There is an obvious reason: miracles may all have the same nature, but not all miracles have the same purpose. Augustine wrote the *City of God* to steer Christians away from expecting those miracles that had been thought to prove God favored one kind of earthly polity over another. The miracles that he now celebrated were ones that affected individuals, not states: miracles of healing and demon expulsion that had always been the most common form of Christian encounter with the supernatural, as they continue to be right down to the present day (think of the example of Sally in chapter 1); they say nothing about the fate of nations.

The difference is telling. The miracles that I have focused on in this book were understood to mean God wanted the pagan Roman Empire to become a Christian Roman Empire. They may be called imperial miracles, in the sense that they established or confirmed the importance of Christianity to the security of the Roman state. The miracles of Constantine and Theodosius that bookend this century are the most obvious ones of this sort, but even the miracles of this period that do not fit so readily into that mold—from Helena's finding of the True Cross to Antony's shedding of the earthly concerns that weigh down ordinary humans; from the thunderbolts that Ambrose and Symmachus hurled at each other to Julian's successful crowing and inglorious defeat—take on additional meaning because they were refracted through the lens of those imperial victories. It is the rise and fall of this type of miracle that sets the century of miracles apart.

It might not be a coincidence that, just at the time when miracle as proof of God's wishes for earthly domain lost its efficacy, Augustine saw the importance of replacing it with a more traditional type of miracle. In any case, such miracles should not distract us from what the bishop accomplished in the *City of God*.

A unique combination of circumstances fueled the power of miracle stories in the fourth century: a string of political and military successes by Christian rulers, the ease with which such successes could be folded into traditional thinking about the relations between gods and humans, the ideology of kingship, and the emergence of bishops as authoritative arbiters of Christian belief, whose authority extended even to the meaning of miracles. The sack of Rome ended that unique moment, and the *City of God* thoroughly and irrevocably destroyed the theoretical foundation built by Lactantius and Eusebius at the beginning of the century on which Ambrose still relied at its close.

By cleaving the tie between Christianity and the Roman Empire, Augustine set Western Christianity onto a course that eventually led to that clear, conceptual difference between religious and secular institutions that we now summarize as church and state. But the greatest impact of the *City of God* is the unique way it fused the scriptural message of salvation with Platonic idealism, thereby creating a standard for the ideal Christian. In so doing, the book exposed with relentless clarity the shortcomings of a faith built on worldly success. It makes a pale mockery of the complacent triumphalism that fueled so many of the miracles in these pages. The *City of God* is a masterwork, a cornerstone of the new civilization growing on the foundations of old Rome.

It is also the tombstone for a century of miracles.

Chapter 11

Epilogue

The Story of Titus

In the second half of the fifth century, the eastern emperor Leo I (r. 457–474) sent one of his officers, a Gaul by the name of Titus, to seek a blessing from Daniel the Stylite, one of those curious holy men who spent their lives on little platforms atop columns that reached fifty feet and more into the air (Figure 11.1). Instead of returning suitably blessed, however, Titus took an unexpected path. According to the author of a *Life of Daniel*,

> Titus, beholding the holy man, marveled at the strangeness
> of his appearance and his endurance and just as good earth
> when it has received the rain brings forth much fruit, so this
> admirable man Titus was illuminated in mind by the teach-
> ing of the holy and just man and no longer wished to leave
> the enclosure, for he said, "The whole labor of man is spent
> on growing rich and acquiring possessions in this world and
> pleasing men; yet the single hour of his death robs him of all
> his belongings; therefore it is better for us to serve God rather
> than men."[1]

Figure 11.1. Image of Daniel the Stylite (409–493) on his pillar. Such pillars could reach as high as fifty feet, with a platform of about one square yard for the saint to stand on. Miniature from the eleventh-century Menologion (Book of Saints) of Basil II. Wikimedia Commons.

Outraged, Leo protested the loss of so capable a leader. Daniel was contrite. "Without your approval I never wished to do anything," he wrote in reply. But, he also said, "You yourself need no human aid; for owing to your perfect faith in God you have God as your everlasting defender; do not therefore covet a man who today is and tomorrow is not; for the Lord doeth all things according to His will. Therefore dedicate thy servant to God Who is able to send your Piety in his stead another still braver and more useful." In reply, Leo wrote, "To crown all your good deeds there yet remained this good thing for you to do. Let the man, then, remain under your authority, and may God accept his good purpose" (*Life of Daniel* 61).

At this point, the story takes a further twist. Once inside Daniel's compound, Titus started to spy on the saint, convinced there was some trick to his apparent indifference to things of the flesh, that while others slept the saint gorged himself on food and drink. When his surveillance failed to uncover such cheating, Titus finally confronted the holy man, at which point Daniel tells him there is no secret: "Believe me, brother, I both eat and drink sufficiently for my needs; for I am not a spirit nor disembodied, but I too am a man and am clothed with flesh." Daniel then offered the novice some disarmingly rational advice. Explaining that it took him many years to reach the point where his body required so little to survive, he counseled Titus not to rush his own ascetic program, "for if you load a ship beyond its usual burden, it will readily be sunk by its weight."

But that is not what Titus wanted to hear. Instead, he set himself on a fast track to sainthood. Picking out a corner of the oratory, the former officer "hung himself up by ropes under his armpits so that his feet did not rest upon the ground, and from one evening to another he would eat either three dates or three dried figs and drink the ration of wine. He also fixed a board against his chest on which he would sometimes lay his head and sleep and at others place a book and read" (*Life of Daniel* 62).

For a while, the author of the *Life of Daniel* tells us, Titus succeeded in his program, to the point where the emperor himself would also ask his former officer to bless him whenever he came to see the saint. But the prudence of Daniel's advice soon became clear:

> And it pleased the Lord to call him [Titus] while he was at prayer, with his eyes and his face turned upwards and heavenwards, and thus it was that he breathed his last. The brethren looking at him thought he was praying as usual. When evening had fallen, the two brethren came who had formerly been his servants and now ministered unto him and brought him all he required, and they discovered that he was dead. . . . And as one looked on the corpse of this saintly champion it showed the departed soul's longing for God.

LESSONS

The story of Titus holds many lessons. The first, and most obvious: miracles were not unique to the fourth century; they did not
end with the sack of Rome in 410, any more than they had begun
with Constantine's vision in 312. Holy men like Daniel continued to
perform the miracles of healing and demon expulsion that were the
bread and butter of Christian encounters with the supernatural.[2]
This book has been about one particular kind of miracle, the battlefield miracle that promised victory in return for pious behavior. But
not exactly just this kind, for even battlefield miracles continued to
have what one scholar has called "a long and happy life," occurring
as recently as World War I.[3] It has been about what might be called
"imperial miracles," a series of divine interventions that were understood either to promise or confirm Christian belief that their God
supported making Christianity the religion of the Roman Empire.

Their uniqueness in this century is due to a particular convergence of circumstances. It was not just the battlefield miracles,
powerful as they were, that set this century apart, but the fact that
they occurred as part of a seemingly unbroken series of divine
interventions. Combined with the prevailing belief that a deity
could, and would, intervene directly in human affairs in response
to the appeal of a religiously potent favorite, and that the cosmic
struggle of different divinities was reflected in their relative success or failure in earthly encounters, these miracle accounts created a heady cocktail of Christian triumphalism—especially when
the apparent failure of the old gods to protect their followers, or
even themselves, was added to the mix. It was a great time to be a
Christian. Once this formula was broken, as happened in 410, and
many times thereafter, Christians had to temper their joy with the

realization—long held by the Jews—that the ways of their God were truly unknowable.

So it is the unbroken string of successes that makes the miracles of this period unique, along with the way these successes fused so readily with ancient concepts about the role and function of a deity, all of which seemed to be confirmed by unparalleled growth in Christian power and control. Add to this the spectacular failures of the old gods, and it is easy to see how the miracles of this century proved to contemporary Christians that their God wanted them to make Christianity the religion of the empire.

To an age that firmly believed a deity took a direct hand in the outcome of human affairs, these successes, combined with the perceived failures of enemies, confirmed for Christians the truth of their faith. Even more than the verbal gymnastics of Augustine's *City of God*, the story of Titus explains how that faith persisted even when the century of imperial miracles ended.

But how? Ultimately, the point of studying history is to find out about ourselves. But to do this, we have to learn how to understand people who were often very different from us—how to meet them on their terms, not ours. But how are we ever going to understand, much less sympathize with, people who engaged in practices that, to our eyes, were so self-destructive, and a culture that honored them for doing so? Sure, we can grasp intellectually the importance of demons in that age, but there are not many people today who see such forces at work in our own affairs—at least not enough for demons to seem realistic, instead of simply more proof of superstition.

The way to gain the insight we seek from this age is to forget about means and concentrate on ends. That is what the story of Titus can help us do.

A COMMON DENOMINATOR

Is his story proof of an age mired in superstition? Perhaps. But consider the initial response of the emperor Leo to the loss of a promising officer: he bitterly rebuked Daniel for costing him a precious asset, exactly as we would expect any leader in our world to do. But while his response thus reinforces the common scholarly claim that Christianity drained the empire of much-needed manpower resources at a critical point in its history, it also suggests that reason, as we understand the word, had not fled from this world.

Yet if that is so, how must we understand Leo's reaction when the saint sent a humble and contrite reply? At this point, instead of seizing his advantage (and his officer), Leo backed down. Why? Perhaps because he had the good sense to realize he was holding a losing hand, and the only gambit open to him was to engage in an exercise of what Maude Gleason has called "one downsmanship."[4] Yet just because Leo's initial response seems more sensible to our age, we should not rule out the possibility that, once reminded, the emperor was sincere in his belief that the prayers of holy men like Daniel were a surer guarantee of victory than armies and officers. It is a bit humbling to realize that, although the western empire through which we draw our cultural heritage crashed and burned in the fifth century, the eastern empire, piloted by rulers like Leo, lasted an additional thousand years. In an age that believed the intervention of a deity could be decisive in a battle and that prayer could sway that deity's support, Leo might have made a rational decision.

Nor does Daniel fit the profile of a half-crazed fanatic that our modern minds have created. Indeed, when Titus tried to catch him in a midnight orgy, Daniel's reaction was to advise the novice to do a little at a time, never more than his body could bear. Not much different from the advice a personal trainer today would give. Instead of a pie-eyed lunatic, Daniel seems to be something of a problem-solver. His long career wrestling demons, strange as it seems to us, appears to have won for him serenity and a certain amount of grace.

Then there is Titus himself. In the passage quoted at the start of this chapter, the author tells us that the mere sight of "the strangeness of his [Daniel's] appearance and his endurance" was enough to make Titus "renounce earthly ambition." He "threw himself down before the holy man begging him to receive him and let him be enrolled in the brotherhood." Was it superstition that moved him to abandon a promising military career? There are reasons to think he had other matters on his mind. We are told, for instance, that Titus brought with him from Gaul a legion of his own retainers—a move reminiscent of another ambitious leader, the younger Pompey in the late republic, who Plutarch tells us raised a client army of three legions because he did not want to be just another "empty handed fugitive asking for help."[5] Then there is Titus's rash decision to get on a fast track to sainthood despite Daniel's warning—all signs that he was ambitious, an overachiever with a decidedly competitive nature who had not so much surrendered his ambitions as found a more powerful arena in which to pursue them.

The author of the *Life of Daniel* did not tell the story this way. He clearly admired Titus—there is no hint of irony in his account of this former officer's fatal regimen. He does cluck his tongue about the way Titus stalked his hero, yet even here it is not Titus he faults but "the Devil, the hinderer of good men [who] imbued Titus with a spirit of inquisitiveness."[6] Even though the author of the *Life* believed it was the fleeting nature of human life that motivated Titus, the way he describes the officer's subsequent behavior entitles us to suspect that other thoughts mingled with these. What else would Titus have seen when he arrived at the saint's compound?

The author of the *Life* tells us of the crowds who massed beneath the saint's pillar, seeking healing and blessings. Among them were the highest officials of the state, who had ready access since Daniel had set up shop within easy reach of Constantinople. This, Titus would have seen as well. We also need to take into account his decision to ignore Daniel and charge ahead with his ascetic program in the fastest and most spectacular way possible. Whatever he wanted, he wanted it very badly.

To the author of the *Life*, Titus wanted to achieve perfection, but it is easier for us to see him as part of "the same old story," as the song has it, competing for pre-eminence on a new field of glory. The two goals are not mutually exclusive. In the environment of late antiquity, spectacular feats of self-mortification and self-denial were not ends in themselves. As St. Antony taught in chapter 7, denying the needs of the body was a way to enlarge the soul, making it lighter than air. And a soul purified in this way became a conduit for the cosmic power otherwise beyond the reach of earthbound mortals. Those who had achieved this state were able to make that power visible in this sphere, having gained authority over the powers that be, both mortal and demonic.

Let us say that, when Titus viewed Daniel on his pillar, what he saw was power. Power enough to propel his soul into the next world, to be sure—but while awaiting that judgment, power that would bring him prestige and glory in this one, greater than anything else an ambitious Gaul could ever achieve. It was a type of power that brought even the emperor to kneel before him. That is what Titus wanted and, just as he always had, he risked life and limb to get it.

Power is the way to make contact between the very different faces that Titus presents to Daniel's hagiographer and to us. The idea is not so far-fetched. In the New Testament, "power" (*dunamis*) is the word most often used to describe events we think of as miracles.[7] To our age, extravagant feats of self-mortification and physical denial may still seem a strange and even unhealthy means to achieve anything, but power as an end is something we can understand. It is a concept that allows us to appreciate the fourth century, and perhaps also to discover a new way to think about our own values. Consider, for instance, these reflections on modern life by one experienced and insightful observer: "Our culture is in love with certain kinds of power: military and financial leverage, bullying certainties about politics and ethics, the extraordinary and paradoxical power that comes from clinging to the status of victim—all of them varieties of power that have nothing to do with feeling for and living from the grain of reality."[8]

The insight is this: the methods an ambitious overachiever uses to achieve power may vary from age to age; in ours, power comes from the accumulation of material resources, while in Titus's it came from denying them. But in both, power is the goal. Titus's race to a fast track of asceticism was a means to an end, not an end in itself.

"WE HAVE THE CHILDREN"

There is one other change to consider, which we can see spelled out for us in the *Life* of another fifth-century saint, Porphyry of Gaza (c. 347–420). Porphyry had used some blatantly strong-arm tactics to convert the inhabitants of this fiercely pagan town, and (intriguingly) some of his parishioners evidently still harbored traditional Christian objections to such coercion. When they confronted their bishop with their concerns, Porphyry responded, "It is needful that mankind be admonished by fear and threats and discipline. . . . For even if they come doubting, time is able to soften their hearts, if Christ consent." But there was something else to consider, the saint continued: "even though they be not seen to be worthy of the faith, having been already in a state of evil, they that are born of them can be saved, by having converse with the good."[9] In other words, "no matter what, we have the children."

There are problems with the date and authenticity of this work, but these are of no concern here. Whether or not this exchange actually occurred, it is significant that the author thought it appropriate to put these concerns into the mouths of faithful parishioners, and that he would set down such a Realpolitik response by the bishop, evidently because he thought it an effective answer.[10] It is indeed a shrewd response, reminiscent of what Julian had in mind when he banned Christians from teaching the classics (chapter 8). What we have been witnessing is the most banal of revolutions—that which occurs when a new generation comes of age. The kind of growth Christianity experienced in its early centuries meant that, in any given period, a plurality, if not majority, of its membership had to have been made up of adult converts. The fourth century was a turning point, with members in increasing numbers being born into the church and infant baptism increasingly becoming the norm.[11]

Like all else in the matter of "Christianization," this change did not take place everywhere or overnight. As the *Life of Porphyry* shows, the process was still underway in the fifth century, and it would be many more centuries before the old ways could be declared completely gone. But to more and more young people in each new generation, the old gods were just that—a means of worship with which they had no personal experience—and the fourth century was the tipping point in this process.[12] So what actually is significant about these stories is that they are the ones on which, increasingly, children were being raised, giving them new examples of good and bad, right and wrong, behaviors to be admired and others to be shunned. They represent the "new normal."[13]

A string of game-changing miracles helped too, for they enabled Christians to put together a triumphalist narrative in terms that non-Christians could understand. But this was a narrative that demanded continued victory to succeed, and the failure of their

God to prevent the Gothic sack of Rome in 410 put an end to that string. So the remaining issue is to explain Christianity's ability to shrug off such a colossal challenge to its authority. In the long run, Augustine's *City of God* provides the answer. The book is often, and rightly, identified as a cornerstone of Western thought, and its outline, if not its argument, is known to every student who has ever taken a humanities or civilization course. But the ubiquity of his thought now should not blind us to the fact that few people in his age, or for many ages to come, were literate, and even fewer of those wanted to invest much time in the study of this unique fusion of Platonic and Christian thought.

To understand how ordinary Christians survived the end of the kind of empire-affirming miracles they feasted on in the fourth century, we must look elsewhere. So let me put in a bid here for a more humble answer, in the person of our friend Titus.

THE VALUE OF A GOOD STORY

Alan Cameron, in the course of his vigorous dissection of Theodosius's miracle at the Frigidus River, mused about the difference a victory by Eugenius would have made. In the end, he decided, not very much:

> Even if he had won and restored both subsidies and sacrifice, there is little reason to believe that this would have halted the steady and surely now irreversible spread of Christianity, or that paganism could ever have recovered its hold on the populace at large—or indeed survived much longer than it did.

Echoing the famous debate over whether the fall of Rome was due to internal or external forces, Cameron decided that "Roman paganism was not extinguished on the field of battle or even by imperial laws. It died a natural death, and was already mortally ill before Theodosius embarked on his final campaign."[14]

If Cameron is correct, then it is stories like that of Titus that help explain this "irreversible ... hold on the populace at large." Whatever else his flamboyant bid for sainthood portends, there is no denying that Titus's struggle made for a ripping good story. In this he was far from alone. By the time the fourth century ended, a cottage industry of legends, martyr stories, and fanciful accounts of all types was flourishing, and their proliferation was immense. The author of a meticulous study of saints' lives in the medieval Latin West considered the number of nine thousand given in a standard handbook for that time and place alone to be "far from complete."[15]

Such numbers testify to the widespread popularity of such stories, but their importance goes far beyond mere number. In a world where relatively few people below the elite were literate, these stories popularized and made accessible the more austere thinking of Christian intellectuals; they were the way ordinary Christians understood their faith. It should come as no surprise, therefore, that this century of miracles is also the period in which martyr stories began to incorporate wholesale the trappings of popular literature.[16] These tales are part of the complex process by which historical memory is created. Specifically, what they show us is the way mechanisms were created for remembering and interpreting miracles.

Because they are stories, there is room for imagination. To return to the example in chapter 1 of Sally and her amazing recovery from an incurable illness, consider all the parts that were open to elaboration. Why, for instance, did she go hiking after being told she had so little time left to live? How long was she in that ravine before being rescued? For that matter, who were her rescuers and how did they find her? All these silences are entry points for an artful storyteller, and the details that this writer chooses to flesh out the story will not only make it more interesting but also confirm a particular reading. Suppose, for instance, that Sally went hiking as part of a spiritual journey, and that her rescuers were missionaries directed her way by saints or angels. Throw in a celestial sign or two and an encounter in the ravine with demons who are confounded by Sally's heretofore unappreciated skill at dialectic, and the effect will be to confirm the believer's interpretation and eliminate the alternatives without ever having to discuss them.

This is what one of the master storytellers of our own day meant in the phrase that I used as an epigram for this book. Speaking through one of his characters, Iain Pears wrote that "stories take place in societies, otherwise they cannot exist."[17] As a storyteller, Pears's interest was in the process of creating a world for his story; as historians, our interest is in using a story to capture and understand the world that produced it. That is the value of the miracle stories from late antiquity. In these stories, the Christian hero meets an appropriate enemy (a demon, a torturer, or a magician) and follows a script every bit as formulaic as a modern television drama—a contest between good and evil, replete with angelic interventions, miraculous cures, and the requisite martyrdom.[18] And like popular television fare, these stories required no special skills to be understood. They were fun to read or listen to; they had heroes and villains, practices to admire or scorn. Central to all of them is the meaning Christianity gave to suffering and the promise it held of a better life to come. Even the martyr acts, which portray the brutality of the persecutors in frequently graphic detail, are more interested in the heroic endurance of the martyr, and his or her eventual glory, than on the punishment or suppression of the torturers, who are instead regularly depicted as thwarted and confounded.

Titus's story is not just a good tale; it is also one that confirms the superiority of Daniel's ascetic program. In this sense, what these tales represent is a shift in popular literature from stories about kidnapped princesses and star-crossed lovers to edifying tales of Christian stalwarts. They show how completely a Christian viewpoint had saturated the Roman world, no matter how many still clung to the old ways.

As miracle tales formed an ever more important part of this popular literature, their purpose changed. In the Gospels, miracles served to bring people to the Jesus movement, but by the time the fourth century ended they had clearly started to take on an additional function as entertainment. As with so much else in these early centuries, this development was not a matter of Christian "superstition" replacing classical "rationalism," but a more general development that brought to the fore fantastical elements that already existed at the popular level. Indeed, there seems to have been a lively trade in such elements, with pagans borrowing from Christian stories as much as Christians did from their pagan counterparts.[19]

This literature allows us to witness the creation of a new culture in a way that the power plays of an Ambrose, the fireworks of a Chrysostom, or even the steady soul-searching of an Augustine cannot. Like the rhythms of the Christian calendar, with its sabbaths and feast days, the use of Christian processions to mark a new sacred landscape, and the shrines to local saints that replaced pagan deities at country crossroads, these stories hold the key to the question of how Christianity survived the disaster of 410.[20]

Driven by their own reasoning and imperatives, the miracle accounts in these chapters, and stories like that of Titus and Daniel, show us how the elevated worldview of the Church Fathers played out on the popular level. The miracle stories and other forms of popular literature are thus a way to avoid the trap set by the polemicists who engaged in elite discourse. These stories are first and foremost entertainment, but, as we have seen, they also addressed latent questions and worries among the laity.

EPILOGUE

The battlefield miracles with which this century began and
ended were, above all else, miracles of power; they affirmed, in a
way uniquely suited to the sensibilities of the late antique world, a
divine sanction for the winner's cause. The other miracles in this
book were displays of power as well. The dispute over the Altar of
Victory pitted Christian sensibilities against traditional senatorial values, and Julian's spectacular failure to rebuild the Temple in
Jerusalem and his subsequent death in Persia were taken as proof
of the Christian God's willingness to intervene on behalf of his
people.

While intellectuals were framing conditions for the future,
these stories helped more ordinary Christians, especially new ones,
understand the world of their day. They provided the ballast that
allowed the Christian ship of state to weather the storm of 410,
and eventually the end of Roman rule in the West. In this way, the
story of Titus explains how Christianity survived the disaster of
410. After that date, the spell of the fourth century shattered. But
by then it scarcely mattered. By the time this carefully constructed
narrative came crashing down, generations had grown up knowing
only a Christian world, and these generations were ready to accept
any explanation that conformed to their assumptions about the way
the world worked. So the simple answer is that, by 410, Christians
no longer needed victory-bringing miracles to explain their world
to themselves.

Instead, they had these stories. By the time this string of victories ended with the sack of Rome in 410, these stories had gained
so thoroughgoing a hold that Christians could brush off the failure
with hardly a stutter. Ultimately, the miracle stories in this book
help us think through this connection between miracle, the estab-
lishment of Christianity, and the fall of Rome in a way that makes
sense to us yet still lets us appreciate the way people at the time
understood their problems. In a nutshell, Christianity survived the

fall of Rome because the miracle stories prevailed, even when the empire-affirming miracles that characterized the fourth century stopped. That is how the pagan Roman Empire became a Christian Roman Empire.

With this final lesson, we may now let Titus go to his reward, content in the knowledge that his story is still being told, and pondered, and understood.

NOTES

Chapter 1

1. If, despite all my warnings, you insist on knowing something about miracles, a good place to start would be Twelftree 2011 and Moule 1965a. For more specific studies, see the essays in Nicklas and Spittler 2013. For a good discussion of views on miracles in early modern Europe, see Burns 1981; Shaw 2008. For a more precise discussion of miracle types, see the classic study of Kee 1983, esp. 290–96. Turnabout is fair play. For an attack on science as the new dogma, see another classic, Fort 1919.
2. A good introduction to Diocletian is Rees 2004. See also Corcoran 1996.
3. On the late empire, see Harries 2012; Mitchell 2006; Wienand 2015. On Valens, see Lenski 2002; Matthews 1990. On the continued unity of the two halves, see Millar 2006.
4. I am grateful to Amanda Butt for this updated analogy. See Nock 1947: 102–16, at 104. See also chapter 3 and Maraval 2014; Nuffelen 2011: 4 identifies "an increased tendency to view human society as part of a cosmic hierarchy" as characteristic of this period. For use of macrocosm–microcosm analogies in earlier Greek and Chinese thought, see Raphals 2015: 653.
5. On the persecution, see DePalma Digeser 2012; Twomey and Humphries 2009; Portman 1990; Kolb 1988. Still useful: Frend 1967.
6. Gibbon 1909–1914. The quotation is from chap. 71 (vol. 7: 320).
7. Gibbon 1909–1914, chap. 15 (vol. 2: 3). The remaining reasons were: "II. The doctrine of a future life, improved by every additional circumstance which could give weight and efficacy to that important truth. III. The miraculous

powers ascribed to the primitive church. IV. The pure and austere morals of the Christians. V. The union and discipline of the Christian republic, which gradually formed an independent and increasing state in the heart of the Roman empire."

8. Zecchini 2011.

9. "*Si quis idola fregerit et ibidem fuerit occisus, quatenus in Evangelio scriptum non est neque invenitur sub Apostolis unquam factum, placuit in numero eum non recipi martyrum.*" ("No one who is put to death for destroying an idol should be made a martyr, for we do not find anywhere in Scripture that the Apostles ever countenanced such action.") In Jonkers 1954: 18. The council is usually dated between 300 and 314, but Superbiola Martinez 1987 has argued that the text is actually a compilation of councils that met throughout the fourth century. See esp. his appendix 2.

10. Kahlos 2009: 136. Pettegree 1996: 198 made the "losers" comment while discussing Reformation arguments. The sentiment was never better put than by Macaulay 1849–1865, vol. 1: 196, writing about James II: "He learned by rote the commonplaces which all sects repeat so fluently when they are enduring oppression, and forget so easily when they are able to retaliate it."

11. For the Christian belief in toleration, see Garnsey 1984; Beatrice 1990. I have dealt with this problem at greater length in Drake 1996, Drake 2000, and Drake 2011.

12. Brown 1971: 80–101. For retrospectives on the impact of this article, see Howard-Johnston and Hayward 1999, and thoughts by Brown himself 1998: 353–76. On the problems posed by the term "rational," see Frankfurter 2005a: 256. On the monopoly of knowledge, see Dean 1998: 9. For changes in the meaning of "superstition" and "heresy" in Rome, see Salzman 2017. For a good discussion of these issues, see Boin 2015: 1–7. More recent studies have even turned the old argument on its head, suggesting that practices like divination that were formerly considered "primitive superstition" actually spurred the development of "rationality and legitimacy." See Raphals 2013: 4. For an engaging study of the way the Reformation contributed to the formation of the modern secular state, see Gregory 2012.

13. As put by Weddle 2010: xii–xiii, "an event that is merely puzzling does not constitute a *miracle* in the religious sense. A miracle is an *interpreted* event."

14. Cf. Dean 1998: 11: "The stories Americans tell about space are stories about who we are and who we want to be."

15. The problem is posed succinctly by Shaw 2006: 3: "What are we to do with the great core of religious life, with the supernatural world, where humans may not dominate causality? This is an especially large problem when historians disagree with their subjects as to the possibilities of supernatural beings or supernatural actions, that is, when there is deep ontological dissonance between historians and the past."

16. Hopkins 1999. For a more nuanced understanding of ancient monotheism than I give here, see Fredriksen 2010, esp. 11, 54.

17. Garland 2011: 75: "In the plainest terms, a goal scored from behind the half-way line could, without hyperbole, have been appropriately deemed 'miraculous.'" Cf. Martin 2004: 13: "'the supernatural' did not exist in ancient cultures *as a category*'"; Mount 2013. For some examples of "miracles" performed by pagan holy men, see Fowden 1982: 50.

18. I capitalize the Judaeo-Christian deity mostly out of convention, but also because there are times that it can help avoid confusion over the deity in question.

19. See in general the essays in Nicklas and Spittler 2013; Bowie 2011; Grant 1952.

20. See Moberly 2011. Signer 1999: 117: "The Rabbis would emphasize the source of the miracle rather than the person performing the miracle. The source of these miraculous acts . . . was the God of Israel whose commandments bound Israel in an ever-lasting covenant."

21. Signer 1999; Weddle 2010: 103.

22. Golda Meir to German Chancellor Willy Brandt at a state dinner, June 10, 1973 (*New York Times*, June 11, 1973, 3). For Tevye, see Kanfer 2006: 123.

23. A term used by the sociologist Pierre Bourdieu to represent the social and cultural assumptions that underlay actions and decision making. See Bourdieu 1977.

24. Lizzi Testa 2015: 405. For essays written in the conflict mode, see Momigliano 1963. In a memorable phrase, Dagron 1967: 4 referred to the "night and day" division of Christians and pagans as "une Histoire trop euclidienne."

25. The path-breaking work on diversity in early Christianity is Bauer 1934, also available in English: Bauer 1971. For a succinct introduction, see King 2008, and for a recent, readable study, see Ehrman 2003. On "paganism," see Jürgasch 2016.

26. Cracco Ruggini 1977: 118. For a reflection of the "conflict" view, see Garland 2011: 87.

27. As observed by Swain 2013: 14, "Aristotle's excavation of power and society was not of general interest. . . . General principles and images of correct behaviour were what mattered." Brown 1981 overturned a long-standing scholarly premise that there was a difference between the credulity of "popular religion" and the more rational beliefs of higher classes.

28. North 1992.

29. Price 2008; Moss 2013.

30. Rives 1999; Selinger 2004.

31. See, for example, Guignebert 1923; Bonner 1984: 350 argued that such Christians "cushioned the psychological shock" for new converts. Markus 1990: 33 warned that "the distinction sometimes made between 'Christians' and 'semi-' or 'paganised' Christians . . . is based on the

historian's assumptions about what sort of a culture or life-style is to count as 'Christian.'" Boin 2015: 15-35 provides lively examples.

32. Sauer 2003: 164, after a judicious review of the evidence for destruction of pagan sites, concluded, "It is not monotheism as such which is to blame, but extremism—and not just religious extremism, but also secular ideologies." For an attempt to identify a sociopolitical dynamic, see Drake 1996.

33. See the pioneering work of D. Boyarin 1999, with Boyarin 2009; Janowitz 2000; Jürgasch 2016. For pagans, see Chadwick 1985: 9.

34. Acting under the either–or dichotomy that prevailed in Cold War thinking, an earlier generation of historians interpreted pagan use of this language as refusal to reconcile themselves to the hated name of "Christ" in the aftermath of Constantine's conversion. See, for example, Jones 1962: 82–83: such language "is eloquent of the embarrassment of the pagan orator, forced to avoid all mention of the immortal gods, but averse from sullying his lips with any allusion to the God of the Christians." For pagan monotheism, see Athanassiadi and Frede 1999; Mitchell and van Nuffelen 2010. Edwards 2001 takes exception to the term. On solar cult, see Wallraff 2001a; Halsbergh 1972; Hijmans 2009; Bardill 2012.

35. As observed by Jones 2014: 5–6. Cf. Boin 2014: 194–95: "The emergence of 'pagan' and 'paganism' might now perhaps best be seen as a symptom of growing Christian sectarianism in the fourth century."

36. Bowie 2011: 172.

37. Cameron 2011: 19–25.

38. For an opposing view, see the wide-ranging critique of Ratti 2013; Paschoud 2012a; Jürgasch 2016. For a rich study of use of the term over time, see Marenbon 2015.

Chapter 2

1. Theodoret, *HE* 5.24.

2. The view of this battle as a final confrontation between the two ideologies was particularly appealing during the Cold War (see chapter 1). For a skillful dismantling, see Cameron 2011: 93–131; Salzman 2010.

3. At *obit. Theo.* 3, Ambrose points to Honorius "standing at the altar" (*assistente sacris altaribus*). As Lunn-Rockliffe 2008: 199, n. 46, has observed, giving such prominence to a layman would have been exceptional.

4. *obit. Theo.* 7.

5. *obit. Theo.* 10. The Elisha allusion is to 2 Kings 6:18, where the prophet prays that the enemy army be blinded.

6. Trans. Cameron 2011: 114.

7. Rufinus's version of the miracle is at *HE* 11.3–34 in his continuation of Eusebius of Caesarea's *Church History* published in 402 or 403. The story

is picked up and expanded over the next half century by Augustine in his *City of God* (5.26) and three church historians writing in the East: Socrates, *HE* 5.25; Sozomen, *HE* 7.24; and Theodoret, *HE* 5.24, part of whose account appears at the start of this chapter. The threat about Milan's basilica occurs in Paulinus of Milan, *Life of Ambrose* 31.

8. Alan Cameron, who has done more than any single scholar to overturn the model, began to question the existence of a "pagan revival" half a century ago with Cameron 1966. See also Cameron 1977 and Cameron 2011. For an epitome of the "conflict" approach, see Momigliano 1963.

9. Sozomen, *HE* 7.22. For the stereotype of Christian intolerance, see chapter 1.

10. Cameron 2011: 92 minimizes Eugenius's role in any reversal of previous anti-pagan legislation.

11. Markus 1990: 19.

12. In his *Life of Saint Ambrose*, the bishop's secretary, Paulinus of Milan, tells us that even as a child Ambrose "thought that he was going to be a bishop." *Life of Ambrose* 4. For Ambrose's career, see McLynn 1994: 291–360.

13. On the importance of ceremony, the trailblazing book was McCormack 1981. More recently, Smith 2007. For imperial churchgoing, see McLynn 2004.

14. Ambrose, *Ep.* 75a.36: *imperator enim intra ecclesiam, non supra ecclesiam est.*

15. The circumstances are muddled by tendentious accounts, including Ambrose's own. I here follow the course set by McLynn 1994: 181–96. See also Colish 2002. For a reading of this event through Ambrose's spiritual understanding, see Chin 2010, esp. 548–53.

16. For a detailed and insightful discussion of the battle, see Lenski 2002: 320–67.

17. *Ep.* 74 (40).12: *Sed disciplinae te ratio, imperator, movet. Quit igitur est amplius? disciplinae species an causa religionis? Cedat oportet censura devotioni.*

18. Ambrose recorded his triumph for his sister, and posterity, in a gloating letter that he sent in 388/389. See further McLynn 1994: 298–315. For a translation of the letter, see Liebeschuetz and Hill 2005: 262–69. Paulinus of Milan gives a developed version of the confrontation in his *Life of Ambrose* 24; what might be called the canonical version appears in Theodoret, *HE* 5.17.

19. McLynn 1994: 109, referring to the opening sentences of Ambrose's *de fide*.

20. Liebeschuetz and Hill 2005: 27–46.

21. Sozomen, *HE* 7.25. It was evidently customary in Constantinople for the emperor to celebrate mass with the priests. On the phenomenon of child emperors, see McEvoy 2013.

22. McGoldrick 1995.

23. Shaw 2011: 412–13. Cf. Diefenbach 2015: 354, pointing out that, "by appealing to biblical texts and martyr acts, Christian discourses tapped a new reservoir of cultural models that could be deployed to delegitimate the emperor." On Ambrose's sermons, see Lunn-Rockliffe 2008;

Graumann 1997. On sermons more generally, see MacMullen 1966; MacMullen 1989.

24. Los Angeles *Times* 1997. On the importance of coins for conveying imperial messages, see Levick 1982; Crawford 1983; Laurence 1994; Wienand 2015a.

25. On the importance of sermons, see Graumann 1997; MacMullen 1966.

26. For text and translation, see n. 3 in this chapter.

27. For classical parallels to these themes, see Raspanti 2009. The "cardinal virtues" are those inscribed on a shield presented by the Roman Senate to the first emperor, Augustus, because of his "courage, clemency, justice, and piety" (*virtutis clementiaeque iustitiae et pietatis causa*). See Augustus, *Res Gestae* 34 and Charlesworth 1937. For a caution against treating these as "cardinal virtues," see Wallace-Hadrill 1981.

28. *De obit. Theo.* 34.

29. For examples in a sermon by Eusebius of Caesarea, see Smith 1989.

30. 2 Kings 2:13.

31. *De obit. Theo.* 15.

32. *De obit. Theo.* 38.

33. As one of the greatest church historians of the twentieth century once put it, "That the right form of worship is essential if heaven is to be propitious is an axiom of ancient society." Chadwick 1980: 10.

34. A classic study remains Fustel de Coulanges 1864.

35. A point made by Diefenbach 2015.

36. Paulinus, *Life of Ambrose* 3. For the parallel with Jesus, see Luke 13:11.

37. Paulinus, *Life of Ambrose* 11, 54. For similar incidents, see chaps. 18, 20, 34, 37.

38. *Expositio Psalmi* CXVIII, 15.15. Tr. Riaian 1998: 216, modified. See further Roukema 2014: 209.

39. Paulinus, *Life of Ambrose* 5. On the significance of martyrs, see chapter 7.

40. McLynn 1994: 209–16.

41. Ambrose, *Ep.* 74 (40).22; Jews: 74 (40).15, 18; Christ: 74 (40).22.

42. *De fide* 1 Prol. 3.

43. Ambrose, *Ep.* 73 (18).34.

Chapter 3

1. *De obit. Th.* 40.

2. As did one of the seminal thinkers about Constantine when he wrote that the first Christian emperor's "ideal State would be hampered by no fetters of toleration." Baynes 1939: 686.

3. "The image of a society neatly divided into 'Christian' and 'pagan' is the creation of late fourth-century Christians, and has been too readily taken at its face value by modern historians." Markus 1990: 28.

4. For a theoretical framework that can serve as a model for future study, see Lenski 2016, esp. 1–23.

5. Eusebius, *Life of Constantine* 1.28.2. Unless otherwise noted, all translations of the *Life* are from Cameron and Hall 1999. In antiquity, midday was considered the "witching hour" for supernatural encounters, just as midnight is now. See, with examples, Bremmer 2013: 6.

6. Lactantius, *De mortibus persecutorum* 44.5. Hereafter *DMP*. For the date, see Barnes 1973.

7. Bruun 1966: 364; Alföldi 1932: 9–32; Kraft 1954–1955: 151–78; Ehling 2011. On coins as propaganda, see chapter 2, n. 24.

8. As argued by Bleckmann 2015: 325–27.

9. As argued by Bruun 1997. See also Bruun 1966: 61–64.

10. Grégoire 1930: 258. Moreau 1954: 433–35 accepted the emendation in his edition for Sources Chrétiennes. See also Sulzberger 1925: 406–7; Marrou 1959. Contra: Black 1970.

11. Bhola, 2015: 291–312 argues for redating this panegyric to 309. For present purposes the difference is not significant, so I have stayed with 310 to avoid unnecessary confusion.

12. Nixon and Rodgers 1994 includes the 1964 Latin text of R. A. Mynors. For this panegyric, see 211–67. Unless otherwise indicated, all quotations are from this translation.

13. *Confessions* 6.3.

14. An example survives under the name of one Menander Rhetor. See Russell and Wilson 1981.

15. *PL* VI (VII). 14.1: *De quo ego quemadmodum dicam adhuc ferme dubito et de nuto numinis tui exspecto consilium.* Trans. Nixon and Rodgers, 237.

16. *PL* VI (VII). 3.1: *imperium nascendo meruisti.*

17. *PL* VI (VII).3–5. The "most beautiful temple" is thought to have been the sanctuary at Grand, which housed a cult statue of the Gallic Apollo Grannus, often portrayed holding a laurel wreath. Woolf 2003: 145.

18. Long 2009. Although halo phenomena had been mentioned in earlier works, the first systematic study was conducted by Peter Weiss 1993. An English translation by A. R. Birley is available in Weiss 2003. Weiss's argument has been widely accepted, but see the critique by Harris 2005.

19. As Weddle 2010: xii–xiii pointed out, "an event that is merely puzzling does not constitute a *miracle* in the religious sense. A miracle is an *interpreted* event, set within a tradition's broader system of beliefs and understood as signifying something about transcendent reality." Cf. Harris 2007: 24: "a truly historical and critical interpretation must respect the integrity and purpose of its original author(s)."

20. See Sumi 2005: 128, with further citations. I am grateful to Jacob Latham for this reference. See also Woods 2012; Drijvers 2009.

21. Nock 1933: 7–8, paraphrasing James 1902. For the variety of conversion experiences, see Jacobs 2012: 27–47.
22. For an argument that Constantine had been born a Christian, see Elliott 1987, developed in Elliott 1997.
23. It is "a sense of perceiving truths not known before, a sense of clean and beautiful newness . . . [often] accompanied by hallucinatory or quasi-hallucinatory phenomena," in the classic study by Nock 1933: 266. For a discussion of the importance of socialization, see Stark 1993: 172. See further Morrison 1992; Crook 2004; Bremmer, van Bekkum, and Molendijk 2006.
24. Van Dam 2003; Flower 2012.
25. *Life* 2.12.1–2. I have modified Cameron and Hall 1999, which reads "a revelation from God" for θεοφανείας.
26. As part of a speech to Constantine that he appended to the *Life*, Eusebius spoke of "the countless manifestations of your Savior and his countless personal visits during sleep." Eus., *SC* 18.1–3. For Eusebius's speeches, see chapter 4.
27. See Stewart 2004: 44: "the broad populace . . . thought that dreams contained divinatory messages (perhaps sent by the gods)." Cf. Potter 1994: 20: "The 'mainstream' philosophic view of dream prediction, enunciated most clearly in Stoic thought was that in sleep the mind might travel free of the body to make contact with the divine."
28. For a noteworthy exception, see Harries 2012.
29. The document has become a football—or, maybe better, hand grenade—in the debate over Constantine's sincerity. For a review, see Drake 2014.
30. *et Christianis et omnibus liberam potestatem sequendi religionem quam quisque voluisset, quo quicquid <est> divinitatis in sede caelesti. DMP* 48.2.
31. Diocletian's junior emperor and successor Galerius wrote in 311, when he decided to tolerate Christians after all, that they had been persecuted because "we saw that these same people were neither offering worship and due religious observance to the gods nor practising the worship of the god of the Christians" (*videremus nec diis eosdem cultum ac religionem debitam exhibere nec Christianorum deum observare*): *DMP* 43.4.
32. On the imperial *comes*, see chapter 1, n. 4. See further Nock 1930. Two important, and competing, works on the ideology of the late empire are now available in English translation: Peterson 2011; Schmitt 2008. Translated earlier, Schmitt 1985. Significant recent studies include den Boer 1972; Kloft 1979; Lassandro 2000; Noreña 2011; Wienand 2012.
33. *Oration to the Saints* 22.2. On public support, see *OC* 25.3: "the emperor's decision could not prevail over the good sense of the people." Eusebius tells us of his intention to append this document as an example of the emperor's speech-making activities: *Life* 4.32. Arguments that the speech was not written by the emperor were dismissed by Barnes 1981: 74.

34. See, for example, *OC* 11.7, Christ's "innate benevolence" and the "astonishing miracle" of his willingness to put up with error, and *OC* 15.34, the "heavenly wisdom" that violence merely begets more violence. See also his argument for diversity in chap. 13 and his contrast of Christian benevolence with the violent acts of the persecutors in chap. 23.

35. Sibyl: *OC* 19; Vergil: *OC* 19–21.

36. As observed by Fürst 2010: 84, "There was a high degree of convergence between Christian belief in one God and philosophical ideas of unity, and there was a 'monotheistic' consensus in the matter of whether God was singular or plural, in so far as this question addressed theoretical principles and was deemed to be about the first principle of all reality."

37. *Life* 2.60.1. Cf. 2.59: "Let mankind, all of us, take advantage of the common heritage of good bequeathed to us, that is the blessing of peace."

38. See n. 8 above.

Chapter 4

1. As observed by Dagron 2003: 148: "The Constantine legend was not intended only to rewrite history and to make the first Christian emperor a paragon of virtue; it identified problems and explored possible routes forward, most of which were judged dangerous by the institutional Church." Cf. Wallraff 2001b, esp. 267–68.

2. *Life* 4.24.

3. Constantine's claim is at *OC* 11.2. For the Christian makeup of this audience, see Barnes 2001: 34.

4. Athanasius used the title liberally in his path-breaking *Life of Antony*. See, for example, 70.2, 71.1, 93.1. A casual search of the online *Thesaurus Linguae Graecae* (stephanus.tlg.uci.edu, s.v. θεοῦ ἄνθρωπος) found some two hundred uses, almost all of which applied only to monks and bishops. See further Steidle 1956.

5. For Paul's vision, see *Acts of the Apostles*, 9. Paul's claim to direct contact is at Galatians 1:1: "From Paul, an apostle, not by human appointment or human commission, but by commission from Jesus Christ and from God the Father who raised him from the dead." Compare Constantine in *OC* 11.2: "We, however, have received no aid from human instruction; nay, whatever graces of character are esteemed of good report by those who have understanding, are entirely the gift of God." Eusebius describes the emperor's burial arrangements at *Life* 4.60. See further Staats 2008; Dagron 2003: 143–44; Montgomery 1968: 84–109; Gillman 1961. For the use of *Isapostolos* starting in the fifth century, see Meier 2003: 139.

6. For the pagan orator, see *PL* 9 (12).2.5. For imperial ideology, see chapter 3, 66–70 with n. 32 and chapter 1, n. 4.

7. See Creed 1984: xxix–xxx.
8. Jerome, *De viris illustribus,* 80.
9. Lactantius, *DMP* 33–35. See Momigliano 1963b: 79. On Lactantius's treatment of Galerius, see further chapter 9.
10. *Contra Celsum* 8.39.
11. DePalma Digeser 1994. We know from Eusebius's *Life* 4.55 that later in life Constantine held a regular salon where philosophers debated such issues, so it is reasonable to presume that he held similar gatherings at this earlier date. For the purpose, see DePalma Digeser 2000.
12. Lact., *DI* 5.1.15–16: "This is the principal reason why holy scripture lacks the trust of the wise, both scholars and princes of this world: its prophets have spoken to suit ordinary folk, in plain and ordinary language; they thus earn the contempt of people who will not read or hear anything not polished and eloquent." For his aim, see Lact., *DI* 5.1.14. He takes note of Christian waverers at *DI* 5.1.9.
13. Lact., *DI* 5.13.13–14. For the story of Mucius, see Livy 2.12–13. Regulus, twice consul (267, 256 BCE), was a historical figure but his self-sacrifice, as celebrated by Horace, *Carmina* 3.5, is considered a legend. For Roman judicial practices in the late empire, see MacMullen 1986.
14. *Contra Celsum* 3.44.
15. Lact., *DI* 5.19.10–13.
16. Garnsey 1984. Less convinced of the sincerity of the Christian argument is Kahlos 2009. See further chapter 8.
17. Schott 2008: 112–13. For an English translation of Constantine's oration, see Edwards 2003. See further Drake 2006.
18. Hanson 1980; Miller 1994; Shulman and Stroumsa 1999; Weber 2000; Demandt 2007; Harris 2009.
19. Warmington 1998: 266. Barnes 1981 remains a foundational study, with redating by Burgess 1997.
20. The path-breaking work was Bauer 1934 (English translation Bauer 1971).
21. Viz. Barnes 1981: 254–55, where this phrase is cited as proof of the oration's "aggressively Christian content." For the date and circumstances of Eusebius's speeches, see Drake 1976: 40–45.
22. On the trend toward monotheistic thought in late antiquity, see Athanassiadi and Frede 1999; Mitchell and van Nuffelen 2010. There is some debate over whether the term "monotheism" applies to pagan religion. See Edwards 2004; Gordon 2014.
23. A turning point was established when Barnes 1981: 266 determined that Eusebius could only be put in Constantine's presence on four occasions. Equally important: Av. Cameron 1983; Av. Cameron 1997. There has been an explosion of new interest in Eusebius. From a large list, see Inowlocki and Zamagni 2011; Johnson and Schott 2013; Singh 2015.

24. This speech, "On Christ's Sepulchre" (*De Sepulchro Christi*, hereafter *SC*), has come down in manuscripts as chaps. 11–18 of Eusebius's other speech, "In Praise of Constantine" (*laus Constantini*, hereafter *LC*). For their separate occasions, see Drake 1976: 30–44.

25. In the *Life* 4.33.1, Eusebius says that the emperor listened to the *SC* "with rapt attention" and "made a shrewdly considered critique of the speech."

26. *SC* 11.1. The quotation is from Galatians 1:1.

27. In "Silver Blaze," Holmes solves the disappearance of a prize racehorse by observing that the watchdog did not bark as it should have, which meant that it knew the thief. The story appeared in Doyle 1894.

28. *Life* 1.12, preceded by *HE* 9.9.5–7. See further *Life* 1.20, 1.38–39. At *Life* 2.12, Constantine's tabernacle and prayers in battle also evoke Moses, though not by name. Finally, as Moses revealed he was not meant to enter the Promised Land, so Constantine on his deathbed reveals that God had denied his wish to be baptized in the Jordan River (*Life* 4.62). Smith 2016: 62 observes, "Without question, the comparison of Constantine to Moses was Eusebius's narrative innovation. It was a historiographical creation necessary for constructing a new sort of emperor who, nevertheless, had deep roots in the past." See further Becker 1910; Hollerich 1989; Rapp 1998a; Damgaard 2013.

29. See, for example, *Deut.* 17:18–19. Greenslade 1973: 5–14. For Moses's dual role, see Pearce 2004; Rapp 1998b.

30. *LC* 2.3, 6.21.

31. *Life* 1.32.1–3.

32. Cf. the private oration that Eusebius delivered in Constantine's presence the previous fall. Here, he disavowed any notion of teaching the emperor himself, who had been taught by God, and even used St. Paul's words in Galatians 1:1 to support his claim: "These revelations are not intended to initiate you, who have been instructed by God," he said, "nor to lay bare secrets for you, to whom well before our account God Himself, 'not by men nor through men' but by means of the Common Savior Himself and frequent enlightening visions of His Divinity revealed and uncovered the secrets of the holy rites." *SC* 11.1.

33. *Life* 1.44.1–2. Constantine is quoted at *Life* 4.24.

34. *Life* 4.54.2–3. Eusebius's discretion led to Louis Duchesne's famous characterization of the *Life* as "a triumph of reticence and circumlocution" ("le triomphe de la réticence et de la circonlocution"). Duchesne 1910: 191. On the importance of silence in an autocracy, see Timonen 2004 and, more generally, Ahl 1984.

35. For the argument that Eusebius died before completing the *Life*, see Pasquali 1910: 369–86. More recently, L. Pietri has minimized the number and importance of these shortcomings. See Pietri and Rondeau 2013: 18–20.

36. Mango 1990: 581 cf. Angelova 2015: 133. But see Weinreich 1916: 3–14. Similar controversy surrounds the statue Constantine put up in Constantinople, with his own features carved onto a statue of Apollo, which calls to mind his gold medallion of 313 (Figure 2.4). Preger 1901: 457–69 remains foundational, despite a heroic effort by Barnes 2011: 23 to discard this evidence. See Bardill 2012.

37. Dagron 2003: 143.

38. Eusebius, *Life* 2.71.

39. On the trend toward monotheistic thought in late antiquity, see Athanassiadi and Frede 1999; Mitchell and van Nuffelen 2010. There is some debate over whether the term "monotheism" applies to pagan religion. See Edwards 2004; Gordon 2014. On misunderstanding caused by vague language, see the important article by Ando 1996.

40. "I come forth to sing you the royal praises in a newer strain . . . 'spurning the beaten path of mankind,' [I] shall travel the pristine one . . . ," *LC* Prol. 2 (the quotation is from *Iliad* 6.202). On the emperor as the link between humans and the divine, see Iossif, Chankowski, and Lorber, 2011. On kingship theory itself, see Kolb 2000. For Eusebius in particular, see Chesnut 1986, esp. 231–51. See also Nuffelen 2011, Bardill 2012.

41. The phrase *virtutis clementiaeque iustitiae et pietatis causa*, translated by M. Charlesworth as "bravery, clemency, justice, and sense of duty," was engraved on a golden shield dedicated by the Roman Senate to the first emperor, Augustus. See Charlesworth 1937: 111–12. Wallace-Hadrill 1981 calls the existence of such a precise canon into question.

42. As Cracco Ruggini 1977: 110 put it, "piety (*eusebeia*) became the emperor's most important quality." The virtues that were engraved on a golden shield presented by the Senate to the first emperor, Augustus, were *virtus* (bravery), *clementia* (mercy), *iustitia* (justice), and *pietas* (duty). See further Noreña 2011; Wienand 2015a.

43. On the implications of Eusebius's usage, see Drake 2015.

44. Nuffelen 2011: 19, 114 identifies this aim to situate human society in a cosmic hierarchy as a particular feature of post-Hellenistic kingship theory. For examples of Eusebius's picture of a cosmic struggle, see *LC* 2.3: "our common Universal Savior, by invisible and divine power, keeps the rebellious powers—all those who used to fly through the earth's air and infect men's souls—at a distance, just as a good shepherd keeps wild beasts from his flock. And His friend, armed against his enemies with standards from Him above, subdues and chastises the visible opponents of truth by the law of combat." Cf. Ledegang 2014: 73: "Eusebius, however, puts his [Constantine's] wars in a religious framework. . . . His wars are interpreted by Eusebius as religious wars. This emperor is an instrument of God in his struggle against the demons. As a monarch he fights for the Christian monotheism and against polytheism."

45. See *SC* 16.5–6. The correlation between empire and Christ was first made in the second century by Bishop Melito of Sardis. See Eus., *HE* 4.26.
46. Iossif, Chankowski, and Lorber 2011.

Chapter 5

1. *obit. Theo.* 47–48. On the role of this story in Ambrose's political thought, see Consolino 1984.
2. See Liebeschuetz and Hill 2005: 176–77; Lunn-Rockliffe 2008: 196; Favez 1932.
3. Mannix 1925: 46–64 (Helena is on 59–61). Theodosius's miracle is in chap. 7.
4. *obit. Theo.* 42. This tradition is a likely source for a later account in which Constantine is the product of a one-night stand between his mother and the future emperor Constantius I. See Heydenreich 1879. Ambrose's story had significant impact. See Jaritz 2016. Ambrose brings in Constantine to welcome Theodosius at *obit. Theo.* 40, but otherwise he only appears as the recipient of Helena's wisdom (chap. 41) and gifts (chap. 47). She is linked to the Virgin at chaps. 46–47.
5. *Life* 3.25–28. On *martyrion*, see Grabar 1972; Ousterhout 1990: 46.
6. Biddle 1999: 64. In Biddle 1994: 100–103, Biddle demolished efforts to cast doubt on the location by Wharton 1992 and Taylor 1993. See further Hunt 1997; Ousterhout 1990; Walker 1990; Bahat 1986; Drake 1985.
7. Hebrews 3:12; John 19:41–2.
8. Hamrick 1977.
9. *Life* 3.30–32.
10. For the description: *Life* 3.33–40; for the dedication: *Life* 4.43–45.
11. Matt. 27:60; Mark 15:46; Luke 23:53.
12. Twain 1869, chap. 53. Reprinted in Neider 1966, vol. 1: 369–80.
13. Coüasnon 1974: 40 refers to the distance as "a stone's throw away." As the Catholic architect on the site for more than twenty years, Père Coüasnon was intimately familiar with the building.
14. "Skull," rendered into Greek as "kephalion," thence Latin "Calvary." Late Jewish legend identified it as so named because it was the place where Adam was buried. See Morris 2005: 25. Earlier, but still useful, is Jeremias 1926.
15. Conant and Downey 1956: 6, 21. For a model of the different stages of construction, see his Plate III. Conant 1958: 21 compared ancient and modern attitudes toward preservation.
16. *Life* 3.33–40.
17. Donner 1994.
18. Gibbon 1909–1914, vol. 2: 481, n. 66.

19. *Life* 3.38 τὸ κεφάλαιον τοῦ παντὸς ἡμισφαίριον. Coüasnon 1974: 44 thought the term referred to an apse, though he admitted it would be difficult for such a space to hold the twelve columns described by Eusebius. In 1945, A. Piganiol 1945: 9–10, 13 suggested that it was a reference to an *omphalos*, such as at Delphi, but noted that it was also a term used for a cupola. Either, he thought, would have been intended to mark the place of Jesus's death, as the tomb marked the Resurrection.

20. Conant and Downey 1956: 6 point out that a "monumental jeweled cross" can be seen in a mosaic in the Church of Santa Pudenziana in Rome, dated to the 390s. But something was in place earlier. The pilgrim Egeria, who was in Jerusalem between 381 and 384, makes several references to it. See, for example, 25.1: "The people assemble in the Great Church built by Constantine on Golgotha Behind the Cross." Wilkinson 1981: 125. Coins depicting the cross atop a stepped monument started to appear around 420. See Holum 1977.

21. See Conant 1958: 17: "It seems evident that the Calvary served to identify the Holy Sites." Cf. Hunt 1997: 413: "By linking the basilica solely to the symbolism of the Tomb Eusebius has misrepresented not only the actual topography of the site, but equally, it appears, the intentions of Constantine."

22. For an engaging account of restoration efforts, see Cohen 2008.

23. Coüasnon 1974: 41. Conant and Downey 1956: 21–22 speculated that Eusebius's attention was focused on "the splendid Constantinian works at the site; in the new arrangement, Calvary probably remained plain at first, and, despite its importance, rather effaced in the southeast corner of the Great Court."Coüasnon 1974: 2 shows the various plans that have been put forth over the years.

24. Catech. 14.9 (re the tomb).

25. In Catech. 4.10, Cyril offers as proof "this visible place itself, this blessed Golgotha." Cf. Catech. 13.4, "Golgotha here, close to which we are now gathered" and 13.39, "this holy Golgotha . . . the sepulchre nearby, where he was laid." In Catech. 10.19, he points to the "many true testimonies" by which the initiates were surrounded, including Gethsemane, Golgotha, the Holy Sepulchre, and the Mount of Olives, adding Sion, where the Holy Spirit descended on the Apostles at Pentecost, at Catech. 16.4. For the intense schedule of Lenten preparation, see Wills 2012: 85–133.

26. Catech. 4.10, 10.19, 13.4. His claim that the wood was visible "even to this day" is at Catech. 10.19.

27. Letter to Constantius, 3. On the letter, see Irshai 1996; Drijvers 1999. On its date, see Barnes 1993: 107.

28. Rubin 1982.

29. Walker 1990: 256. Conant and Downey 1956: 6.

30. At *Life* 2.8, Eusebius repeats stories that he says he heard from the emperor himself about the miraculous qualities of this standard. A contest between

miracle and magic was already the centerpiece of the second-century apocryphal Acts of Peter, in which the Apostle engages in a prolonged contest with
the arch-heretic Simon Magus. See Schneemelcher 1992: 271–321. On this
work, see further chapter 8. In the *Life of Antony* 78.5, the holy man claims,
"Wherever one sees the sign of the cross, magic loses its power and sorcery
has no effect."

31. Calvin 1964: 419–20. Fleury 1870: 52–59 estimated that all known pieces
of the cross added up to about two-thirds the size of a beam that would have
been used for the Crucifixion. On magic, see Aune 1980.

32. See, for example, *Life* 1.37, 1.40, 2.4. See further Storch 1970.

33. For Constantine's letter, see Eusebius, *Life* 3.30–32. In his state oration,
Eusebius dwelt on the importance Constantine attached to the symbol of the
cross. See *LC* 9.

34. Guthrie 1966; Austin 1980; Pohlsander 1984; Potter 2013: 244–45.

35. On the importance of Theodosius's penance, see McLynn 1994: 315–30. See
further Brown 1992; Gleason 1995; Harris 2001; Davis 2006.

36. *Life* 3.44–45, 3.47.

37. Rufinus, *Historia Ecclesiastica* 10.7–8.

38. Nuffelen 2002.

39. Canon 36 of the Council of Elvira, which probably met early in the fourth
century (see chapter 1, n. 9), forbade the painted images in churches lest they
become objects of worship. But as Brink 2007: 698 observed, Constantine
"serenely ignored" other conventions of the time. Baumstark 1913: 229–30,
seconded by Herzog zu Sachsen 1913: 258. Conant and Downey 1956: 10
accepted the idea of "a mosaic or fresco in the apse" depicting the crucifixion.

40. In a masterful study, Heid 1989 did not go so far as to blame the legend on
tour guides, but he did stress the importance of pilgrims in development
of the legend. For the way miracle reports circulated in a later period, see
Finucane 1977: 152–60.

41. *Life* 4.45.1.

42. Conant and Downey 1956: 45.

43. *Life* 3.41–45.

44. Blaauw 1997; Linder 1975: 69.

45. Duchesne 1889: 417; he added the caveat in Febretti 1890: 176–77.

46. *Catechesis* 13.40.

47. No law survives, but one is reported by a fourth-century author, Aurelius
Victor, *De Caesaribus* 41.4, repeated in the fifth century by the Church his-
torian Sozomen, *HE* 1.8.13. For a full discussion and review of sources, see
Cook 2014.

48. On theology, see Leach 1973: 8. As a sign of Christian allegiance, see Jacobs
2014: 207.

49. Carroll 2001: 164. On the impact, see Storch 1970; Drijvers 2011: 147.

50. Quinn 1962. See also n. 14 in this chapter.
51. Baert 2004; Ashton 1887.
52. Alexander Monachos, *De inventione vivificae crucis*, trans. Scott 2004. For connections between Alexander's work and the legend, see Drake 2012.

Chapter 6

1. For a recent review of the evidence, see Drijvers 2011; for a more detailed account, see Drijvers 1992. See also chapter 5.
2. The Judas story is told in dozens of surviving manuscripts—Latin, Greek, and Syriac, as well as vernacular—all with interesting variants. For convenience, and to make a consistent narrative, I use the account of Jacobus de Varagine in his *Legenda Aurea*, even though it is quite late (thirteenth century). On this work, see further next note. For a likely date of the early fifth century for the story's origin, see H. and J.-W. Drijvers 1997: 20.
3. Jacobus de Varagine, *Legenda aurea* 68. On Jacobus, see Reames 1985. Schechner 1997: 29 observes that Jacobus's work was "more widely owned by merchants and artisans than the Bible."
4. *Leg. aur.* 68.
5. *Leg. aur.* 68.
6. Jan-Willem Drijvers, who has traced the origins of his story to the first decades of the fifth century, has observed, "The Judas Kyriakos legend became the best known and most widespread version of the *inventio crucis* tradition." Drijvers 2011: 159.
7. Jacobus 68 notes, "However, it does not seem credible to us that the father of this Judas could have been alive at the time of the Passion of Christ, for from his day to the time of Helena two hundred and seventy years had passed, unless, on the other hand, men lived longer in those days than in our time."
8. As Andrew Jacobs has proposed: Jacobs 2016: 2.
9. As observed by Verheyden 2008: 144, citing Dummer 1973. For a study of the role medical metaphors played in Christian discourse, see Fournier 2016. I am grateful to Prof. Fournier for providing me with an advance copy of this chapter.
10. See Simon 1979.
11. For a discussion of Epiphanius's use of the term, see Goranson 1990: 19–20.
12. Epiphanius, *Panarion* 30.
13. *Panarion* 30.4.1–12.9. After reconstructing Epiphanius's chronology, Goranson 1990: 72 concluded that Epiphanius probably met the historical Joseph. See also Thornton 1990; Goranson 1999.
14. Thornton 1990: 61.
15. For a moving account of anti-Semitism in the Catholic Church, see Carroll 2001.

16. As observed by Ronchey 2014: 153. See also Rutgers 1995.
17. The term "anti-Semitic" developed in nineteenth-century Germany as a response to arguments about the superiority of the "Aryan race." See Levy 2005; Cohen 1986: 43–47. For present-day difficulties with the term, see Marcus 2015. For the problem with "pagan" as a label, see chapter 1.
18. Stroumsa 2007; Schwartz 2001; Schäfer 1998; Lieu, Rajak, and North 1992; Linder 1987.
19. McGing 2002.
20. Johnson 1989: 423–24. For an excellent survey of conditions, see Fredriksen and Irshai 2006.
21. Dothan 1983: 42. Dothan's reading of imperial coins depicting the emperor in the guise of Sol is standard, but this identification has been astutely challenged by Hijmans 2009: 89. Hijmans in general plays down the importance of the Sol Invictus cult.
22. For a detailed description of the mosaic, see Dothan 1983: 39–40.
23. See Levine 2012: 327 for a summary of the various interpretations.
24. For a discussion of the use of archaeology to identify elements of nonrabbinic Judaism, see Fine 2005: 35–46; Rutgers 1992.
25. Stroumsa 2007: 168.
26. See Dölger 1918 and Dölger 1920. See also Arneth 2000; Wallraff 2001a.
27. Fine 2005: 196–97; Levine 2012: 319.
28. Kühnel 2000; for Beit Alpha, see Levine 2012: 280–93; Fine 2005: 92, 196.
29. As Jacobs 2004: 48 observed, Epiphanius's Joseph also stands as a bulwark against heresy: "Whereas the Ebionites combine all manner of heresy, Joseph remains pure in his Christian orthodoxy. He embodies the knowledge of Jew and Christian necessary to define and combat heresy."
30. In the words of Frances Young, "Epiphanius represents the fanatical, slogan-shouting mind that could not distinguish central from peripheral matters or think through fundamental theological issues." Young 1983: 124. See also Young 1982. For a more positive view, see Kim 2015; Jacobs 2016.
31. As observed by Verheyden 2008: 172.
32. On Epiphanius as a reflection of broader trends, see Jacobs 2016.
33. Shaw 2011: 308–9.
34. *Ep.* 74 (40).10, 18, 19.
35. *Ep.* 74 (40).20.
36. *Discourses Against Judaizing Christians* 1.1.6, 1.4.1,1.6.7, 1.7.5, 1.2.6. See further Roukema 2014.
37. As early as Eusebius, who in *Life* 4.27 praises the emperor for forbidding "prophet-slayers and Christ-killers" from owning Christian slaves. For use of the phrase in Antioch, see Wilken 1983: 125–26.
38. For a vivid picture of the way preachers like Chrysostom would interact with their audience, as well as a discussion of the techniques of ancient rhetoric, see Wilken 1983: 95–127; Mayer 1997.

NOTES TO PAGES 129–133

39. John Chrysostom, *Discourses Against Judaizing Christians*. For Greek rather than Jewish criticism, see Wilken 1983: 152. For examples of the Jewish practices followed by John's "Judaizers," see Fredriksen and Irshai 2006: 1005; Mayer and Allen 2000: 148 (with a translation of the first discourse at 149–67). Shepardson 2014: 92–128 studies the *Adversus Judeios* sermons as part of Chrysostom's broader program of defining orthodox belief and behavior.

40. For hatred as a unifying instrument, see Posner 1999: 211: "It is bracing to have an enemy. Indeed, without an enemy to inspire enough fear to submerge differences on lesser issues, it is difficult to hold a coalition together."

41. *Against Judaizing Christians* 1.6l; cf. Wilken 1983: 160.

42. As Bowersock 2006: 119 put it, these mosaics "open up a Judaism that hardly anyone would have credited a hundred years ago." A pioneering article by Reuther 1972 touched off a wave of new thinking. Kinzig 1991 draws a useful distinction between different levels of separation. See further Cohen 1999; Fredriksen 2003; Boyarin 2004 and 1999; and the discussion in Levine 2012: 207.

43. Boyarin 2009: esp. 12–20. Cf. Schwartz 2003: 210, noting an "increasingly unambiguous Jewishness" as a particular trait of Jewish culture in late antiquity.

44. See Wilken 1983: 95–127, especially 105–6, for a vivid picture of the setting of an ancient sermon. For the influence of the philosophical schools, see Johnson 1989: 429, and succinctly at 436: "Jews and Christians alike are so inured to such 'attacks on idolatry' that they simply do not hear the inflammatory nature of this language." Cf. for Ambrose Liebeschuetz and Hill 2005: 96: the bishop's language was "perhaps not as shockingly irresponsible as it would seem, because extreme rhetorical exaggeration was assumed by everybody, and allowance made for it."

45. *Confessions* 5.13.

46. Johnson 1989: 424.

47. *Discourse on Blessed Babylas*, 13.

48. As Dagron 2003: 148 observed, such practices "allowed into the Christian literature of the fifth century a strain of ferocious polemic which has continued to our day." So, too, Frankfurter 2005b: 148 observes that legends "assume a different resonance in subsequent centuries. . . . Thus we can speak of further functions to legends of violence when the tellers are no longer emergent sectarians in conflict but rather troubadours, friars, official readers of festival cycles, festival actors, burghers, and lay rumormongers."

49. Or, as put by Henry 2005: 362, "Historically, Judaism has been Christianity's bad conscience, an unremitting, silent threat to the substance of Christianity's identity. . . . Ironically, the so-called 'Jewish question' may, after all, really be the 'Christian question.'"

50. See, for instance, *obit. Theo.* 9, where Ambrose refers to Abraham, Isaac, and Jacob as "our elders." A striking example is the way Chrysostom and Augustine argued that the Maccabean martyrs died for Christ. See Rouwhorst 2005.

Chapter 7

1. *Life of Antony* 14.7: "he [Antony] persuaded many to choose the monastic life. And so monastic dwellings came into being in the mountains and the desert was made a city by monks." The Israeli statement, attributed to Shimon Peres among others, has not gone uncontested. See George 1979.
2. See Rapp 2006; Sizgorich 2007.
3. Chitty 1966.
4. Walbank 1969.
5. As Williams 2008: 146 put it, "Late-antique Christian biography challenged its readers to accept the miraculous as a component of the everyday world."
6. For the full story, see Jones 1978; English 2012. For illustrations showing the development of Santa's iconography, see Smith 1991/1992.
7. *Life of Antony* 5.4–5.
8. *Life of Antony* 10.1–4.
9. For an excellent introduction to Antony and his monastery, see Vivian 2002. If you ever have the urge to visit, here are directions, to be found in Vivian 2005: 62: "We left Cairo the afternoon of the 29th and traveled east on Highway 44 for 118 kilometers, turning south short of Suez. The traditional route, taken by earlier travelers who have left accounts ... was to take the highway south from Cairo to Beni Suef, then turn east. . . . The coastal route, however, seems to be preferred now. Near Suez, we traveled another 106 kilometers south until we reached the lighthouse at Zafarana, where we turned west at a military checkpoint onto Highway 54 for 45 kilometers. This highway cuts through the Wadi Arabah that lies between the northern and southern Galala mountain ranges. About half an hour later we came to a marker (a set of benches under a roof) with the sign of Deir Anba Antonius, written in Arabic and English, hanging above the entrance, like those used by ranchers in the western United States to identify their property. We turned southwest towards the monastery, now 17 kilometers distant, and in ten to fifteen minutes reached Saint Antony's."
10. *Life of Antony* 14.7. For the size of his monastery, see Rubenson 2007: 649, n. 22.
11. Much credit is due to the path-breaking work of E. Patlagean. See, for example, Patlagean 1968 (Eng. trans. Patlagean 1983). Basic rules for treating these works were laid out by Delehaye 1934.

12. C. Rapp 1998c: 432.
13. As Bartlett 2013: 510 put it, "It was an absolute commonplace of hagiographic literature that saints provided examples to be followed: 'the individual Passions of saints are nothing other than lessons in the Christian life.'" Alvarez 1988: 101–2 identified four purposes in the *Life of* Antony: (1) "to set up a model for monastic life," (2) to show the role of the monk in the broader church "by focusing on the monk as martyr," (3) to show pagans the superiority of Christianity, and (4) as a polemic against heretics. On religious literature more generally, see Campany 2017.
14. Rubenson 1990; Brakke 1995; Goehring 1997.
15. *Confessions* 8.6–7. At 8.7, Augustine provides a date of c. 385 for this episode.
16. Cf. Frilingos 2009: 827: "Scholars now regard the discourse of martyrdom— 'the ideology of death as the necessary fulfillment of the love of God'—as crucial to the self-definition of ancient Christians and Jews." For this reason, Moss 2013 risks throwing out the baby with the bathwater. For a broader range of assessments, see the essays in Gemeinhardt and Leemans 2012.
17. Williams 2008: 191. See also Gemeinhardt and Leemans 2012: 5: "Christians are not the victims of a persecution but they are the winning party in a combat with cosmological proportions, a combat between persecutors and persecuted."
18. For the interplay of Christianity with classical philosophy, see A. Brown 2007: 248–52. Plato describes the philosopher-king in Book Five of the *Republic*.
19. *On the Life of Plotinus* 1. See also Stern-Gillet 1997.
20. For pagan mysticism, see Fowden 1982: 37; Porphyry, *Life of Plotinus* 23. For natural wisdom, see Fowden 1982: 38: "The fact that the pagan holy man was almost by definition a philosopher does not of course mean that late paganism altogether lacked the concept of natural, inborn wisdom." For a Christian example, see Eusebius of Caesarea, *Preparation for the Gospel* 7.6: the original Hebrew patriarchs "enjoyed a free and unfettered mode of religion, being regulated by the manner of life which is in accordance with nature," with which compare the future emperor Julian, *Oration II* 82AB: "it seems to me that the ancients, employing a wondrous sagacity of nature, since their wisdom was not like ours a thing acquired, but they were philosophers by nature, not manufactured, perceived the truth of this."
21. *Life of Antony* 7.9, 45.5. Cf. 1 Cor. 9:27. Christians never went as far as others in distinguishing the soul from the body, a point forcibly made by Chin 2010: 554.
22. Fowden 1982: 50.
23. *Life of Antony* 38.1–2.
24. For a detailed discussion of the stages in this development, see Malone 1950, summarized in Malone 1956.

25. For Constantine: Eusebius, *LC* 2.3. For Antony's powers, see, for example, *Life of Antony* 54 and *passim*. For the prevalence of this link between cosmic and earthly spheres in late antiquity, see Nuffelen 2011: 107-8.

26. *Comparison* 1. On traditional virtues of the good king, see chapter 3.

27. On Pachomius, see Rousseau 1985; Goehring 1996.

28. Palladius tells the story of Melania the Elder in his *Lausiac History*, chap. 46; see also chap. 54 and, for Melania the Younger, chap. 61. For Drepanum, see Jones, Avi-Jonah, et al. 1971: 165-66.

29. For "ascetic tourism," see Rubenson 2007: 649. On pilgrimages to saints more generally, see Frank 2000. See further Chin and Schroeder 2016.

30. Doran 1992. See further Harvey 1988: 376-94. On pillar saints, see Frankfurter 1990. For the local roots of Syrian monasticism, see Brock 1973. For life of Simeon, see *Theodoret, Historia Religiosa*, trans. Price 1985: 160-72. A classic study is Delehaye 1923. A standard work is Voöbus 1957-1988.

31. A path-breaking study was Brown 1971, which applied anthropological methods. Brown has since broadened and deepened his approach. See esp. Brown 1998.

32. Libanius, *Or.* 30.8; Eunapius, *vit. phil.* 472; Rutilius Namatianus, *de reditu suo* ll. 444-46.

33. Gibbon 1909-1914, vol. 2: 102, n. 65. Gibbon has often been said to have lived his sex life in his footnotes, a remark usually attributed to the early twentieth-century author and wit Philip Guedalla. On Gibbon's use of humor, see Clive 1976.

34. The classic work is Walbank 1969.

35. See, for example, North 1992. For late antiquity, see Caner 2006.

36. Iannaccone 1998, but see also the critique of Montgomery 1996 and the rich selection of topics in Oslington 2014.

37. *Life of Antony* 21.2. See Alvarez 1988.

38. *Life of Antony* 10.2.

39. Brakke 2006. See also Alvarez 1988.

40. Sulpicius, *Life of Martin*, chaps. 7-8, 12, 16-19; *Dialogue* 2.

41. *Life of Antony* 48, 54. The Mosaic miracle occurs at Exodus 17.

42. As Baynes 1954: 7 observed, the *Life of Antony* "lets us see the outstanding importance which the Devil and his demons held for the monks of Egypt in the fourth century."

43. The theater and circus are major targets of Chrysostom's "On Vainglory and the Right Way for Parents to Bring Up Their Children," trans. Laistner 1951: 85-122. See also Moss 1935.

44. *Life of Antony* 29-30. For the importance of Job to Augustine, see chapter 9.

45. Harris 2001. On the importance of deportment, see Gleason 1995: esp. 55-81. On health care, see Crislip 2005.

46. *Life of Antony* 78-79.

47. *Life of Antony* 72.
48. Augustine, *Confessions* 8.6. On the language of miracle, see Moule 1965b.

Chapter 8

1. The legend traditionally has been dated a century later: Sessa 2010: 84. But Ehrhardt 1959–1960: 292 held that an "archetype" would have existed no later than 415; cf. Pohlkamp 1992. On Constantine and Silvester, see Sessa 2017.

2. For the life of Silvester, attributed (falsely) to Eusebius of Caesarea, see De Leo 1974: 151–221. The story of the debate is told at 179–221. For the different versions of Constantine's baptism, see Amerise 2005.

3. M. Stokes, ed. and trans., *Apology of Socrates* (Warminster, 1997); Apuleius, *Pro se de magia*, ed. Hunink 1997. For a translation, Hunink 2001.

4. Origen, *Contra Celsum* Pref. 1. The account of Jesus's silence is in Matt. 26.59–63, Mark 14:55–61. In a path-breaking book, Lim 1995 identified the fourth century as the time when the classical practice of establishing truth through open debate and competition changed to a system where truth was handed down from on high and doled out by authorities who could not be challenged. But see the critique by Nuffelen 2014.

5. In this conflict, which takes place before the Roman citizenry in the Forum, Simon Magus makes a boy drop dead by whispering in his ear; Peter then resurrects him (for good measure, Peter also performs a couple of encores). See Schneemelcher 1992: 306–9.

6. On the continued use of classical argument, see Av. Cameron 2014: esp. 23–38. For a concise overview of the theological controversies, see Chadwick 1998. For more detailed studies, see (from a large literature), Ayres 2004; Barnes and Williams 1993; Hanson 1988.

7. Libanius, *Oration* 30.9. For an analysis of this speech as a defense of classical culture, see Sizgorich 2007.

8. *Relatio III*, 10.

9. Themistius, *Oration* 5.68AB. Nuffelen 2014: 168 has characterized this speech as "the most eloquent and extended praise of religious competition from the whole of Antiquity." See also Swain 2013. On Themistius more generally, see Heather 1998; Vanderspoel 1995. Still useful: Downey 1957.

10. *Or.* 30.29.

11. *Or.* 30.21.

12. For the older view, see Robinson 1915. The *locus classicus* is Bloch 1945, with Bloch 1963. A big hole was blown in this position by Cameron in a series of landmark articles, now conveniently collected (along with others) in Cameron 2016a.

13. See Di Maio, Arnold, and Arnold 1992; Burgess 2008.

14. Peninah Walpo, "Julian Recast: Failure of a Cultural Entrepreneur." Paper delivered at Fifth International Borderlands International Graduate Student Conference, March 13, 2016. I am grateful to Ms. Walpo for permission to quote this passage. Cf. Swain 2013: 86, who suggests that Julian's inability to deal with the views and needs of others places him "somewhere on the autistic spectrum." Tougher 2007 is a useful introduction with a selection of documents. For recent studies, see Baker-Brian and Tougher 2012; Smith 1995; Bowersock 1978. Bidez 1930 remains indispensible.

15. On the sheer volume of Julian's writing, see Teitler 2017; on his self-reflection, cf. the observation of Bouffartigue 1978: 15.

16. *Caesares* 336AB (I have slightly modified Wright's translation).

17. *Ag. Gal.* 159E, trans. Wright 1913–23, vol. 3: 319–427.

18. *Ag. Gal.* 335CD. For the serious impact of Julian's gibes, see Hunt 2012.

19. Ward-Perkins 1966.

20. See, for example, *Ag. Gal.* 238CD: "But though their lawgiver forbade them to serve all the gods save only that one, whose 'portion is Jacob, and Israel an allotment of his inheritance'; [Deut. 32.9] though he did not say this only, but methinks added also 'Thou shalt not revile the gods'; yet the shamelessness and audacity of later generations, desiring to root out all reverence from the mass of the people, has thought that blasphemy accompanies the neglect of worship. This, in fact, is the only thing that you have drawn from this source; for in all other respects you and the Jews have nothing in common."

21. Ammianus 22.12.6–7. On philosophy, cf. Martin 2004: 204: "The third- and fourth-century Neoplatonism of the likes of Porphyry and Iamblichus rejected much about Christianity, but it could no longer differentiate its own 'science' from the 'superstition' of Christianity on the basis of demonology."

22. *Ep.* 22, To Arsacius, High Priest of Galatia, 429D. For questions about the authenticity of this letter, see n. 26 in this chapter.

23. *Ep.* 20, To the High Priest Theodorus, 452A–454B.

24. Fragment of a letter to a Priest 300C, 304C, 305A.

25. *Ep.* 22, To Arsacius, High Priest of Galatia, 429D–431A.

26. Doubted by Nuffelen 2002, supported by McLynn 2014: 133–34; defended by Bouffartigue 2005, supported by Aceto 2008.

27. Steinbeck 1957.

28. The edict survives in the *Theodosian Code*, 13.3.5.

29. *Ep.* 36, On Christian Teachers, 422A–424A.

30. *Ag. Gal.* 229C; *Ep.* 36, 423B–D.

31. As argued by McLynn 2014.

32. For an appreciation of the continued importance of rhetorical training to Christians, see Nuffelen 2015.

33. Tertullian, *de praescriptione haereticorum* 7.

34. Jerome described his dream at *Ep.* 22.30. Jerome did not consistently hold to this position. As Markus 1974: 5 observed, "Jerome himself pointed out that even the prophets warn us not to take dreams seriously."
35. Basil of Caesarea, *To Young Men* 4, 10. As a reaction to Julian, see Moffatt 1972.
36. Ammianus 22.10.7. Swain 2003: 361 called attention to Julian's "extreme Hellenism." On Julian's atypical concept of classical literature, see Cameron 1993.
37. Elm 2012. In this book, Elm showed that Gregory's orations were only delivered after Julian's death (all things considered, the safest time to pick a fight with a Roman emperor).
38. For Jerome's dream, *Ep.* 22.30 and n. 34 earlier. On the altar, see Evenepoel 1998–1999; Rosen 1994; Klein 1972.
39. As noted by Lizzi Testa 2015: 418. Regarding the temples more generally, cf. Sizgorich 2007.
40. *Rel.* 3.8.
41. As observed by Chuvin 1990: 1–9.
42. Cameron 2016b: 70 calculated that fully one-half of the correspondents in the more than nine hundred letters of Symmachus were Christians.
43. Brown 1995: 47 thought nothing "would have been more distressing . . . than the suggestion that 'pagan' and 'Christian' were designations of overriding importance in their style of life and in their choice of friends and allies."
44. Chenault 2016.
45. As Evenepoel 1998–1999: 301 put it, "Setbacks and successes revealed whether a people enjoyed the favour of the divine."
46. Paschoud 1983. On different premises of Christians and pagans, see Ando 1996; Av. Cameron 2014.
47. *Rel.* 3.3, trans. Barrow 1973 (slightly amended).
48. *Ep.* 73 (18).35–37.
49. *Epp* 83, 114.436c, 115.424c. See Penella 1993: 31–32.
50. Eusebius reveals the presence of "one of those so-called [pagan] intellectuals" (τινα τῶν δοκησισόφων) at *Life* 4.55.2. In *Ep.* 26, Julian invited Basil of Caesarea, whom he had met when both studied in Athens, to come to his court. *Ep.* 35 is an example of the invitation he extended to philosophers. For Ammianus's low opinion of some of these invitees, see n. 21 earlier. Woods 2006 argues that the philosophers at Constantine's court were converts.

Chapter 9

1. Or, as Cameron 2011: 130 put it, "The temptation to make prophecies and predictions more accurate by retroactively adjusting them against the historical record is almost irresistible."

2. *DMP* 33. Eusebius tells a similar story at *HE* 8.16–17. Less concerned than Lactantius with the details of Galerius's illness, Eusebius took even greater pains to show that this outcome was not due to "any human agency," but "solely due to the oversight of Divine Providence" (8.16.2). For the edict, see *DMP* 34. Eusebius gives a Greek translation at *HE* 8.17.

3. See 2 Macc. 9; Paschoud 2012b; Africa 1982.

4. A comprehensive presentation of education from grammar school to post-graduate training survives in the *Institutiio Oratoria* of the first-century author Quintilian. See esp. Bks. 10–12.

5. Caesar, *Civil War* 3.83. For rhetorical strategies in the *Commentaries*, see Rambaud 1966, esp. 177–242, 349–52.

6. Paulinus, *Life of Ambrose* 31.

7. Dunkle 1967; Dunkle 1971. On changes, see Barnes 1996.

8. Eus., *HE* 8.14.1. The most extreme argument for Maxentius's Christianity is that of Donciu 2012. For a more restrained view, see Decker 1968; Pezzela 1967. Still useful: Schoenebeck 1939.

9. *DMP* 44.8.

10. Herodotus, *Histories* 1.53.

11. *Life* 2.5.3. See further Montgomery 2000. For a kinder view of Licinius, see Smith 1997; Corcoran 1993.

12. Oration 4.11.

13. Or. 4.58, 61.

14. *DI* 5.10.10–13. At *DI* 5.11.11, Lactantius indicates that officials used the same blandishments in his day: "The worst sort is a man who lulls you with a bogus appearance of mercy; the butcher who decides to kill no one is the really harsh and cruel man." But in this case, his persecutors tortured their victims as well.

15. Socrates, *HE* 3.12.16; Gaddis 2005: 92. See further Drake 2011.

16. The story of Mark is in Sozomen, *HE* 5.10; cf. Theodoret, *HE* 3.6. For a thorough discussion, denying that Julian himself was responsible for any martyrdoms, see Teitler 2017. Earlier: Penella 1993.

17. Ammianus 22.12.6–7. On Julian and the gods, see Elm 2012: 286–327; Smith 1995.

18. *Life of Antony* 30–35.

19. *Oration II to Constantius* 91C. Many scholars take these musings as Julian's thinking about his own kingship. For an irreverent look at this work, see Drake 2012.

20. Vision: Ammianus 20.5.10; Persia: Ammiaunus 22.12.6. On Julian's misreading of omens, see Elm 2012: 446–50.

21. For a thorough review of ancient sources and modern studies, see Levenson 2004. See also his earlier study, Levenson 1990. Also useful: Aziza 1978; Freund 1992; Drijvers 1992; Penella 1999; Simmons 2006.

22. *Life* 3.33.1–2.
23. Wilken 1983: 137.
24. Wilken 1983: 141; Fredriksen and Irshai 2006.
25. Bradbury 1995; cf. Salzman 2011.
26. In a letter to the Jewish community, Julian praised Jehovah as "the Most High God, the Creator." *Ep.* 51, 297C, trans. Wright (1913–1923), vol. 3:179. But in his letter to an unnamed priest, he chided the Jews for having prophets who were "unwise" and poorly educated: Wright 1913–1923, vol. 2: 315. For Jehovah as another ethnic god, see *Against the Galilaeans* 100C, trans. Wright (1913–1923), vol. 3: 345; Penella 1999: 25.
27. Ammianus 23.1.2, Rolfe trans. 1950-1952, slightly modified.
28. For discussion and examples, see Wilken 1983: 128–60.
29. Ammianus 23.1.3.
30. Rufinus, *HE* 10.38.
31. Socrates, *HE* 3.20; Levenson 2004 analyzes forty-seven sources from the fifth through fourteenth centuries that discuss the event. The biblical references are to Rom. 11:25 and 2 Cor. 3:14.
32. Russell 1980.
33. For a summary of Christian sources, see Penella 1993, esp. 32, for Jerome's claim about sacrificing Christians.
34. *II Or. Const.* 75D–76A.
35. Curtin 1995.
36. For Julian's last moments, see Ammianus 25.3.15–21; Theodoret, *HE* 3.25. On his death and legacy, see Baynes 1937; Hahn 1960; Elm 2012: 444–45; Woods 2015.
37. Socrates, *HE* 3.14.
38. Gregory Nazianzen laments the Christians who left "for the sake of temporary gain, or court favour, or brief power." *Oration 4*, chap. 11. For Julian's lasting effect, see Wilken 1983: 128.
39. *Acts of the Apostles* 11:26.
40. Elm 2012: 269–335; Sandwell 2007. See further Kalleres 2015; Shepardson 2014; Limberis 2000.
41. Viz. Swain 2013: 86: "The response in his satire, the *Beard Hater*, to the Antiochenes' disregard of his idea of religion and conduct and their lack of gratitude to him is one of the best examples not simply of how Julian got things wrong but of how he completely failed to understand why." On *Misopogon* as a literary work, see Hawkins 2011; Gleason 1986; Long 1993; Alonso-Núñez 1979.
42. Ammianus 22.12.6, 22.10.7. A useful but obviously biased source for Babylas is John Chrysostom's "Discourse on Blessed Babylas," trans. Schatkin and Harkins 1985. See Shepardson 2009.
43. "On Vainglory and the Right Way for Parents to Bring Up Their Children," trans. Laistner 1951b.

44. As Brown 1982: 85 put it, "the cloud [of Julian] had cast such a chill shadow that, from then onwards, Christian bishops never let the Emperor out of their sight for a moment." For the increasing emphasis on suppression, see Baynes 1968: 12–13. For a full discussion of Julian's reform effort, see Renucci 2000; Scrofani 2010. On Julian's lasting impact, see Wilken 1983: 128.

Chapter 10

1. Augustine, *De excidio urbis Romae sermo* 3.
2. There has been a resurgence of interest in the question of Rome's fall in recent years. Noteworthy titles include Brown 2012; Heather 2012; Kelly 2009; Ward-Perkins 2005; Wood 2008; Ando 2008; Halsall 2008; Ward-Perkins 2005; Wickham 2005; McCormick 2001.
3. The story is told by the sixth-century Byzantine historian Procopius, *Vandal Wars* 3.2.25–26, trans. Dewing 1916, vol. 3: 17.
4. Orosius, *Historiarum Adversum Paganos* 7.35.19, as cited by Heather 2005: 212.
5. So Ambrose in *De fide* 2.16. This is, ironically, the same passage in which Ambrose predicted a great victory for the orthodox Gratian. See chapter 2.
6. Jerome, *Ep.* 127.12 (dated to 412), trans. Wright 1980. The quotation is from Vergil, *Aeneid* 2.361–65. See further Salzman 2009. On "the crisis of identity" more generally, see Markus 1990: 21–43.
7. Bruyn 1993. For the effect on Christians, see Mommsen 1951: 368.
8. Bruyn 1993: 115, and 113–14 for pagans and "bad Christians."
9. Brown 2000 remains a standout in a very crowded field. For Augustine in Milan, see Wills 2012.
10. On the conference, see Ubiña 2013. On Donatism, Shaw 2011 has largely superseded the longtime standard, Frend 1952, which is still useful. More broadly, Rébillard 2012 makes interesting methodological suggestions.
11. For a good introduction to aspects of Augustine's thought, see Wetzel 2012.
12. The phrase comes from Augustine's *Retractations* (2.68.1), an annotated list of his works that he put together near the end of his life, in which he included notice of ways his thinking had changed.
13. *City of God* (*Civ. Dei*) 1.1, trans. Marcus Dods, 1887.
14. Heather 2005: 227. Orosius 7.39, trans. Raymond 1936: 388. For a recent study, see Nuffelen 2012.
15. As Conybeare 2014: 139 noted, Augustine chose the word *civitas* "over the more common and creditable biblical words *populus* or *regnum*."
16. *Civ. Dei* 14.1, 15.1.
17. *Epistle to Diognetus* 5.9, 6.1. For Christians as a third race, see Galatians 3:28. See further Johnson 2006; Buell 2001.
18. Aelius Aristides, *To Rome* 59.

19. *Remota itaque iustitia quid sunt regna nisi magna latrocinia? Civ. dei* 4.4. For criticism of Plato, see 8.4–13 and Clark 2009: 122–23.
20. *Republic* 473d.
21. *Civ. Dei* 5.25.
22. *Civ. Dei* 4.33. See, more broadly, Salamito 2012.
23. Mommsen 1951: 360.
24. *Civ. Dei* 22.8. The stoning of Stephen is at *Acts* 7:54. On this part of *Civ. Dei*, see Ward 1999: 133; Bartlett 2013: 22–26.
25. *True Religion* 47. See C. Brown 2011: 275; Williams 2008: 191–95.

Chapter 11: Epilogue

1. *Life of Daniel the Stylite,* chap. 60. The Titus episode is in chaps. 60–64. On the *Life of Daniel,* see Lane Fox 1997; M. R. Vivian 2010.
2. As observed by Bremmer 2010: 14: "there can be no doubt that miracles figure prominently in the Christian tradition of the first centuries. . . . The nature of these miracles is well summarized by *Matthew* (10.8): 'Cure the sick, raise the dead, cleanse the lepers, cast out demons.'"
3. Bremmer 2008: 367 (discussing a reported epiphany of St. George to British troops at Mons in 1915).
4. Gleason 1998: 508. Cf. Wortley 1992: 383–404.
5. Plutarch, *Life of Pompey* 6. Titus's two retainers stayed with him after he dismissed the rest of his troops: see *Life of Daniel* 60.
6. *Life of Daniel* 62.
7. Moule 1965b: 235.
8. Rowan Williams, a specialist on fourth-century Christianity and former archbishop of Canterbury, in Vivian and Athanassakis 2003: xvi.
9. Mark the Deacon, *The Life of Porphyry, Bishop of Gaza,* chaps. 72–73. For a more up-to-date translation (unfortunately, not including this passage), see Rapp 2001. On Porphyry, see Van Dam 1985; Durliat 1990.
10. For these issues, see MacMullen 1997: 174, n. 68. Commenting more generally, Shaw 2011: 346 observed, "Where parishioners were hesitant to take violent action (probably in most cases), the preacher's role was crucial."
11. As observed by Stark 1987: 24. For infant baptism, see Louth 2014: 110.
12. As observed by Watts 2015: 150.
13. See Rapp 1998c.
14. Cameron 2011: 131. Arguing for a Rome that fell because of overwhelming external pressures, the great French historian André Piganiol 1947: 422 exclaimed, "Roman civilization did not die a natural death; it was assassinated" ("La civilisation Romaine n'est pas morte de sa belle mort, elle est assassinée").

15. Bartlett, 2013: 504, citing the *Bibliotheca Hagiographia Latina*. On the significance of the fourth-century accounts, see Williams 2008: 229: "Christian biographies, and their authors, represented themselves as possessing an authority that had otherwise been restricted to the scriptures."

16. As observed by Moss 2013: 234: "The fourth century becomes the turning point for martyrdom literature. We are no longer dealing with stories that are authentic. We are teetering precariously on the cusp of crude plagiarism and fanciful invention." Cf. Gemeinhardt and Leemans 2012, which takes note of the influence of paintings and other art works.

17. Pears 2017: 10.

18. See Bowersock 1995b: 46: "An important setting for the final days of a martyr's teaching was the local prison, in which the martyr was confined pending interrogation and execution. There was usually a captive audience of other Christians as well as police officers and prison guards in the employ of the city. But others came voluntarily, including pagans who wanted to dispute with the master teacher."

19. As observed by Bowersock 1995a. For an overview of the interplay between classical standards and Christian thinkers, see Neil 2007. On changing use of miracles, see Bremmer 2013: 18–19. On "superstition" versus "rationalism," see Frankfurter 2005.

20. On the importance of the calendar, see Salzman 2004. On processions, see Latham 2016: 186–91; Latham forthcoming. On shrines, a classic work is Brown 1981. See further Henig and King 1986; Hahn 1997.

PRIMARY SOURCES

(for full entries see the main bibliography)

Actus Petri cum Simone (Acts of Peter and Simon)
  ed. Lipsius and Bonnet 1959, vol. 1: 45–103.
  trans. Schneemelcher 1992.

Actus Silvestri
  ed. Mombritius 1974.

Aelius Aristides
To Rome
  ed. Keil in Oliver 1953: 982–91.
  trans. Oliver 1953.

Alexander Monachos
De inventione vivificae crucis
  ed. Pennacchini 1913.
  trans. Scott 2004.

Ambrose of Milan
Oratio De Obitu Theodosii
  ed. Faller 1955.
  trans. Liebeschuetz and Hill 2005.
Epistles 73, 74, 75a
  ed. Zelzer 1990–1996.
  trans. Liebeschuetz and Hill 2005.

Expositio Psalmi CXVIII.
  ed. Petschenig 1923.
  trans. Riain 1998

Ammianus Marcellinus
Res Gestae
  ed. and trans. Rolfe 1950–1952.

Apuleius
Pro se de magia
  ed. Hunink 1997.
  trans. Hunink 2001.

Athanasius of Alexandria
vita Antonii (Life of Antony)
  ed. Bartelink 1993.
  trans. Vivian and Athanassakis 2003.

Augustine of Hippo
Confessions
  ed. and trans. Watts 2006.
City of God (civ. dei)
  ed. Dombart and Kalb 1955.
  trans. Dods 1887.

De excidio urbis Romae sermo 3
    ed. and trans. O'Reilly 1955.
Retractations
    ed. Mutzenbecher 1984.
    trans. Bogan 1968.
De vera religione (On True Religion)
    ed. Daur 1962.
    trans. Burleigh 1953

Augustus
Res Gestae
    ed. and trans. Ehrenberg et al. 1967.

Aurelius Victor
De Caesaribus
    ed. Pichlmayr and Gruendel 1970.
    trans. Bird 1994.

Basil of Caesarea
To Young Men
    ed. Wilson 1975.
    trans. Deferrari 1934.

Constantine I
*Oration to the Saints (Oratio ad coetum
    sanctorum) = OC*
    ed. Heikel 1902: 149–92.
    trans. Edwards 2003.

John Chrysostom
*Discourses Against Judaizing
    Christians*
    ed. *Pat. Gr.* 48: 843–942.
    trans. Harkins 1979.
Discourse on Blessed Babylas
    ed. Schatkin et al. 1990.
    trans. Schatkin 1985.
*A Comparison Between a King
    and a Monk*
    ed. *Pat. Gr.* 47: 387–92.
    trans. Hunter 1988.
On Vainglory
    ed. Exarchos 1952.
    trans. Laistner 1951.

Cyril of Jerusalem
Catechesis (Catech.)
    ed. Piédagnel and Paris 1966.
    trans. McCauley and Stephenson
    1969 and 1970.
Letter to Constantius II
    ed. Bihain 1973.
    trans. McCauley and Stephenson
    1970: 232.

Egeria
Itinerarium
    ed. Francheschini and Weber
    1965
    trans. Wilkinson 1981.

Epiphanius
Panarion
    ed. Holl et al. 2013.
    trans. Amidon 1990; Williams
    1987–1994.

Epistle to Diognetus
    ed. and trans. Jefford 2013.

Eunapius
*vitae sophistarum (Lives of the
    Philosophers)*
    ed. Giangrande 1956.
    trans. Wright 1921.

Eusebius of Caesarea
*Historia ecclesiastica (Church
    History)*
    ed. Bardy 1952–1960.
    trans. Williamson 1965.
*De vita Constantini (Life of
    Constantine)*
    ed. Winkelmann 1975.
    trans. Cameron and Hall 1999.
*laus Constantini (In Praise of
    Constantine)*
    ed. Heikel 1902: 195–223.
    trans. Drake 1976: 83–102.

De sepulchro Christi (On Christ's Sepulchre) = chaps. 11–18 of LC
  ed. Heikel 1902: 223–59.
  trans. Drake 1976: 103–27.
Preparation for the Gospel
  ed. Mras 1954–1956.
  trans. Gifford 1903.

Gregory of Nazianzus
Orations 4–5
  ed. Bernardi 1984.
  trans. King 1888: 1–121.

Jacobus de Voragine
Legenda Aurea
  ed. Maggioni 1998.
  trans. Ryan and Ripperger 1941.

Jerome
De viris illustribus (On Illustrious Men)
  ed. Bernoulli 1895.
  trans. Halton 1999.
Epistle CXXVII
  ed. Hilberg 1910–1918.
  trans. Wright 1980.

Julian
Against the Galilaeans
  ed. and trans. Wright 1913–1923, vol. 3: 319–427.
Letters
  ed. and trans. Wright 1913–1923, vol. 3.
Second Oration to Constantius (II Or. Con.)
  ed. and trans. Wright 1913–1923, vol. 1: 133–269.
The Caesars
  ed. and trans. Wright 1913–1923, vol. 2: 345–415.

Lactantius
De mortibus persecutorum (On the Deaths of the Persecutors) (DMP)
  ed. and trans. Creed 1984.
Divinarum institutionum (The Divine Institutes) (DI)
  ed. Heck and Wlosok 2005–2011.
  trans. Bowen and Garnsey 2003.

Libanius
Oration 30
  ed. and trans. Norman 1977.

Life of Daniel the Stylite
  ed. H. Delehaye 1913.
  trans. Dawes and Baynes 1948: 7–71.

Mark the Deacon
The Life of Porphyry, Bishop of Gaza
  ed. Usener and SPBS 1895
  trans. Hill 1913; Rapp 2001

Origen
Contra Celsum
  ed. Marcovich 2001.
  trans. Chadwick 1953.

Orosius
Historiarum Adversum Paganos Libri VII
  ed. Arnaud-Lindet 1990–1991.
  trans. Raymond 1963.

Palladius
Lausiac History
  ed. and trans. Petersen 1996.

Paulinus of Milan
Life of Ambrose
  ed. Kaniecka 1928.
  trans. Ramsey 1997.

PL = XII Panegyrici Latini
  ed. Mynors 1964.
  trans. Nixon and Rodgers 1994.

Plato
Apology of Socrates
  ed. and trans. Stokes 1997.
Republic
  ed. Adam 1965.
  trans. Lee 1955.

Porphyry of Gaza
On the Life of Plotinus
  ed. Henry and Schwyzer 1964.
  trans. Edwards 2000: 1–53.

Procopius
History of the Wars
  ed. and trans. Dewing 1814–1928.

Quintilian
Institutio Oratoria
  ed. and trans. Russell 2001.

Rufinus
Historia Ecclesiastica libri duo
  ed. *Pat. Lat.* 21: 461–540.
  trans. Amidon 1997.

Rutilius Namatianus
de reditu suo
  ed. and trans. Keene and
    Savage-Armstrong 1907.

Socrates Scholasticus
Historia Ecclesiastica (Church History)
  ed. Hansen 1995.
  trans. Zenos 1890–1900.

Sozomen
Historia Ecclesiastica (Church History)
  ed. Bidez and Hansen 1960.
  trans. Hartranft 1890–1900.

Sulpicius Severus
vita Martini
  ed. Fontaine 1967–1969.
  trans. Hoare 1995.
Dialogues
  ed. Fontaine and Dupré
    2006.
  trans. Roberts 1894.

Symmachus
Relatio III
  ed. Klein 1972.
  trans. R. H. Barrow 1973.

Tertullian
de praescriptione haereticorum
  ed. Refoulé 1954.
  trans. Holmes 1885–1896.

Themistius
Oration 5
  ed. Schenkl and Downey
    1965.
  trans. Heather and Moncur
    2001: 159–73.

Theodoret of Cyrrus
Historia Ecclesiastica (Church History)
  ed. Scheidweiler and
    Parmentier 1954.
  trans. Jackson 1892.
Historia Religiosa (A History of the Monks of Syria)
  ed. Canivet and Leroy-Milinghen
    1977–1979.
  trans. Price 1985.

BIBLIOGRAPHY

Aceto, F. 2008. "Note sull' autenticita dell' Ep. 84 di Giuliano imperatore." *Rivista di cultura classica e medioevale* 50: 187–206.

Adam, J., ed. 1965. *The Republic of Plato.* 2nd ed. 2 vols. Cambridge: Cambridge University Press.

Africa, T. W. 1982. "Worms and the Death of Kings: A Cautionary Note on Disease and History." *Classical Antiquity* 1: 1–17.

Ahl, F. 1984. "The Art of Safe Criticism in Greece and Rome." *American Journal of Philology* 105: 174–208.

Alföldi, A. 1932. "The Helmet of Constantine with the Christian Monogram." *Journal of Roman Studies* 22: 9–32.

Alonso-Núñez, J. M. 1979. "The Emperor Julian's *Misopogon* and the Conflict Between Christianity and Paganism." *Ancient Society* 10: 311–24.

Alvarez, P. 1988. "Demon Stories in the Life of Antony by Athanasius." *Cistercian Studies* 23: 101–18.

Amerise, M. 2005. *Il battesimo di Costantino il Grande. Storia di una scomoda eredità.* Hermes Einzelschrift 95. Stuttgart: Franz Steiner,.

Amidon, P., trans. 1990. *The Panarion of St. Epiphanius, Bishop of Salamis, Selected Passages.* New York: Oxford University Press.

Amidon, P., trans. 1997. *The Church History of Rufinus of Aquileia: Books 10 and 11.* New York: Oxford University Press.

Ando, C. 1996. "Pagan Apologetics and Christian Intolerance in the Ages of Themistius and Augustine." *Journal of Early Christian Studies* 4: 171–207.

Ando, C. 2008. "Decline, Fall, and Transformation." *Journal of Late Antiquity* 1: 31–60.

Angelova, D. 2015. *Sacred Founders: Women, Men, and Gods in the Discourse of Imperial Founding, Rome Through Early Byzantium*. Berkeley: University of California Press.

Arnaud-Lindet, ed. and trans. 1990–1991. *Orose: Histoires (Contre les Païens)*. 3 vols. Paris: Belles Lettres.

Arneth, A. 2000. *"Sonne der Gerechtigkeit": Studien zur Solarisierung der Jahwe-Religion im Lichte von Psalm 72*. Beihefte zur Zeitschrift für Altorientische und Biblische Rechtsgeschichte 1. Wiesbaden: Harrassowitz.

Ashton, J. 1887. *The Legendary History of the Cross. A Series of 64 Woodcuts from a Dutch Book Published by Veldener, AD 1483*. New York: A.C. Armstrong & Son.

Athanassiadi, P., and M. Frede, eds. 1999. *Pagan Monotheism in Late Antiquity*. New York: Oxford University Press.

Attridge, H., et al., eds. 1990. *Of Scribes and Scrolls: Studies on the Hebrew Bible, Intertestamental Judaism and Christian Origins, Presented to John Strugnell on the Occasion of His Sixtieth Birthday*. Lanham, MD: University Press of America.

Aune, D. 1980. "Magic in Early Christianity." In Haase 1980: 1507–57.

Austin, N. J. E. 1980. "Constantine and Crispus, AD 326." *Acta Classica* 23: 133–38.

Ayres, L. 2004. *Nicaea and Its Legacy: An Approach to Fourth-Century Trinitarian Theology*. New York: Oxford University Press.

Aziza, C. 1978. "Julien et le judaisme." In Braun and J. Richer 1978: 141–58.

Baert, B. 2004. *A Heritage of Holy Wood: The Legend of the True Cross in Text and Image*, trans. L. Preedy. Leiden: Brill, 2004.

Bahat, D. 1986. "Does the Holy Sepulchre Church Mark the Burial of Jesus?" *Biblical Archaeology Review* 12: 26–45.

Baker-Brian, N., and S. Tougher, eds. 2012. *Emperor and Author: The Writings of Julian the Apostate*. Swansea.

Bardill, J. 2012. *Constantine, Divine Emperor of the Christian Golden Age*. Cambridge: Cambridge University Press.

Bardy, G., ed. and trans. 1952–1960. *Eusèbe de Césarée Histoire ecclésiastique et Les Martyrs en Palestine*. 4 vols. Sources chrétiennes. Paris: Éditions du Cerf.

Barnes, M. R., and D. H. Williams, eds. 1993. *Arianism After Arius: Essays on the Development of the Fourth Century Trinitarian Conflicts*. Edinburgh: T & T Clark.

Barnes, T. D. 1973. "Lactantius and Constantine." *Journal of Roman Studies* 63: 29–46.

Barnes, T. D. 1981. *Constantine and Eusebius*. Cambridge, MA: Harvard University Press.

Barnes, T. D. 1993. *Athanasius and Constantius: Theology and Politics in the Constantinian Empire*. Cambridge, MA: Harvard University Press.

Barnes, T. D. 1996. "Oppressor, Persecutor, Usurper: the Meaning of 'Tyrannus' in the Fourth Century." In Bonamente and Mayer 1996: 55–65.

Barnes, T. D. 2001. "Constantine's *Speech to the Assembly of the Saints*: Place and Date of Delivery." *Journal of Theological Studies*, n.s. 52: 26–36.

Barnes, T. D. 2011. *Constantine: Dynasty, Religion and Power in the later Roman Empire.* Chichester, England: Wiley-Blackwell.

Barrow, R. H., trans. 1973. *Prefect and Emperor: The Relationes of Symmachus, A.D. 384.* Oxford: Clarendon Press.

Bartelink, G., ed. and trans. 1993. *Athanase d'Alexandrie: Vie d'Antoine.* Sources chrétiennes, no. 400. Paris: Éditions du Cerf.

Bartlett, J. R., ed. 2002. *Jews in the Hellenistic and Roman Cities.* London: Routledge.

Bartlett, R. 2013. *Why Can the Dead Do Such Great Things? Saints and Worshippers from the Martyrs to the Reformation.* Princeton: Princeton University Press.

Baslez, M.-F., ed. 2014. *Chrétiens persécuteurs. Destructions, exclusions, violences religieuses au IVe siècle.* Paris: A. Michel.

Bauer, W. 1934. *Rechtgläubigkeit und Ketzerei im ältesten Christentum.* Tübingen: Mohr.

Bauer, W. 1971. *Orthodoxy and Heresy in Earliest Christianity.* Philadelphia: Fortress.

Baum, G., E. Cunitz, E. Reuss, A. Erichson, eds. 1863–1900. *Joannis Calvini Opera quae supersunt omnia.* 35 vols. Brunswig: C.A. Schwetschke.

Baumstark, A. 1913. "Konstantiana aus syrischer Kunst und Liturgie." In Dölger 1913: 217–54.

Baynes, N. H. 1937. "The Death of Julian the Apostate in a Christian Legend." *Journal of Roman Studies* 2: 22–29.

Baynes, N. H. 1939. "Constantine." In S. A. Cook et al., eds., *Cambridge Ancient History* vol. 12: 678–99. Cambridge: Cambridge University Press.

Baynes, N. H. 1954. "St. Antony and the Demons." *Journal of Egyptian Archaeology* 40: 7–10.

Baynes, N. H. 1968. *The Political Ideas of St. Augustine's De Civitate Dei,* The Historical Association Pamphlet, 1st ser., 104. rev. ed. London: Historical Association.

Beatrice, P. 1990. "L'intolleranza cristiana nei confronti dei pagani: un problema storiographico." *Cristianesimo nella storia* 11: 441–48.

Becker, A., and A. Reed, eds. 2003. *The Ways That Never Parted: Jews and Christians in Late Antiquity and the Early Middle Ages.* Tübingen: Mohr Siebeck.

Becker, E. 1910. "Konstantin der Grosse, der 'neue Moses': Die Schlacht am Pons Milvius und die Katastrophe am Schilfmeer." *Zeitschrift für Kirchengeschichte* 31: 161–71.

Berger, D., ed. 1986. *History and Hate: The Dimensions of Anti-Semitism.* Philadelphia: Jewish Publication Society.

Bernardi, J., ed. and trans. 1984. *Grégoire de Nazianze: Discours 4-5 contre Julien.* Sources chrétiennes, no. 309. Paris: Éditions du Cerf.

Bernoulli, C. A., ed. 1895. *Hieronymus: De viris illustribus.* Freiburg: Mohr.

Bhola, R. K. 2015. *A Man of Visions: A New Examination of the Vision(s) of Constantine (Panegyric VI, Lactantius' De mortibus persecutorum and Eusebius' De vita Constantini).* PhD dissertation, University of Ottawa.

Biddle, M. 1994. "The Tomb of Christ: Sources, Methods and a New Approach." In Painter 1994: 73–197.

Biddle, M. 1999. *The Tomb of Christ.* Stroud, England: Sutton.

Bidez, J. 1930. *La vie de Julien.* Paris: Les Belles Lettres.

Bidez, J., and G. C. Hansen, eds. 1960. *Sozomenus Kirchengeschichte.* 2nd ed. GCS, 50. Berlin: Akademie Verlag.

Bihain, E. 1973. "L'épitre de Cyrille de Jérusalem à Constance sur la vision de la Croix. Tradition manuscrite et édition critique." *Byzantion* 43: 264–96.

Binns, J. W., ed. 1974. *Latin Literature of the Fourth Century.* London: Routledge.

Bird, H. W., trans. 1994. *Aurelius Victor: De Caesaribus.* Translated Texts for Historians. Philadelphia: University of Pennsylvania Press.

Bjornlie, S., ed. 2017. *The Life and Legacy of Constantine: Traditions Through the Ages.* London: Routledge.

Blaauw, S. de. 1997. "Jerusalem in Rome and the Cult of the Cross." In Colella et al. 1997: 55–73.

Black, M. 1970. "The Chi-Rho Sign—Christogram and/or Staurogram?" In Gasque and Martin 1970: 219–27.

Bleckmann, B. 2015. "Constantine, Rome, and the Christians." In Wienand 2015b: 309–29.

Bloch, H. 1945. "A New Document of the Last Pagan Revival in the West." *Harvard Theological Review* 38: 199–244.

Bloch, H. 1963. "The Pagan Revival in the West at the End of the Fourth Century." In Momigliano 1963a: 193–218.

Bogan, M. I., trans. 1968. *Augustine: The Retractations.* Fathers of the Church, vol. 60. Washington, DC: Catholic University of America Press.

Boin, D. 2014. "Hellenistic 'Judaism' and the Social Origins of the 'Pagan-Christian' Debate." *Journal of Early Christian Studies* 22: 167–96.

Boin, D. 2015. *Coming Out Christian in the Roman World: How the Followers of Jesus Made a Place in Caesar's Empire.* London: Bloomsbury.

Bolman, E., ed. 2002. *Monastic Visions: Wall Paintings in the Monastery of St. Antony at the Red Sea.* New Haven, CT: Yale University Press.

Bonamente, G., and A. Nestori, eds. 1988. *I Cristiani e l'Impero nel IV secolo: atti del convegno sul Cristianesimo nel mondo antico (Macerata, 17-18 dicembre 1987).* Roma: EGLE.

Bonamente, G., and M. Mayer, eds. 1996. *Historiae Augustae Colloquium Barcinonense.* Bari: Edipuglia.

Bonamente, G., N. Lenski, and R. Lizzi Testa, eds. 2012. *Costantino prima e dopo Costantino*. Bari: Edipuglia.

Bonner, G. 1984. "The Extinction of Paganism and the Church Historian." *Journal of Ecclesiastical History* 35: 339–57.

Bouffartigue, J. 1978. "Julien par Julien." In Braun and Richer 1978: 15–30.

Bouffartigue, J. 2005. "L'authenticité de la Letter 84 de l'empereur Julien." *Revue de philologie, de littérature et d'histoire anciennes*, 3 ser 79: 231–42.

Bourdieu, P. 1977. *Outline of a Theory of Practice*, trans. R. Nice. Cambridge: Cambridge University Press.

Bowen, A., and P. Garnsey, trans. 2003. *Lactantius: The Divine Institutes*. Translated Texts for Historians, 40. Liverpool: Liverpool University Press.

Bowersock, G. W. 1978. *Julian the Apostate*. Cambridge, MA: Harvard University Press.

Bowersock, G. W. 1995a. *Fiction as History. Nero to Julian*. Berkeley.

Bowersock, G. W. 1995b. *Martyrdom and Rome*. Cambridge: Cambridge University Press.

Bowersock, G. W. 2006. *Mosaics as History. The Near East from Late Antiquity to Islam*. Cambridge: Cambridge University Press.

Bowie, F. 2011. "Miracles in Traditional Religions." In Twelftree 2011: 167–83.

Boyarin, D. 1999. *Dying for God: Martyrdom and the Making of Christianity and Judaism*. Palo Alto: Stanford University Press.

Boyarin, D. 2004. *Border Lines: The Partition of Judaeo-Christianity*. Philadelphia.

Boyarin, D. 2009. "Rethinking Jewish Christianity: An Argument for Dismantling a Dubious Category (to Which Is Appended a Correction of My Border Lines)." *Jewish Quarterly Review* 99: 7–36.

Bradbury, S. 1995. "Julian's Pagan Revival and the Decline of Blood Sacrifice." *Phoenix* 49: 331–56.

Brakke, D. 1995. *Athanasius and the Politics of Asceticism*. New York: Oxford University Press.

Brakke, D. 2006. *Demons and the Making of the Monk: Spiritual Combat in Early Christianity*. Cambridge, MA: Harvard University Press.

Brakke, D., D. Deliyannis, and E. Watts, eds. 2012. *Shifting Cultural Frontiers in Late Antiquity*. Farnham: Ashgate.

Braun, R., and J. Richer, eds. 1978. *L'Empereur Julien: de l'histoire à la légende (331–1715)*. Groupe de Recherches de Nice, vol. I. Paris: Belles Lettres.

Bremmer, J. N. 2008. "Close Encounters of the Third Kind: Heliodorus in the Temple and Paul on the Road to Damascus." In Houtman et al. 2008: 367–84.

Bremmer, J. N. 2010. *The Rise of Christianity Through the Eyes of Gibbon, Harnack and Rodney Stark: A Valedictory Lecture on the Occasion of His Retirement from the Chair of Religious Studies in the Faculty of Theology*. 2nd ed. Gröningen: Barkhuis.

Bremmer, J. N. 2013. "Richard Reitzenstein's *Hellenistische Wunderzählungen.*" In Nicklas and Spittler 2013: 1–19.

Bremmer, J. N., W. J. van Bekkum, A. L. Molendijk, eds. 2006. *Paradigms, Poetics and Politics of Conversion.* Leuven: Peeters.

Brink, B. 2007. "Art and *propaganda fide*: Christian Art and Architecture, 300-600." In Cassiday and Norris 2007: 691–725.

Brock, S. 1973. "Early Syrian Asceticism." *Numen* 20: 1–19.

Bromley, D., and P. Hammond, eds. 1987. *The Future of New Religious Movements.* Macon, GA: Mercer University Press.

Brooke, C. N. L. et al., eds. 1983. *Studies in Numismatic Method Presented to Philip Grierson.* Cambridge: Cambridge University Press.

Brown, A. 2007. "The Intellectual Debate Between Christians and Pagans." In Cassiday and Norris 2007: 248–95.

Brown, C. 2011. "Issues in the History of the Debates on Miracles." In Twelftree 2011: 273–90.

Brown, P. R. L. 1971. "The Rise and Function of the Holy Man in Late Antiquity." *Journal of Roman Studies* 61: 80–101.

Brown, P. R. L. 1981. *The Cult of the Saints: Its Rise and Function in Latin Christianity.* Chicago: University of Chicago Press.

Brown, P. R. L. 1982. "The Last Pagan Emperor: Robert Browning's *The Emperor Julian.*" In P. R. L. Brown, *Society and the Holy in Late Antiquity,* 83–102. Berkeley: University of California Press.

Brown, P. R. L. 1992. *Power and Persuasion in Late Antiquity: Towards a Christian Empire.* Madison, WI: University of Wisconsin Press.

Brown, P. R. L. 1995. *Authority and the Sacred. Aspects of the Christianisation of the Roman World.* Cambridge: Cambridge University Press.

Brown, P. R. L. 1998. "The Rise and Function of the Holy Man in Late Antiquity, 1971-97." *Journal of Early Christian Studies* 6: 353–76.

Brown, P. R. L. 2000. *Augustine of Hippo, A Biography.* Rev. ed. Berkeley: University of California Press.

Brown, P. R. L. 2012. *Through the Eye of a Needle: Wealth, the Fall of Rome, and the Making of Christianity in the West, 350-550 AD.* Princeton: Princeton University Press.

Bruun, P. 1997. "The Victorious Signs of Constantine: A Reappraisal." *Numismatic Chronicle* 157: 41–59.

Bruun, P., ed. 1966. *Constantine and Licinius, A.D. 313-337.* Roman Imperial Coinage, vol. 7. London: Spink and Son.

Bruyn, T. S. de. 1993. "'Ambivalence Within a Totalizing Discourse': Augustine's Sermons on the Sack of Rome." *Journal of Early Christian Studies* 1: 405–21.

Buell, D. 2001. "Rethinking the Relevance of Race for Early Christian Self-Definition." *Harvard Theological Review* 94: 449–76.

Burgess, R. W. 1997. "The Dates and Editions of Eusebius' Chronici canones and Historia Ecclesiastica." *Journal of Theological Studies,* n.s. 48: 471–504.

Burgess, R. W. 2008. "The Summer of Blood: The 'Great Massacre' of 337 and the Promotion of the Sons of Constantine." *Dumbarton Oaks Papers* 62: 5–51.

Burleigh, J. H. S., trans. 1953. "On True Religion." In *Augustine: Earlier Writings*, Library of Christian Classics, vol. 6: 225–83. Philadelphia: Westminster Press.

Burns, R. M. 1981. *The Great Debate on Miracles: From Joseph Danville to David Hume*. Lewisburg, PA: Bucknell Unversity Press.

Burrus, V., ed. 2005. *A People's History of Christianity*, vol. 2: *Late Ancient Christianity*. Minneapolis: Fortress.

Cain, A., and N. Lenski, eds. 2009. *The Power of Religion in Late Antiquity*. Aldershot: Ashgate.

Calvin, Jean. 1543. "Advertissement tresutile du grand proffit qui revendroit à la Chrestienté s'il se faisoit inventoire de tous les corps sainctz et reliques . . ." In Baum, Cunitz, Reuss, and Erichson 1863–1900, vol. 6: 405–52.

Cameron, A. 1966. "The Date and Identity of Macrobius." *Journal of Roman Studies* 56: 25–38.

Cameron, A. 1977. "Paganism and Literature in Late Fourth Century Rome." In Fuhrmann 1977: 31–40.

Cameron, A. 1993. "Julian and Hellenism." *Ancient World* 24: 25–29.

Cameron, A. 2011. *The Last Pagans of Rome*. New York: Oxford University Press.

Cameron, A. 2016a. *Wandering Poets and Other Essays on Late Greek Literature and Philosophy*. New York: Oxford University Press.

Cameron, A. 2016b. "Were Pagans Afraid to Speak Their Minds in a Christian World?" In Salzman, Sághy, and Lizzi Testa 2016: 64–111.

Cameron, Av. 1983. "Eusebius of Caesarea and the Rethinking of History." In Gabba 1983: 71–88.

Cameron, Av. 1997. "Eusebius' *Vita Constantini* and the Construction of Constantine." In Edwards and Swain 1997: 145–74.

Cameron, Av. 2014. *Dialoguing in Late Antiquity*. Cambridge, MA: Harvard University Press.

Cameron, Av., and P. Garnsey, eds. 1998. *The Late Empire A.D. 337–425*, Cambridge Ancient History 13. Cambridge: Cambridge University Press.

Cameron, Av., and S. G. Hall, trans. 1999. *Eusebius of Caesarea: Life of Constantine*. Oxford: Clarendon Press.

Campany, R. 2017. " 'Buddhism Enters China' in Early Medieval China." In Poo, Drake, and Raphals 2017: 13–34.

Caner, D. 2006. "Towards a Miraculous Economy: Christian Gifts and Material 'Blessings' in Late Antiquity." *Journal of Early Christian Studies* 14: 329–77.

Canivet, P., and A. Leroy-Molinghen, eds. and trans. 1977–1979. *Theodoret: Philotheos historia*. 2 vols. Sources chrétiennes, nos. 234, 257. Paris: Éditions du Cerf.

Carroll, J. 2001. *Constantine's Sword: The Church and the Jews, a History*. Boston.

Cassiday, A., and F. W. Norris, eds. 2007. *Constantine to 600,* The Cambridge History of Christianity, vol. 3. Cambridge: Cambridge University Press.

Cavadini, J., ed. 1999. *Miracles in Jewish and Christian Antiquity: Imagining Truth.* Notre Dame: University of Notre Dame Press.

Ceccini, A., and Ch. Gabrielli, eds., 2011. *Politiche religiose nel mondo antico e tardoantica: poteri e indirizzi, forme del controllo, idee e prassi di tolleranza,* Atti del Convegno, Firenzi, 24–36 settembre 2009. Bari: Edipuglia.

Chadwick, H., trans. 1953. *Origen: Contra Celsum.* Cambridge: Cambridge University Press.

Chadwick, H. 1980. *The Role of the Christian Bishop in Ancient Society,* Center for Hermeneutical Studies, Berkeley, Protocol of the Thirty-Fifth Colloquy: 25 February 1979. Berkeley: The Center.

Chadwick, H. 1985. "Augustine on Pagans and Christians: Reflections on Religious and Social Change." In D. Beales and G. Best, eds., *History, Society and the Churches: Essays in Honour of Owen Chadwick*: 9-27. Cambridge: Cambridge University Press.

Chadwick, H. 1998. "Orthodoxy and Heresy from the Death of Constantine to the Eve of the First Council of Ephesus." In Cameron and Garnsey 1998: 561–600.

Charlesworth, M. P. 1937. "The Virtues of a Roman Emperor: Propaganda and the Creation of Belief." *Proceedings of the British Academy* 23: 105–33.

Chenault, R. 2016. "Beyond Pagans and Christians: Politics and Intra-Christian Conflict in the Controversy over the Altar of Victory." In Salzman, Sághy, and Lizzi Testa 2016: 46–63.

Chesnut, G. 1986. *The First Christian Histories.* 2nd ed. Macon, GA: Mercer University Press.

Chin, C. 2010. "The Bishop's Two Bodies: Ambrose and the Basilicas of Milan." *Church History* 79: 531-55.

Chin, C., and C. Schroeder, eds. 2016. *Melania: Early Christianity Through the Life of One Family.* Berkeley: University of California Press.

Chitty, D. 1966. *The Desert a City. An Introduction to the Study of Egyptian and Palestinian Monasticism Under the Christian Empire.* London: Mowbrays.

Chuvin, P. 1990. *A Chronicle of the Last Pagans,* trans. B. A. Archer. Cambridge, MA: Harvard University Press.

Clark, G. 2009. "Can We Talk? Augustine and the Possibility of Dialogue." In Goldhill 2009: 117–34.

Clive, J. 1976. "Gibbon's Humor." *Daedalus* 105 (3): 27–36.

Cohen, R. 2008. *Saving the Holy Sepulchre: How Rival Christians Came Together to Rescue Their Holiest Shrine.* New York: Oxford University Press.

Cohen, S. J. D. 1986. "Anti-Semitism in Antiquity: The Problem of Definition." In Berger 1986: 43–47.

Cohen, S. J. D. 1999. *The Beginnings of Jewishness: Boundaries, Varieties, Uncertainties.* Berkeley: University of California Press.

Colella, R. L., et al., eds. 1997. *Pratum Romanum. Richard Karautheimer zum 100. Geburtstag.* Wiesbaden: L. Reichert.

Colish, M. 2002. "Why the Portiana? Reflections on the Milanese Basilica Crisis of 386." *Journal of Early Christian Studies* 10: 361–72.

Conant, K. 1958. "The Holy Sites at Jerusalem in the First and Fourth Centuries AD." *Proceedings of the American Philosophical Society* 102: 14–24.

Conant, K., and G. Downey. 1956. "The Original Buildings at the Holy Sepulchre in Jerusalem." *Speculum* 31: 1–48.

Consolino, E. 1984. "Il significato dell' inventio crucis nel De obitu Theodosii." *Annali della facoltà di lettere e filosofia dell' università di Siena* 5: 161–80. Firenze.

Conybeare, C. 2014. "The City of Augustine: On the Interpretation of *Civitas.*" In Harrison, Humfress, and Sandwell 2014: 139–55.

Cook, J. 2014. *Crucifixion in the Mediterranean World.* Tübingen: Mohr Siebeck.

Corcoran, S. 1993. "Hidden from History: The Legislation of Licinius." In Harries and Wood 1993: 97–119.

Corcoran, S. 1996. *The Empire of the Tetrarchs: Imperial Pronouncements and Government AD 284–324.* New York: Oxford University Press.

Coüasnon, C. 1974. *The Church of the Holy Sepulchre in Jerusalem*, trans. J.-P. and C. Ross. London: Oxford University Press for the British Academy.

Cracco Ruggini, L. 1977. "The Ecclesiastical Histories and the Pagan Historiography: Providence and Miracles." *Athenaeum*, n.s. 55: 107–26.

Crawford, M. 1983. "Imperial Coin Types and the Formation of Public Opinion." In Brooke et al. 1983: 47–64.

Creed, J. L., ed. and trans. 1984. *Lactantius, De mortibus persecutorum.* Oxford: Clarendon Press.

Crislip, A. 2005. *From Monastery to Hospital: Christian Monasticism and the Transformation of Health Care in Late Antiquity.* Ann Arbor, MI: University of Michigan Press.

Crook, Z. 2004. *Reconceptualizing Conversion. Patronage, Loyalty, and Conversion in the Religions of the Ancient Mediterranean*, Beihefte zur Zeitschrift für die neutestamentliche Wissenschaft und die Kunde der älteren Kirche, 130. Berlin: De Gruyter.

Curtin, F. 1995. "Atticism, Homer, Neoplatonism, and *Fürstenspiegel*: Julian's Second Panegyric on Constantius." *Greek, Roman and Byzantine Studies* 36: 177–211.

Dagron, G. 1967. *L'Empire romain d'Orient et les traditions politiques de l'Hellenisme: le témoignage de Themistios*, Centre de Recherche d'histoire et civilization byzantines, Travaux et Mémoires 3. Paris: De Boccard.

Dagron, G. 2003. *Emperor and Priest: The Imperial Office in Byzantium*, trans. J. Birrell. Cambridge: Cambridge University Press.

Damgaard, F. 2013. "Propaganda Against Propaganda: Revisiting Eusebius' Use of the Figure of Moses in the *Life of Constantine.*" In Johnson and Schott 2013: 115–49.

Daur, Kl.-D., ed. 1962. *De vera religione*. In *Sancti Aurelii Augustini: Opera*, pars. IV: 2. CCSL 32. Turnholt: Brepols.

Davis, J. 2006. "Teaching Violence in the Schools of Rhetoric." In Drake 2006: 197–204.

Dawes, E. and N. H. Baynes, trans. 1948. *Three Byzantine Saints: Contemporary Biographies of St Daniel the Stylite, St Theodore of Sykeon and St John the Almsgiver*. Oxford: Blackwell.

De Leo, P. 1974. *Il Constitutum Constantini: compilazione agiografica del sec. VIII: note e documenti per una nuova lettura*. Reggio Calabria: Editori meridionali riuniti.

Dean, J. 1998. *Aliens in America: Conspiracy Cultures from Outerspace to Cyberspace*. Ithaca: Cornell University Press.

Decker, D. de. 1968. "La politique religieuse de Maxence." *Byzantion* 38: 472–562.

Deferrari, R., trans. 1934. "To Young Men, on How They Might Derive Profit from Pagan Literature." In *Basil of Caesarea: The Letters*. 4 vols. 4: 378–435. LCL. Cambridge, MA: Harvard University Press.

Delehaye, H., ed. 1913. "Vita S. Danielis Stylitae." *Analecta Bollandiana* 32: 121–216.

Delehaye, H. 1923. *Les saints stylites*. Bruxelles: Societé des Bollandistes.

Delehaye, H. 1934. *Cinq Leçons sur la Méthode Hagiographique*. Subsidia Hagiographica 21. Bruxelles: Societé des Bollandistes.

Demandt, A. 2007. "Wenn Kaiser träumen—Die Visionen Konstantins des Großen." In A. Demandt and J. Engemann, eds., *Konstantin der Grosse: Geschichte, Archäologie, Rezeption*, 49–59. Trier: Rheinisches Landesmuseum.

Den Boeft, J., et al., eds. 1992. *Cognitio gestorum: The Historiographic Art of Ammianus Marcellinus*. Amsterdam: Royal Netherlands Academy of Arts and Sciences.

Den Boer, W., ed. 1972. *Le culte des souverains dans l'Empire romain*, Fondation Hardt Entretiens sur l'antiquité classique, 19. Geneva: Fondation Hardt.

DePalma Digeser, E. 1994. "Lactantius and Constantine's Letter to Arles: Dating the *Divine Institutes*." *Journal of Early Christian Studies* 2: 33–52.

DePalma Digeser, E. 2000. *The Making of a Christian Empire: Lactantius and Rome*. Ithaca: Cornell University Press.

DePalma Digeser, E. 2012. *A Threat to Public Piety: Christians, Platonists, and the Great Persecution*. Ithaca: Cornell University Press.

Dewing, H. B., ed. and trans. 1914–1928. *Procopius: History of the Wars*, 5 vols. LCL. Cambridge, MA: Harvard University Press.

Di Maio, M., M. Arnold, and W. H. Arnold. 1992. "*Per Vim, per Caedem, per Bellum*: A Study of Murder and Ecclesiastical Politics in the Year 337 A.D." *Byzantion* 62: 158–211.

Diefenbach, S. 2015. "A Vain Quest for Unity: Creeds and Political (Dis) Integration in the Reign of Constantius II." In Wienand 2015b: 353–78.

Dods, M., trans. 1887. *Augustine: The City of God*. In Schaff 1886–1890, vol. 2: 7–511.

Dölger, F., ed. 1913. *Konstantin der Gross und seine Zeit.* Römische Quartalschrift, Supplementheft 19. Freiburg: Herder'sche.

Dölger, F. J. 1918. *Die Sonne der Gerechtigkeit und der Schwarze, eine religions-geschichtliche Studie zum Taufgelöbnis.* Liturgiegeschichtliche Forschungen 2. Münster: Aschendorff.

Dölger, F. J. 1920. *Sol Salutis, Gebet und Gesang im christlichen Altertum,* Liturgiegeschichtliche Forschungen, 4–5. Münster: Aschendorff.

Dombart, B., and A. Kalb, eds. 1955. *Augustine: De civitate Dei.* 2 vols. CCSL, 47–48. Turnholt: Brepols.

Donciu, R. 2012. *L'empereur Maxence.* Bari: Edipuglia.

Donner, H. 1994. *The Mosaic Map of Madaba. An Introductory Guide.* Palestina Antiqua 7. Kampen: Pharos.

Doran, R., trans. 1992. *The Lives of Simeon Stylites.* Cistercian Studies 112. Kalamazoo, MI: Cistercian Publications.

Dothan, M. 1983. *Hammath Tiberias. Early Synagogues and the Hellenistic and Roman Remains.* Jerusalem: Israel Exploration Society.

Downey, G. 1957. "Themistius and the Defense of Hellenism in the Fourth Century." *Harvard Theological Review* 50: 259–74.

Doyle, A. C. 1894. *The Memoirs of Sherlock Holmes.* New York: A. Burt.

Drake, H. A., trans. 1976. *In Praise of Constantine: A Historical Study and New Translation of Eusebius' Tricennial Orations.* Berkeley: University of California Press.

Drake, H. A. 1985. "Eusebius on the True Cross." *Journal of Ecclesiastical History* 36: 1–22.

Drake, H. A. 1996. "Lambs into Lions: Explaining Early Christian Intolerance." *Past and Present*, no. 153: 3–36.

Drake, H. A. 2000. *Constantine and the Bishops: The Politics of Intolerance.* Baltimore: Johns Hopkins University Press.

Drake, H. A. 2006a. "'Measure Our Religion Against Yours': Constantine's Concept of Christianity in the Oration to the Saints." *Studia Patristica* 42: 107–12.

Drake, H. A., ed. 2006b. *Violence in Late Antiquity: Perceptions and Practices.* Aldershot, England: Ashgate.

Drake, H. A. 2011. "Intolerance, Religious Violence and Political Legitimacy in Late Antiquity." *Journal of the American Academy of Religion* 79: 193–235.

Drake, H. A. 2012. "Where High and Low Culture Meet: The Legend of the Cross." In Brakke, Deliyannis, and Watts 2012: 65–71.

Drake, H. A. 2014. "The Edict of Milan: Why We Still Need It." In V. Vachkova and D. Dimitrov, eds., *Serdica Edict (AD 311): Concepts and Realizations of The Idea of Religious Toleration*, 61–76. Sofia: Tangra.

Drake, H. A. 2015. "Speaking of Power: Christian Redefinition of the Imperial Role in the Fourth Century." In Wienand 2015b: 291–308.

Drijvers, H. 1999. "Promoting Jerusalem, Cyril and the True Cross." In Drijvers and Watt 1999: 79–95.

Drijvers, H., and J. W. 1997. *The Finding of the True Cross: The Judas Kyriakos Legend in Syriac. Introduction, Text and Translation.* Corpus Scriptorum Christianorum Orientalium 565, Subsidia 93. Louvain: Peeters.

Drijvers, J. W. 1999. "The Rebuilding of the Temple in Jerusalem." In den Boeft et al. 1992: 19–26.

Drijvers, J. W. 2009. "The Power of the Cross: Celestial Cross Appearances in the Fourth Century." In Cain and Lenski 2009: 237–48.

Drijvers, J. W. 2011. "Helena Augusta, the Cross and the Myth: Some New Reflections." *Millennium* 8: 125–74.

Drijvers, J. W., and J. W. Watt, eds. 1999. *Portraits of Spiritual Authority: Religious Power in Early Christianity, Byzantium, and the Christian Orient.* Leiden: Brill.

Duchesne, L. 1889. "Une inscription chrétienne trouvée aux environs de Sétif par MM. Letaille et Audollent." *Comptes rendus des séances de l'Académie des Inscriptions et Belles-Lettres* 33 (6): 417.

Duchesne, L. 1910. *Histoire ancienne de l'Église.* 4th ed. Paris: Fontemoing & cie.

Dummer, J. 1973. "Ein naturwissenschaftliches Handbuch als Quelle für Epiphanius von Constantia." *Klio* 55: 289–99.

Dunkle, J. R. 1967. "The Greek Tyrant and Roman Political Invective of the Late Republic." *Transactions of the American Philological Society* 98: 151–71.

Dunkle, J. R. 1971. "The Rhetorical Tyrant in Roman Historiography: Sallust, Livy, Tacitus." *Classical World* 65: 12–20.

Durliat, J. 1990. *De la ville antique à la ville byzantine: le problème des subsistances.* Rome: École française de Rome.

Edwards, M., trans. 2000. *Neoplatonic Saints: The Lives of Plotinus and Proclus by Their Students.* Translated Texts for Historians, 35. Liverpool: Liverpool University Press.

Edwards, M., trans. 2003. *Constantine and Christendom: The Oration to the Saints, the Greek and Latin Accounts of the Discovery of the Cross, the Edict of Constantine to Pope Silvester.* Translated Texts for Historians, 39: 1–62. Liverpool: Liverpool University Press.

Edwards, M. 2004. "Pagan and Christian Monotheism in the Age of Constantine." In Swain and Edwards 2004: 211–34.

Edwards, M., and S. Swain, eds. 1997. *Portraits: Biographical Representation in the Greek and Latin Literature of the Roman Empire.* Oxford: Clarendon Press.

Ehling, K. 2011. "Das Christogramm als magisches Siegeszeichen—Zum konstantiniscen Silbermedaillon des Jahres 315." In Ehling and Weber 2011: 27–32.

Ehling, K., and G. Weber, eds. 2011. *Konstantin der Große: Zwischen Sol und Christus.* Darmstadt: Phillipp von Zabern.

Ehrenberg, V., A. H. M. Jones, P. A. Brunt, and J. M. Moore, eds. and trans. 1967. *Res Gestae Divi Augusti. The Achievements of the Divine Augustus.* Oxford: Oxford Scholarly Editions.

Ehrhardt, A. 1959–1960. "Constantine, Rome and the Rabbis." *Bulletin of the John Rylands Library* 42: 288–312.

Ehrman, B. 2003. *Lost Christianities: The Battles for Scripture and the Faiths We Never Knew.* New York: Oxford University Press.

Eidinow, E., and J. Kindt, eds. 2015. *Oxford Handbook of Ancient Greek Religion.* New York: Oxford University Press.

Elliott, T. G. 1987. "Constantine's Conversion: Do We Really Need It?" *Phoenix* 41: 420–38.

Elliott, T. G. 1997. *The Christianity of Constantine the Great.* Scranton, PA: University of Scranton Press.

Elm, S. 2012. *Sons of Hellenism, Fathers of the Church: Emperor Julian, Gregory of Nazianzus, and the Vision of Rome.* Berkeley: University of California Press.

Engels, D., and P. van Nuffelen, eds. 2014. *Religion and Competition in Antiquity,* Collection Latomus, 343. Bruxelles: Éditions Latomus.

English, A. 2012. *The Saint Who Would Be Santa Claus: The True Life and Trials of Nicholas of Myra.* Waco, TX: Baylor University Press.

Evenepoel, W. 1998–1999. "Ambrose vs. Symmachus: Christians and Pagans in AD 384." *Ancient Society* 29: 283–306.

Exarchos, B. K., ed. 1952. *Johannes Chrysostomos: Über Hoffart und Kindererziehung.* Munich: Max Huber.

Faller, O., ed. 1955. *Sancti Ambrosii Opera,* pars 7. CSEL 73. Vienna: Hoelder-Pichler-Tempsky.

Favez, Ch. 1932. "L'épisode de l'invention de la croix dans l'Oraison Funèbre de Théodose." *Revue des Etudes Latins* 10: 423–29.

Fear, A., J. Fernández Ubiña, and Mar Marcos, eds. 2013. *The Role of the Bishop in Late Antiquity: Conflict and Compromise.* London: Bloomsbury.

Febretti, A. 1890. "Acquisition de la pierre phénicienne découverte par feu Anglay." In *Comptes rendus des séances de l'Académie des Inscriptions et Belles-Lettres,* 34: 176–77.

Fine, S. 2005. *Art and Judaism in the Greco-Roman World: Toward a New Jewish Archaeology.* Cambridge: Cambridge University Press.

Finian, T., and V. Twomey, eds., 1995. *Scriptural Interpretation in the Fathers: Letter and Spirit.* Dublin: Four Courts Press.

Finucane, R. 1977. *Miracles and Pilgrims: Popular Beliefs in Medieval England.* London: J.M. Dent.

Fleury, R. de. 1870. *Mémoire sur les Instruments de la Passion de notre Sauveur Jesus Christ.* Paris: Librairie Liturgique Catholique.

Flower, R. 2012. "Visions of Constantine." *Journal of Roman Studies* 102: 287–305.

Fontaine, J., ed. and trans. 1967–1969. *Sulpice Sévère. Vie de Saint Martin.* 3 vols. Sources chrétiennes, nos. 133–135. Paris: Éditions du Cerf.

Fontaine, J., and N. Dupré, ed. and trans. 2006. *Gallus: dialogues sur les "vertus" de saint Martin.* Sources chrétiennes, no. 510. Paris: Éditions du Cerf.

Fort, C. 1919. *The Book of the Damned*. New York: H. Liveright.

Fournier, E. 2016. "Amputation Metaphors and the Rhetoric of Exile: Purity and Pollution in Late Antique Christianity." In Hillner, Enberg, and Ulrich 2016: 47–65.

Fowden, G. 1982. "The Pagan Holy Man in Late Antique Society." *Journal of Hellenic Studies* 102: 33–59.

Frakes, R. M., and E. DePalma Digeser, eds. 2010. *The Rhetoric of Power in Late Antiquity: Religion and Politics in Byzantium, Europe and the Early Islamic World*. London: Tauris Academic Studies.

Francheschini, E., and R. Weber, eds. 1965. *Itinerarium Egeriae*. CCSL 175. Turnholt: Brepols.

Frank, G. 2000. *The Memory of the Eyes: Pilgrims to Living Saints in Christian Late Antiquity*. Berkeley: University of California Press.

Frankfurter, D. 1990. "Stylites and Phallobates: Pillar Religions in Late Antique Syria." *Vigiliae Christianae* 44: 168–98.

Frankfurter, D. 2005a. "Beyond Magic and Superstition." In Burrus 2005: 255–312.

Frankfurter, D. 2005b. "Violence and Religious Formation: An Afterword." In Matthews and Gibson 2005: 140–52.

Fredriksen, P. 2003. "What 'Parting of the Ways'? Jews, Gentiles, and the Ancient Mediterranean City." In Becker and Reed 2003: 35–63.

Fredriksen, P. 2010. *Augustine and the Jews: A Christian Defense of Jews and Judaism*. rev. ed. New Haven: Yale.

Fredriksen, P., and O. Irshai. 2006. "Christian Anti-Judaism, Polemics and Policies from the Second to the Seventh Century." In Katz 2006: 977–1035.

Frend, W. H. C. 1952. *The Donatist Church: A Movement of Protest in Roman North Africa*. Oxford: Clarendon Press.

Frend, W. H. C. 1967. *Martyrdom and Persecution in the Early Church: A Study of a Conflict from the Maccabees to Donatus*. New York: Anchor Books.

Freund, R. 1992. "Which Christians, Pagans and Jews? Varying Responses to Julian's Attempt to Rebuild the Temple in Jerusalem in the Fourth Century CE." *Journal of Religious Studies* 18: 67–93.

Frilingos, C. 2009. " 'It Moves Me to Wonder': Narrating Violence and Religion Under the Roman Empire." *Journal of the American Academy of Religion* 77: 825–52.

Fuhrmann, M., ed. 1977. *Christianisme et formes littéraires de l'antiquité tardive en Occident*, Fondation Hardt, Entretiens sur l'antiquité classique, 23. Genève: Fondation Hardt.

Fürst, A. 2010. "Monotheism Between Cult and Politics: The Themes of the Ancient Debate Between Pagan and Christian Monotheism." In Mitchell and van Nuffelen 2010: 82–99.

Fustel de Coulanges, Numa D. 1864. *La cité antique: étude sur le culte, le droit, les institutions de la Grèce et de Rome*. Paris: Hachette.

Gabba, E., ed. 1983. *Tria Corda: Scritti in onore di Arnaldo Momigliano.* Como, Italy: Edizioni New Press.

Gaddis, J. M. 2005. *There Is No Crime for Those Who Have Christ: Religious Violence in the Christian Roman Empire.* Berkeley: University of California Press.

Gannagé, E., P. Crone, M. Aouad, D. Gutas, and E. Schütrumpf, eds. 2004. *The Greek Strand in Islamic Political Thought,* Proceedings of the Conference held at the Institute for Advanced Study, Princeton, 16–27 June 2003. *Mélanges de l'Université Saint-Joseph* 57.

Garland, R. 2011. "Miracles in the Greek and Roman World." In Twelftree 2011: 75–94.

Garnsey, P. 1984. "Religious Toleration in Classical Antiquity." In Shiels 1984: 1–27.

Gasque, W., and R. Martin, eds. 1970. *Apostolic History and the Gospel: Biblical and Historical Essays Presented to F.F. Bruce.* Grand Rapids, MI: Eerdmans.

Geljon, A. C., and R. Roukema, eds., 2014. *Violence in Ancient Christianity: Victims and Perpetrators.* Leiden: Brill.

Gemeinhardt, P., and J. Leemans, eds. 2012. *Christian Martyrdom in Late Antiquity: History and Discourse, Tradition and Religious Identity.* Berlin: DeGruyter.

George, A. 1979. "'Making the Desert Bloom': A Myth Examined." *Journal of Palestine Studies* 8: 88–100.

Giangrande, J. 1956. *Eunapius: vitae sophistarum.* Rome: Typis Publicae Officinae Polygraphicae.

Gibbon, E. 1909–1914. *The History of the Decline and Fall of the Roman Empire,* ed. J. Bury. 7 vols. London: Methuen (originally published 1776–1788).

Gifford, E. H., trans. 1903. *Eusebius of Caesarea: Preparation for the Gospel.* 2 vols. Oxford: Typografio Academico.

Gillman, I. 1961. "Some Reflections on Constantine's 'Apostolic' Consciousness." *Studia Patristica* 4: 422–28.

Gleason, M. 1986. "Festive Satire: Julian's Misopogon and the New Year at Antioch." *Journal of Roman Studies* 76: 106–19.

Gleason, M. 1995. *Making Men: Sophists and Self-Preservation in Ancient Rome.* Princeton: Princeton University Press.

Gleason, M. 1998. "Visiting and News: Gossip and Reputation-Management in the Desert." *Journal of Early Christian Studies* 6: 501–21.

Goehring, J. 1996. "Withdrawing from the Desert: Pachomius and the Development of Village Monasticism in Upper Egypt." *Harvard Theological Review* 89: 297–85.

Goehring, J. 1997. "Monastic Diversity and Ideological Boundaries in Fourth-Century Christian Egypt." *Journal of Early Christian Studies* 5: 61–84.

Goldhill, S., ed. 2009. *The End of Dialogue in Antiquity.* Cambridge: Cambridge University Press.

Goranson, S. 1990. *The Joseph of Tiberias Episode in Epiphanius: Studies in Jewish and Christian Relations.* PhD dissertation, Duke University.

Goranson, S. 1999. "Joseph of Tiberias Revisited: Orthodoxies and Heresies in Fourth Century Galilee." In Meyer 1999: 335–43.

Gordon, R. 2014. "Monotheism, Henotheism, Megatheism: Debating Pre-Constantinian Religious Change." *Journal of Roman Archaeology* 27: 665–76.

Grabar, A. 1972. *Martyrium; Recherches sur le culte des reliques et l'art chrétien antique.* 2 vols. London: Variorum.

Grant, R. M. 1952. *Miracle and Natural Law in Graeco-Roman and Early Christian Thought.* Amsterdam: North Holland Publishing.

Graumann, T. 1997. "St. Ambrose on the Art of Preaching." In *Vescovi e pastori in epoca teodosiana, XXV incontro di studiosi dell'antichità cristiana, Roma, 8–11 maggio 1996,* 2 vols., Studia ephemeridis Augustinianum, 58. vol. 2: 587–600. Roma: Institutum Patristicum Augustinianum.

Graupner, A., and M. Wolter, eds. 2007. *Moses in Biblical and Extrabiblical Traditions.* Beihefte zur Zeitschrift für die alttestamentliche Wissenschaft 372. Berlin: DeGruyter.

Greenslade, S. L. 1954. *Church and State from Constantine to Theodosius.* London: SCM Press.

Grégoire, H. 1930. "La 'conversion' de Constantin." *Revue de l'Univiversité de Bruxelles* 36: 231–72.

Gregory, B. 2012. *The Unintended Reformation: How a Religious Revolution Secularized Society.* Cambridge. MA: Harvard University Press.

Grell, O. P., and B. Scribner, eds. 1996. *Tolerance and Intolerance in the European Reformation.* Cambridge: Cambridge University Press.

Guignebert, C. 1923. "Les demi-Chrétiens et leur place dans l'église antique." *Revue de l'Histoire des Religions* 43: 65–102.

Guthrie, P. 1966. "The Execution of Crispus." *Phoenix* 20: 325–31.

Haase, W., ed. 1980. *Aufstieg und Niedergang der römischen Welt* 2.23.2. Berlin: DeGruyter.

Hahn, C. 1997. "Seeing and Believing: The Construction of Sanctity in Early-Medieval Saints' Shrines." *Speculum* 72: 1079–106.

Hahn, I. 1960. "Der ideologische Kampf um den Tod Julians des Abtrünnigen." *Klio* 38: 225–32.

Halsall, G. 2008. *Barbarian Migrations and the Roman West, 376–568.* Cambridge: Cambridge University Press.

Halsbergh, G. H. 1972. *The Cult of Sol Invictus.* Leiden: Brill.

Halton, T. P., trans. 1999. *Jerome: On Illustrious Men (De viris illustribus).* Fathers of the Church, vol. 100. Washington, DC: Catholic University of America Press.

Hamrick, E. 1977. "The Third Wall of Agrippa I." *Biblical Archaeologist* 40: 18–23.

Hansen, G. C., ed. 1995. *Sokrates Kirchengeschichte*. Griechischen christlichen Schriftsteller der ersten Jahrhunderte, Neue Folge, Bd. 1. Berlin: Akademie Verlag.

Hanson, J. 1980. "Dreams and Visions in the Graeco-Roman World and Early Christianity." In W. Haase, ed., *Aufstieg und Niedergang der römischen Welt* 2.23.2: 1395–1427. Berlin: De Gruyter.

Hanson, R. P. C. 1988. *The Search for the Christian Doctrine of God: The Arian Controversy, 318–381*. Edinburgh: T & T Clark.

Harkins, P., trans. 1979. *John Chrysostom: Discourses Against Judaizing Christians*. Fathers of the Church, vol. 68. Washington, DC: Catholic University of America Press.

Harries, J. 2012. *Imperial Rome AD 284 to 363: The New Empire*. Edinburgh: Edinburgh University Press.

Harries, J., and I. Wood, eds. 1993. *The Theodosian Code: Studies in the Imperial Law of Late Antiquity*. London: Duckworth.

Harris, M. 2007. "How Did Moses Part the Red Sea? Science as Salvation in the Exodus Tradition." In Graupner and Wolter 2007: 5–31.

Harris, W. 2001. *Restraining Rage: The Ideology of Anger Control in Classical Antiquity*. Cambridge, MA: Harvard University Press.

Harris, W. V. 2005. "Constantine's Dream." *Klio* 87: 488–94.

Harris, W. V. 2009. *Dreams and Experience in Classical Antiquity*. Cambridge, MA: Harvard University Press.

Harrison, C., C. Humfress, and I. Sandwell, eds. 2014. *Being Christian in Late Antiquity: A Festchrift for Gillian Clark*. New York: Oxford University Press.

Harrison, S., ed. 2001. *Apuleius: Rhetorical Works*. New York: Oxford University Press.

Hartranft, C., trans. 1890. *The Ecclesiastical History of Sozomen*. In Schaff and Wace 1890–1900, vol. 2: 179–427.

Harvey, P. B. Jr., and C. Conybeare, eds. 2009. *Maxima Debetur Magistro Reverentia. Essays on Rome and the Roman Tradition in Honor of Russell T. Scott*. Biblioteca di Athenaeum 54. Como: New Press.

Harvey, S. A. 1988. "The Sense of a Stylite: Perspectives on Simeon the Elder." *Vigiliae Christianae* 42: 376–94.

Harvey, S., and D. Hunter, eds. 2008. *The Oxford Handbook of Early Christian Studies*. New York: Oxford University Press.

Hawkins, T. 2011. "Jester for a Day, Master for a Year: Julian's *Misopogon* and the Kalends of 363 CE." *Archiv für Religionsgeschichte* 13: 161–73.

Head, T., ed. 2001. *Medieval Hagiography: An Anthology*. New York.

Heather, P. 1988. "Themistius: A Political Philosopher." In Whitby 1998: 125–50.

Heather, P. 2005. *The Fall of the Roman Empire: A New History of Rome and the Barbarians*. New York: Oxford University Press.

Heather, P. 2012. *Empires and Barbarians: The Fall of Rome and the Birth of Europe.* New York: Oxford University Press.

Heather, P., and D. Moncur, trans. 2001. *Politics, Philosophy, and Empire in the Fourth Century. Select Orations of Themistius.* Translated Texts for Historians, vol. 36. Liverpool: Liverpool University Press.

Heck, E., and A. Wlosok, eds. 2005–2011. *Lactantius: Divinarum institutionum libri septem.* 4 vols. Munich/Leipzig: Teubner.

Heid, S. 1989. "Der Ursprung der Helenalegende im Pilgerbetrieb Jerusalems." *Jahrbuch für Antike und Christentum* 32: 41–71.

Heikel, I. A., ed. 1902. *Eusebius Werke,* I. GCS, 7. Leipzig: Hinrichs.

Henig, M., and A. King, eds. 1986. *Pagan Gods and Shrines of the Roman Empire.* Oxford: Oxford University Committee for Archaeology.

Henry, M. D. 2005. "Christianity and Anti-Semitism." *Irish Theological Quarterly* 70: 362.

Henry, P., and H.-R. Schwyzer, eds. 1964. "Porphyrii Vita Plotini." In *Plotini Opera,* vol. 1: 1-38. Oxford: Clarendon Press, 1964.

Herzog zu Sachsen, Johann Georg. 1913. "Konstantin der Grosse und die hl. Helena in der Kunst der christlichen Orients." In Dölger 1913: 255–58.

Heydenreich, E., ed. 1879. *Incerti auctoris de Constantino Magno eiusque matre Helena libellus.* Leipsig: Teubner.

Hijmans, S. 2009. *Sol: The Sun in the Art and Religions of Rome.* PhD dissertation, Proefschrift Rijksuniversiteit Groningen.

Hilberg, J., ed. 1910–1918. *Sancti Eusebii Hieronymi Epistulae.* 3 vols. CSEL 54–56. Vienna: F. Tempsky.

Hill, G. F., trans. 1913. *Mark the Deacon: The Life of Porphyry, Bishop of Gaza.* Oxford: Clarendon Press.

Hillard, T., et al., eds. 1998. *Ancient History in a Modern University: Proceedings of a Conference Held at Macquarie University, 8–13 July, 1993.* 2 vols. Grand Rapids, MI: Eerdmans.

Hillner, J., J. Enberg, and J. Ulrich, eds. 2016. *Clerical Exile in Late Antiquity.* Frankfurt am Main: Peter Lang.

Hoare, F. R., trans. 1995. *The Life of Saint Martin of Tours.* In Noble and Head 1995: 1–29.

Holl, K., C.-F. Collatz, M. Bergermann, and C. Markschies, eds. 2013. *Epiphanius' Ancoratus und Panarion Haer. I-XXXIII.* 2nd ed. 2 vols. Berlin: Akademie Verlag.

Hollerich, M. 1989. "The Comparison of Moses and Constantine in Eusebius of Caesarea's Life of Constantine." *Studia Patristica* 10: 80–85.

Holmes, P., trans. 1885–1896. "The Prescription Against Heretics." In Roberts, Donaldson, and Coxe 1885–1896, vol. 3: 243–65.

Holum, K. 1977. "Pulcheria's Crusade A.D. 421–22 and the Ideology of Imperial Victory." *Greek, Roman, and Byzantine Studies* 18: 153–72.

Hopkins, K. 1999. *A World Full of Gods: Pagans, Jews and Christians in the Roman Empire*. London: Weidenfeld & Nicolson.

Houtman, A., et al., eds. 2008. *Empsychoi Logoi: Religious Innovations in Antiquity, Studies in Honour of Pieter Willem van der Horst*. Leiden: Brill.

Howard-Johnston, L., and P. A. Hayward, eds. 1999. *The Cult of the Saints in Late Antiquity and the Middle Ages: Essays on the Contribution of Peter Brown*. New York: Oxford University Press.

Hunink, V., ed. 1997. *Apuleius: Pro se de magia: apologia*. 2 vols. Amsterdam: J.C. Gieben.

Hunink, V., trans. 2001. "Apuleius, *Pro se de magia*." In Harrison 2001: 25–121.

Hunt, D. 2012. "The Christian Context of Julian's 'Against the Galileans.'" In Baker-Brian and Tougher 2012: 251–61.

Hunt, E. D. 1997. "Constantine and Jerusalem." *Journal of Ecclesiastical History* 48: 405–24.

Hunter, D., trans. 1988. *A Comparison Between a King and a Monk; Against the Opponents of the Monastic Life: Two Treatises*. Lewiston, NY: E. Mellen Press.

Iannaccone, L. 1998. "Introduction to the Economics of Religion." *Journal of Economic Literature* 36: 1465–95.

Inowlocki, S., and C. Zamagni, eds. 2011. *Reconsidering Eusebius: Collected Papers in Literary, Historical, and Theological Issues*, Vigiliae Christianae Supp. 107. Leiden: Brill.

Iossif, P., A. Chankowski, and C. Lorber, eds. 2011. *More Than Men, Less Than Gods: Studies on Royal Cult and Imperial Worship. Proceedings of the International Colloquium Organized by the Belgian School at Athens (November 1-2, 2007)*. Louvain: Peeters.

Irshai, O. 1996. "Cyril of Jerusalem: the Apparition of the Cross and the Jews." In Limor and Stroumsa 1996: 85–104.

Jackson, B., trans. 1892. *The Ecclesiastical History, Dialogues, and Letters of Theodoret*. In Schaff and Wace 1890–1900, vol. 3: 1–348.

Jacobs, A. 2004. *Remains of the Jews: The Holy Land and Christian Empire in Late Antiquity*. Palo Alto: Stanford University Press.

Jacobs, A. 2012. "Matters (Un-)Becoming; Conversions in Epiphanius of Salamis." *Church History* 81: 27–47.

Jacobs, A. 2016. *Epiphanius of Cyprus: A Cultural Biography of Late Antiquity*. Berkeley: University of California Press.

Jacobs, I. 2014. "A Time for Prayer and a Time for Pleasure. Christianity's Struggle with the Secular World." In Engels and van Nuffelen 2014: 192–219.

James, W. 1902. *The Varieties of Religious Experience: A Study in Human Nature*. New York: Longmans.

Janowitz, N. 2000. "Re-thinking Jewish Identity in Late Antiquity." In Mitchell and Greatrex 2000: 205–19.

Jaritz, G. 2016. "Constantine in Late Medieval Western Art: Just the Son of a Holy Mother?" In Bjornlie 2017: 198–225.

Jefford, C., ed. and trans. 2013. *The Epistle to Diognetus (with the Fragment of Quadratus): Introduction, Text and Commentary.* Oxford: Oxford University Press.

Jeremias, J. 1926. *Golgotha.* Leipzig: E. Pfeiffer.

Johnson, A. 2006. *Ethnicity and Argument in Eusebius' Praeparatio Evangelica.* New York: Oxford University Press.

Johnson, A., and J. M. Schott, eds. 2013. *Eusebius of Caesarea: Traditions and Innovations.* Washington, DC: Center for Hellenic Studies.

Johnson, L. 1989. "The New Testament's Anti-Jewish Slander and the Conventions of Ancient Polemic." *Journal of Biblical Literature* 108: 419–41.

Jones, A. H. M. 1962. *Constantine and the Conversion of Europe.* Rev. ed. New York: Collier.

Jones, A. H. M., M. Avi-Jonah, et al. 1971. *The Cities of the Eastern Roman Provinces,* 2nd ed. Oxford: Clarendon Press.

Jones, C. 1978. *Saint Nicholas of Myra, Bari and Manhattan. Biography of a Legend.* Chicago: University of Chicago Press.

Jones, C. 2014. *Between Pagan and Christian.* Cambridge, MA: Harvard University Press.

Jonkers, E., ed. 1954. *Acta et symbola conciliorum quae saeculo quarto habita sunt,* Textus minores, XIX. Leiden: Brill.

Jürgasch, T. 2016. "Christians and the Invention of Paganism in the Late Roman Empire." In Salzman, Sághy, and Lizzi Testa 2016: 115–38.

Kahlos, M. 2009. *Forbearance and Compulsion: The Rhetoric of Religious Tolerance and Intolerance in Late Antiquity.* London: Duckworth.

Kalleres, D. 2015. *City of Demons: Violence, Ritual, and Christian Power in Late Antiquity.* Berkeley: University of California Press.

Kalmin, R., and S. Schwartz, eds. 2003. *Jewish Culture and Society Under the Christian Roman Empire.* Leuven: Peeters.

Kanfer, S. 2006. *Stardust Lost: The Triumph, Tragedy, and Mishugas of the Yiddish Theater in America.* New York: Knopf.

Kaniecka, M. S., ed. 1928. *Paulinus Milanensis: Vita sancti Ambrosii.* Patristic Studies, 16. Washington, DC: Catholic University of America.

Katz, S., ed. 2006. *The Late Roman-Rabbinic Period.* The Cambridge History of Judaism, vol. 4. Cambridge: Cambridge University Press.

Kee, H. C. 1983. *Miracle in the Early Christian World. A Study in Socio-Historical Method.* New Haven, CT: Yale University Press.

Keene, C., and G. F. Savage-Armstrong, ed. and trans. 1907. *Rutilius Claudius Namatianus, De Reditu Suo.* London: George Bell & Sons.

Kelly, C. 2009. *The End of Empire: Attila the Hun and the Fall of Rome.* New York: Norton.

Kim, Y. 2015. *Epiphanius of Cyprus: Imagining an Orthodox World.* Ann Arbor, MI: University of Michigan Press.

King, C. W., trans. 1888. *Julian the Emperor, Containing Gregory Nazianzen's Two Invectives and Libanius' Monody with Julian's Extant Theosophical Works.* London: G. Bell and Sons.

King, K. L. 2008. "Which Early Christianity?" In Harvey and Hunter 2008: 66–84.

Kinzig, W. 1991. "'Non-Separation': Closeness and Co-Operation between Jews and Christians in the Fourth Century." *Vigiliae Christianae* 45: 27–53.

Klein, R., ed. 1972. *Der Streit um den Victoriaaltar; die dritte Relatio des Symmachus und die Briefe 17, 18 und 57 des Mailänder Bischofs Ambrosius. Einführung, Text, Übersetzung und Erläuterungen.* Darmstadt: Wissenschaftliche Buchgesellschaft.

Kloft, H., ed. 1979. *Ideologie und Herrschaft in der Antike.* Darmstadt: Wissenschaftliche Buchgesellschaft.

Knust, J., and Z. Várhelyi, eds. 2011. *Ancient Mediterranean Sacrifice.* New York: Oxford University Press.

Kolb, F. 1988. "L'ideologia tetrarchica e la politica religiosa di Diocleziano." In Bonamente and Nestori 1988: 17–44.

Kolb, F. 2000. *Herrscherideologie in der Spätantike.* Berlin.

Kraft, K. 1954–1955. "Das Silbermedallion Constantins des Grossen mit dem Christus-monogramm auf der Helm." *Jahrbuch für Numismatik und Geldgeschichte* 5–6: 151–78.

Kühnel, B. 2000. "The Synagogue Floor Mosaic in Sepphoris: Between Paganism and Christianity." In Levine and Weiss 2000: 31–43.

Laistner, M. J. W. 1951a. *Christianity and Pagan Culture in the Later Roman Empire.* Ithaca.

Laistner, M. J. W., trans. 1951b. "On Vainglory and the Right Way for Parents to Bring Up Their Children." In Laistner 1951: 85–122.

Lane Fox, R. 1997. "The *Life of Daniel.*" In Edwards and Swain 1997: 175–225.

Lassandro, D. 2000. *Sacratissimus Imperator. L'immagine del princes nell' oratoria tardoantica,* Quaderni di "invigilata Lucernis" 8. Bari.

Latham, J. A. 2016. *Performance, Memory, and Processions in Ancient Rome: The Pompa Circensis from the Late Republic to Late Antiquity.* Cambridge: Cambridge University Press.

Latham, J. A. forthcoming. "Ritual and the Christianization of Urban Space." In Uro, Day, DeMaris, and Roitto forthcoming.

Laurence, R. 1994. "Rumour and Communication in Roman Politics." *Greece & Rome* 41: 62–75.

Leach, E. 1973. "Melchisedech and the Emperor: Icons of Subversion and Orthodoxy." *Proceedings of the Royal Anthropological Institute,* 1972: 5–14. London: The Institute.

Ledegang, F. 2014. "Eusebius' View on Constantine and His Policy." In Geljon and Roukema 2014: 56–75.

Lee, H. D. P., trans. 1955. *Plato: The Republic*. Baltimore: Penguin.

Leemans, J., and J. Mettepenningen, eds. 2005. *More Than a Memory: The Discourse of Martyrdom and the Construction of Christian Identity in the History of Christianity*, Annua nuntia Lovaniensis, 5. Leuven: Peeters.

Lenski, N. 2002. *Failure of Empire: Valens and the Roman State in the Fourth Century A. D.* Berkeley: University of California Press.

Lenski, N. 2016. *Constantine and the Cities: Imperial Authority and Civic Politics*. Philadelphia: University of Pennsylvania Press.

Levenson, D. 1990. "Julian's Attempt to Rebuild the Temple: An Inventory of Ancient and Medieval Sources." In Attridge et al. 1990: 261–79.

Levenson, D. 2004. "The Ancient and Medieval Sources for the Emperor Julian's Attempt to Rebuild the Jerusalem Temple." *Journal for the Study of Judaism in the Persian, Hellenistic and Roman Period* 35: 408–60.

Levick, B. 1982. "Propaganda and the Imperial Coinage." *Antichthon* 16: 104–16.

Levine, L. 2012. *Visual Judaism in Late Antiquity: Historical Contexts of Jewish Art*. New Haven, CT: Yale University Press.

Levine, L., and Z. Weiss, eds. 2000. *From Dura to Sepphoris: Studies in Jewish Art and Society in Late Antiquity*. Journal of Roman Archaeology Supplement 40. Portsmouth, RI.

Levy, R. 2005. "Antisemitism, Etymology of." In R. Levy, *Antisemitism: A Historical Encyclopedia of Prejudice and Persecution*. 2 vols. (Santa Barbara, CA: ABC Clio), vol. 1: 24–25.

Liebeschuetz, J. H. W. G., and C. Hill, trans. 2005. *Political Letters and Speeches by Ambrose*. Translated Texts for Historians, 43. Liverpool: Liverpool University Press.

Lieu, J., T. Rajak, and J. North, eds. 1992. *The Jews Among Pagans and Christians in the Roman Empire*. London: Routledge.

Lim, R. 1995. *Public Disputation, Power and Social Order in Late Antiquity*. Berkeley: University of California Press.

Limberis, V. 2003. "'Religion' as the Cipher for Identity: The Cases of Emperor Julian, Libanius, and Gregory Nazianzus." *Harvard Theological Review* 93: 373–400.

Limor, O., and G. Stroumsa, eds. 1966. *Contra Iudaeos. Ancient and Medieval Polemics between Christians and Jews*. Tübingen: Mohr.

Linder, A. 1975. "The Myth of Constantine the Great in the West: Sources and Hagiographic Commemoration." *Studi Medievali*, ser. 3, 16: 43–95.

Linder, A., ed. and trans. 1987. *The Jews in Roman Imperial Legislation*. Detroit: Wayne State University Press.

Lipsius, R. A., and M. Bonnet, eds. 1959. *Acta apostolorum apocrypha*. 3 vols. Hildesheim: Olms.

Lizzi Testa, R. 2015. "The Famous 'Altar of Victory Controversy' in Rome: The Impact of Christianity at the End of the Fourth Century." In Wienand 2015b: 405–19.

Long, J. 1993. "Structures of Irony in Julian's Misopogon." *Ancient World* 24: 15–23.

Long, J. 2009. "How to Read a Halo: Three (or More) Versions of Constantine's Vision." In Cain and Lenski 2009: 227–35.

Los Angeles *Times* 1997. "British Priest's Situation Ethics: Location Decides if Theft's Immoral." March 16: A6

Louth, A. 2014. "*Fiunt, non nascuntur Christiani*: Conversion, Community, and Christian Identity in Late Antiquity." In Harrison, Humfress, and Sandwell 2014: 109–19.

Lunn-Rockliffe, S. 2008. "Ambrose's Imperial Funeral Sermons." *Journal of Ecclesiastical History* 59: 191–207.

Macaulay, T. B. 1849–1865. *The History of England, From the Accession of James II.* 5 vols. New York: Harper & Bros.

MacMullen, R. 1966. "A Note on Sermo Humilis." *Journal of Theological Studies,* 2 ser, 17: 108–12.

MacMullen, R. 1986. "Judicial Savagery in the Roman Empire." *Chiron* 147–66.

MacMullen, R. 1989. "The Preacher's Audience (AD 350-400)." *Journal of Theological Studies*, n.s. 40: 503–11.

MacMullen, R. 1997. *Christianity and Paganism in the Fourth to Eighth Centuries.* New Haven, CT: Yale University Press.

Maggioni, G. P., ed. 1998. *Jacobus da Varagine: Legenda Aurea.* 2nd ed. 2 vols. Sismel: Galluzzo.

Malone, E. 1950. *The Monk and the Martyr.* Studies in Christian Antiquity, 12. Washington, DC: Catholic University of America Press.

Malone, E. 1956. "The Monk and the Martyr." In Steidle 1956: 201–28.

Mango, C. 1990. "Constantine's Mausoleum and the Translation of Relics." *Byzantinische Zeitschrift* 83: 51–62.

Maraval, P. 2014. "Le devoir religieux des empereurs: de la tolérance à la repression." In Baslez 2014: 37–62.

Marcone, A., U. Roberto, and I. Tantillo, eds. 2014. *Tolleranza religiosa in età tardoantica, IV-V secolo.* Cassino: Edizioni Università di Cassino.

Marcovich, M., ed. 2001. *Origen: Contra Celsum libri VIII.* Vigiliae Christianae Supplement, 54. Leiden: Brill.

Marcus, K. L. 2015. *The Definition of Anti-Semitism.* New York: Oxford University Press.

Marenbon, J. 2015. *Pagans and Philosophers: the Problem of Paganism from Augustine to Leibniz.* Princeton: Princeton University Press.

Markus, R. A. 1974. "Paganism, Christianity and the Latin Classics in the Fourth Century." In Binns 1974: 1–21.

Markus, R. A. 1990. *The End of Ancient Christianity.* Cambridge: Cambridge University Press.

Marrou, H. I. 1959. "Autour du monogramme constantinien." In *Mélanges offerts à Étienne Gilson*, 403–14. Paris: J. Vrin.

Martin, D. 2004. *Inventing Superstition from the Hippocratics to the Christians.* Cambridge, MA: Harvard University Press.

Matthews, J. F. 1990. *Western Aristocracies and Imperial Court, AD 364-425.* Oxford: Clarendon Press.

Matthews, S., and E. L. Gibson, eds. 2005. *Violence in the New Testament.* New York: T & T Clark.

Mayer, W. 1997. "The Dynamics of Liturgical Space: Aspects of the Interaction Between John Chrysostom and his Audiences." *Ephemerides Liturgicae* 111: 104–15.

Mayer, W., and P. Allen. 2000. *John Chrysostom.* New York: Routledge.

McCauley, L., and A. Stephenson, trans. 1969. *Cyril of Jerusalem: Lenten Lectures: Procatechesis, Catecheses 1–12.* Fathers of the Church, vol. 61. Washington, DC: Catholic University of America Press.

McCauley, L., and A. Stephenson, trans. 1970. *Cyril of Jerusalem: Catechetical Lectures 13–18, Mystagogical Lectures, Letter to Constantius.* Fathers of the Church, vol. 64. Washington, DC: Catholic University of America Press

McCormack, S. 1981. *Art and Ceremony in Late Antiquity.* Berkeley: University of California Press.

McCormick, M. 2001. *Origins of the European Economy: Communications and Commerce, AD 300-900.* Cambridge: Cambridge University Press.

McEvoy, M. A. 2013. *Child Emperor Rule in the Late Roman West, AD 367-455.* Oxford: Oxford University Press.

McGing, B. 2002. "Population and Proselytism: How Many Jews Were There in the Ancient World?" In Bartlett 2002: 88–106.

McGoldrick, P. 1995. "Liturgy: The Context of Patristic Exegesis." In Finian and Twomey 1995: 27–37.

McLynn, N. 1994. *Ambrose of Milan: Church and Court in a Christian Capital.* Berkeley: University of California Press.

McLynn, N. 2004. "The Transformation of Imperial Churchgoing in the Fourth Century." In Swain and Edwards 2004: 235–70.

McLynn, N. 2014. "Julian and the Christian Professors." In Harrison, Humfress, and Sandwell 2014: 120–36.

Meier, M. 2003. "Göttlicher Kaiser und christlicher Herrscher? Die christlichen Kaiser der Spätantike und ihre Stellung zu Gott." *Das Altertum* 48: 129–60.

Meyer, E., ed. 1999. *Galilee Through the Centuries.* Duke Judaic Studies, 1. Winona Lake, IN: Eisenbrauns.

Millar, F. 2006. *A Greek Roman Empire: Power and Belief Under Theodosius II, 408-450.* Sather Classical Lectures, 64. Berkeley: University of California Press.

Miller, P. 1994. *Dreams in Late Antiquity: Studies in the Imagination of a Culture.* Princeton: Princeton University Press.

Mills, K., and A. Grafton, eds. 2003. *Conversion in Late Antiquity and the Early Middle Ages: Seeing and Believing.* Rochester: University Rochester Press.

Mitchell, S. 2006. *A History of the Later Roman Empire, A. D. 284-622.* Oxford: Blackwell.

Mitchell, S., and G. Greatrex, eds. 2000. *Ethnicity and Culture in Late Antiquity.* London: Classical Press of Wales.

Mitchell, S., and P. van Nuffelen, eds. 2010. *One God: Pagan Monotheism in the Roman Empire.* Cambridge: Cambridge University Press.

Moberly, R. W. L. 2011. "Miracles in the Hebrew Bible." In Twelftree 2011: 57–74.

Moffatt, A. 1972. "The Occasion of St. Basil's Address to Young Men." *Antichthon* 6: 74–86.

Mombritius, F., ed. 1974. "Vita seu Actus Sancti Silvestri." In De Leo 1974: 151–221.

Momigliano, A., ed. 1963a. *The Conflict Between Paganism and Christianity in the Fourth Century.* Oxford: Clarendon Press.

Momigliano, A. 1963b. "Pagan and Christian Historiography in the Fourth Century A.D." In Momigliano 1963a: 79–99.

Mommsen, T. E. 1951. "St. Augustine and the Christian Idea of Progress: The Background of the City of God." *Journal of the History of Ideas* 13: 346–74.

Montgomery, G. H. 1968. "Konstantin, Paulus und das Lichtkreuz." *Symbolae Osloenses* 43: 84–109.

Montgomery, G. H. 2000. "From Friend to Foe: The Portrait of Licinius in Eusebius." *Symbolae Osloenses* 75: 130–38.

Montgomery, J. 1996. "Contemplations on the Economic Approach to Religious Behavior." *American Economic Review* 86 (2): 443–47.

Moreau, J. 1954. *Lactance: De la mort des persecuteurs.* 2 vols. Paris: Éditions du Cerf.

Morris, C. 2005. *The Sepulchre of Christ and the Medieval West, from the Beginning to 1600.* New York: Oxford University Press.

Morrison, K. 1992. *Understanding Conversion.* Charlottesville: University Press of Virginia.

Moss, C. 1937. "Jacob of Serugh's Homilies on the Spectacles of the Theatre." *Le Muséon* 48: 87–112.

Moss, C. R. 2013. *The Myth of Persecution: How Early Christians Invented a Story of Martyrdom.* New York: Harper.

Moule, C. F. D., ed. 1965a. *Miracles: Cambridge Studies in Their Philosophy and History.* London: A.R. Mowbray.

Moule, C. F. D. 1965b. "The Vocabulary of Miracle." In Moule 1965a: 235–38.

Mount, C. 2013. "Belief, Gullibility, and the Presence of a God in the Early Roman Empire." In Nicklas and Spittler 2013: 85–106.

Mras, K., ed. 1954–1956. *Eusebius Pamphili Praeparatio Evangelica.* 2 vols. Eusebius' Werke VIII: 1–2. GCS, 43. Berlin: Akademie Verlag.

Mullett, M., ed. 2004. *Metaphrastes, or, Gained in Translation: Essays and Translations in Honour of Robert H. Jordan.* Belfast Byzantine Texts and Translations, 9. Belfast: Byzantine Enterprises.

Mutzenbecher, A., ed. 1984. *Augustinus: Retractationum libri II.* CCSL 57. Turnholt: Brepols.

Mynors, R. A., ed. 1964. *XII Panegyrici Latini.* Oxford: Clarendon Press. Reprinted in Nixon and Rodgers 1994: 523–674.

Neil, B. 2007. "Towards Defining a Christian Culture: The Christian Transformation of Classical Literature." In Cassiday and Norris 2007: 317–42.

Nicklas, T., and J. Spittler, eds. 2013. *Credible, Incredible: The Miraculous in the Ancient Mediterranean.* Tübingen: Mohr Siebeck.

Nixon, C. E. V., and B. Rodgers, trans. 1994. *In Praise of Later Roman Emperors: The Panegyrici Latini.* Berkeley: University of California Press.

Noble, T., and T. Head, eds. 1995. *Soldiers of Christ: Saints and Saints Lives from Late Antiquity and the Early Middle Ages.* University Park, PA: Pennsylvania State University Press.

Nock, A. D. 1930. "*A Diis Electa*: A Chapter in the Religious History of the Third Century." *Harvard Theological Review* 23: 251–74.

Nock, A. D. 1933. *Conversion: The Old and the New in Religion from Alexander the Great to Augustine of Hippo.* London: Oxford University Press.

Nock, A. D. 1947. "The Emperor's Divine *Comes*." *Journal of Roman Studies* 37: 102–16.

Noreña, C. 2011. *Imperial Ideals in the Roman West: Representation, Circulation, Power.* Cambridge: Cambridge University Press.

Norman, A. F., ed. and trans. 1977. "Oration 30: To the Emperor Theodosius, for the Temples." *Libanius: Selected Works*, vol. 2: 91–151. LCL. Cambridge, MA: Harvard University Press.

North, J. 1992. "The Development of Religious Pluralism." In Lieu, Rajak, and North 1992: 174–93.

Nuffelen, P. van. 2002. "Deux fausses lettres de Julien l'Apostat: (la lettre aux Juifs, «Ep.» 51 [Wright], et la lettre à Arsacius, «Ep.» 84 [Bidez])." *Vigiliae Christianae* 56: 131–50.

Nuffelen, P. van. 2002. "Gélase de Césarée, un compilateur du cinquième siècle." *Byzantinische Zeitschrift* 95: 621–39.

Nuffelen, P. van. 2011. *Rethinking the Gods. Philosophical Readings of Religion in the Post-Hellenistic Period.* Cambridge: Cambridge University Press.

Nuffelen, P. van. 2012. *Orosius and the Rhetoric of History.* Oxford: Oxford University Press.

Nuffelen, P. van. 2014. "The End of Open Competition? Religious Disputations in Late Antiquity." In Engels and van Nuffelen 2014: 149–72.

Nuffelen, P. van. 2015. "A War of Words: Sermons and Social Status in Constantinople Under the Theodosian Dynasty." In Van Hoof and van Nuffelen 2015: 201–17.

Oliver, J. H. 1953. *The Ruling Power: A Study of the Roman Empire in the Second Century After Christ Through the Roman Oration of Aelius*

Aristides. Transactions of the American Philosophical Society, n.s. 43 (4): 871–1003.

O'Reilly, M. V., ed. and trans. 1955. *Sancti Aurelii Augustini, De excidio urbis Romae sermo.* Washington, DC.

Oslington, P., ed. *The Oxford Handbook of Christianity and Economics.* New York: Oxford University Press.

Ousterhout, R. 1990. "The Temple, the Sepulchre, and the *Martyrion* of the Savior." *Gesta* 29: 44–53.

Painter, K., ed. 1994. *'Churches Built in Ancient Times': Recent Studies in Early Christian Archaeology.* Occasional Papers from the Society of Antiquaries of London, 16. London: Accordia Research Centre, University of London.

Paschoud, F. 1983. "Le rôle du providentialisme dans le conflit de 384 sur l'autel de la Victoire." *Museum Helveticum* 40: 197–206.

Paschoud, F. 2012a. "On a Recent Book by Alan Cameron: *The Last Pagans of Rome,*" trans. A. Birley. *L'Antiquité Tardive* 20: 359–88.

Paschoud, F. 2012b. "Richiamo di una verità offuscata: il secondo libro dei Maccabei quale modello del *de mortibus persecutorum* di Lattanzio." In Bonamente, Lenski, and Lizzi Testa 2012: 373–80.

Pasquali, G. 1910. "Die Composition der Vita Constantini des Eusebius." *Hermes* 45: 369–86.

Patlagean, E. 1968. "Ancienne hagiographie byzantine et histoire sociale." *Annales* 23: 106–26.

Patlagean, E. 1983. "Ancient Byzantine Hagiography and Social History." In Wilson 1983: 101–21.

Pearce, S. 2004. "King Moses: Notes on Philo's Portrait of Moses as an Ideal Leader in the *Life of Moses.*" In Gannagé, Crone, Aouad, Gutas, and Schütrumpf 2004: 37–74.

Pears, I. 2017. *Arcadia.* New York: Vintage.

Penella, R. J. 1993. "Julian the Persecutor in Fifth Century Church Historians." *Ancient World* 24: 31–43.

Penella, R. J. 1999. "Emperor Julian, the Temple of Jerusalem and the God of the Jews." *Koinonia* 23: 15–31.

Pennacchini, P. C., ed. 1913. *Discorso storico dell'invenzione della Croce del monaco Alessandro.* Grottaferrata: Tipografia Italo-Orientale «S. Nilo».

Petersen, J., ed. and trans. 1996. *Handmaids of the Lord: Contemporary Descriptions of Feminine Asceticism in the First Six Christian Centuries.* Cistercian Studies 143. Kalamazoo, MI: Cistercian Publications.

Peterson, E. 2011. *Theological Tractates,* ed. and trans. M. J. Hollerich. Palo Alto: Stanford University Press.

Petshenig, M., ed. 1923. *Expositio Psalmi CXVIII,* S. Ambrosii Opera 5, CSEL 62. Vienna.

Pettegree, A. 1996. "The Politics of Toleration in the Free Netherlands, 1572–1620." In Grell and Scribner 1996: 182–98.

Pezzela, S. 1967. "Massenzio e la politica religiosa di Costantino." *Studi e materiali di Storia delle Religioni* 38: 434–50.

Pichlmayr, Fr., and R. Gruendel, eds. 1970. *Sextus Aurelius Victor: De Caesaribus; Origo gentis Romanae; Liber de viris illustribus urbis Romae; Epitome de Caesaribus.* Leipzig: Teubner.

Pick, D., and L. Roper, eds. 2004. *Dreams and History: The Interpretation of Dreams from Ancient Greece to Modern Psychoanalysis.* New York: Routledge.

Piédagnel, A. and P. Paris 1966. *Cyrille de Jérusalem, Catéchèses mystagogiques.* Sources chrétiennes, no. 126. Paris: Éditions du Cerf.

Pietri, L., and M.-J. Rondeau, trans. 2013. *Eusèbe de Césarée, Vie de Constantin,* Sources chrétiennes, textes grecs, 559. Paris: Éditions du Cerf.

Piganiol, A. 1945. "L'hémisphairion et l'omphalos des lieux saints." *Cahiers archéologique* 1: 7–14.

Piganiol, A. 1947. *l'Empire chrétien, 325-395.* Paris: Presses universitaires de France.

Pohlkamp, W. 1992. "Textfassungen, literarische Formen und geschichtliche Funktionen der römischen Silvester-Akten." *Francia* 19: 115–196.

Pohlsander, H. 1984. "Crispus: Brilliant Career and Tragic End." *Historia* 33: 79–106.

Poo, M., H. Drake, and L. Raphals, eds. 2017. *Old Society, New Belief: Religious Transformation of China and Rome Between the First and Sixth Centuries C.E.* New York: Oxford University Press.

Portman, W. 1990. "Zu den Motiven der Diokletianischen Christenverfolgung." *Historia* 39: 212–48.

Posner, R. 1999. *An Affair of State: The Investigation, Impeachment, and Trial of President Clinton.* Cambridge, MA: Harvard University Press.

Potter, D. 1994. *Prophets and Emperors: Human and Divine Authority from Augustus to Theodosius.* Cambridge, MA: Harvard University Press.

Potter, D. 2013. *Constantine the Emperor.* New York: Oxford University Press.

Preger, Th. 1901. "Konstantinos-Helios." *Hermes* 36: 457–69.

Price, R. M., trans. 1985. *Theodoret, A History of the Monks of Syria/Historia Religiosa.* Kalamazoo, MI: Cistercian Publications.

Price, R. M. 2008. "Martyrdom and the Cult of the Saints." In Harvey and Hunter 2008: 808–25.

Quinn, E. 1962. *The Quest of Seth for the Oil of Life.* Chicago: University of Chicago Press.

Rambaud, M. 1966. *L'art de la defamation historique dans les Commentaires de César.* 2nd ed. Paris: Société d'Édition des Belles Lettres.

Ramsey, B., trans. 1997. *Paulinus of Milan: The Life of Saint Ambrose.* In B. Ramsey, *Ambrose,* 195–218. London: Routledge.

Raphals, L. 2013. *Divination and Prediction in Early China and Ancient Greece.* Cambridge: Cambridge University Press.

Raphals, L. 2015. "China and Greece: Comparisons and Insights." In Eidinow and Kindt 2015: 651–65.

Rapp, C. 1998a. "Comparison, Paradigm and the Case of Moses in Panegyric and Hagiography." In Whitby 1998: 277–98.

Rapp, C. 1998b. "Imperial Ideology in the Making: Eusebius of Caesarea on Constantine as 'Bishop.'" *Journal of Theological Studies*, n.s. 49: 685–95.

Rapp, C. 1998c. "Storytelling as Spiritual Communication in Early Greek Hagiography: The Use of Diegesis." *Journal of Early Christian Studies* 6: 431–48.

Rapp, C., trans. 2001. "Mark the Deacon: *Life of Porphyry of Gaza*." In Head 2001: 53–75.

Rapp, C. 2006. "Desert, City, and Countryside in the Early Christian Imagination." *Church History and Religious Culture* 86: 93–112.

Raspanti, G. 2009. "*Clementissimus Imperator*: Power, Religion, and Philosophy in Ambrose's *De obitu Theodosii* and Seneca's *De clementia*." In Cain and Lenski, 45–55.

Ratti, S. 2013. "Païens et chrétiens au IVe siècle: points de résistance à une doxa." *Antiquité Tardive* 21: 401–10.

Raymond, I. W., trans. 1936. *Orosius: Seven Books of History Against the Pagans*. New York: Columbia University Press.

Reames, S. 1985. *The Legenda aurea: A Reexamination of Its Paradoxical History*. Madison, WI: University of Wisconsin Press.

Rébillard, E. 2012. *Christians and Their Many Identities in Late Antiquity: North Africa, 200–450 C.E.* Ithaca: Cornell University Press, NY.

Rees, R., 1966. *Diocletian and the Tetrarchy*. Edinburgh: Edinburgh University Press.

Refoulé, R., ed. 1954. *De praescriptione haereticorum*. Tertulliani Opera, vol. 1: 185–224. Turnhout: Brepols.

Renucci, P. 2000. *Les idées politiques et le gouvernement de l'empereur Julien*. Collection Latomus, 250. Bruxelles: Latomus.

Reuther, R. 1972. "Judaism and Christianity: Two Fourth Century Religions." *Sciences Religieuses/Studies in Religion* 2: 1–10.

Riain, I. N., trans. 1998. *Homilies of Saint Ambrose on Psalm 118 (119)*. Dublin: Halcyon Press.

Rives, J. 1999. "The Decree of Decius and the Religion of Empire." *Journal of Roman Studies* 89: 135–54.

Roberts, A., trans. 1894. *Sulpicius Severus: Dialogues*. In Schaff and Wace 1890–1900, vol. 11: 24–54.

Roberts, A., J. Donaldson, and A. Cleveland Coxe, eds. 1885–1896. *The Ante-Nicene Fathers*. American ed. 10 vols. Buffalo: Christian Literature Co.

Robinson, D. N. 1915. "An Analysis of the Pagan Revival of the Late Fourth Century with Especial Reference to Symmachus." *Transactions of the American Philological Association* 46: 87–101.

Rolfe, J. C., ed. and trans. 1950–1952. *Ammianus Marcellinus: Rerum Gestarum*. Rev. ed. 3 vols. LCL. Cambridge, MA: Harvard University Press.

Ronchey, S. 2014. "Perché Cirillo assassinò Ipazia?" In Marcone and Tantillo 2014: 135–77.

Rosen, K. 1994. "*Fides contra dissimulationem*. Ambrosius und Symmachus im Kampf um den Victoriaaltar." *Jahrbuch für Antike und Christentum* 37: 29–36.

Rosen, R., ed. 2004. *Time and Temporality in the Ancient World*. Philadelphia: University of Pennsylvania Museum of Archaeology and Anthropology.

Roukema, R. 2014. "Reception and Interpretation of Jesus' Teaching of Love for Enemies in Ancient Christianity." In Geljon and Roukema 2014: 198–214.

Rousseau, P. 1985. *Pachomius: The Making of a Community in Fourth-Century Egypt*. Berkeley: University of California Press.

Rouwhorst, G. 2005. "The Emergence of the Cult of the Maccabean Martyrs in Late Antique Christianity." In Leemans and Mettepenningen 2005: 81–96.

Rubenson, S. 1990. *The Letters of St Antony: Origenist Theology, Monastic Tradition and the Making of a Saint*. Lund: Lund University Press.

Rubenson, S. 2007. "Asceticism and Monasticism, I: Eastern." In Cassiday and Norris 2007: 637–68.

Rubin, Z. 1982. "The Church of the Holy Sepulchre and the Conflict Between the Sees of Caesarea and Jerusalem." *Jerusalem Cathedra* 2: 79–105.

Russell, D. A., ed. and trans. 2001. *Quintilian: Institutio Oratoria*. 5 vols. LCL. Cambridge, MA: Harvard University Press.

Russell, D. A., and N. G. Wilson, eds. and trans. 1981. *Menander Rhetor*. Oxford: Clarendon Press.

Russell, K. W. 1980. "The Earthquake of May 19, A.D. 363." *Bulletin American Schools of Oriental Research* 238: 47–64.

Rutgers, L. 1992. "Archaeological Evidence for the Interaction of Jews and Non-Jews in Late Antiquity." *American Journal of Archaeology* 96: 101–18.

Rutgers, L. 1995. "Attitudes to Judaism in the Greco-Roman Period: Reflections on Feldman's *Jew and Gentile in the Ancient World*." *Jewish Quarterly Review* 85: 361–95.

Ryan, G., and H. Ripperger, trans. 1941. *The Golden Legend of Jacobus de Voragine*. New York: Longmans Green.

Salamito, J.-M. 2012. "Constantin vu par Augustin. Pour un relecture de *Civ.* 5.25." In Bonamente, Lenski, and Lizzi Testa 2012: 549–62.

Salzman, M. R. 2004. "Pagan and Christian Notions of the Week in the 4th Century CE Western Roman Empire." In Rosen 2004: 185–211.

Salzman, M. R. 2009. "Apocalypse Then? Jerome and the Fall of Rome in 410." In Harvey and Conybeare 2009: 175–92.

Salzman, M. R. 2010. "Ambrose and the Usurpation of Arbogastes and Eugenius: Reflections on Pagan-Christian Conflict Narratives." *Journal of Early Christian Studies* 18: 191–233.

Salzman, M. R. 2011. "The End of Public Sacrifice: Changing Definitions of Sacrifice in Post-Constantinian Rome and Italy." In Knust and Várhelyi 2011: 167–84.

Salzman, M. R. 2017. "From *Superstitio* to Heresy: Law and Divine Justice (Fourth-Fifth Centuries CE)." In Poo, Drake, and Raphals 2017: 245-55.

Salzman, M. R., M. Sághy, and R. Lizzi Testa, eds. 2016. *Pagans and Christians in Late Antique Rome: Conflict, Competition, and Coexistence in the Fourth Century.* Cambridge: Cambridge University Press.

Sandwell, I. 2007. *Religious Identity in Late Antiquity: Greeks, Jews and Christians in Antioch.* Cambridge: Cambridge University Press.

Sauer, E. 2003. *The Archaeology of Religious Hatred in the Roman and Early Medieval World.* Charleston, SC: Tempus.

Schäfer, P. 1998. *Judeophobia: Attitudes Toward the Jews in the Ancient World.* Cambridge, MA: Harvard University Press.

Schaff, P. ed. 1886–1890. *A Select Library of Nicene and Post-Nicene Fathers of the Christian Church.* Series 1. 14 vols. New York: Scribner.

Schaff, P., and H. Wace, eds. 1890–1900. *A Select Library of Nicene and Post-Nicene Fathers of the Christian Church.* Series 2. 14 vols. New York: Christian Literature Co.

Schatkin, M., trans. 1985. "Discourse on Blessed Babylas." In Schatkin and Harkins 1985: 75–152.

Schatkin, M., and P. Harkins, trans. *John Chrysostom: Apologist.* Fathers of the Church, vol. 73. Washington, DC: Catholic University of America Press.

Schatkin, M., et al., eds. 1990. *Jean Chrysostome: Discours sur Babylas.* Sources chrétiennes, no. 362. Paris: Éditions du Cerf.

Schechner, S. 1997. *Comets, Popular Culture, and the Birth of Modern Cosmology.* Princeton: Princeton University Press.

Scheidweiler, F., and L. Parmentier, eds. 1954. *Theodoretus: Kirchengeschichte.* 2nd ed. GCS, 44 (19). Berlin: Akademie Verlag.

Schenkl, H., and G. Downey, eds. 1965. "Themistius Oratio V." *Themistii orationes quae supersunt,* vol. 1: 91–104. Leipzig: Teubner.

Schmitt, C. 1985. *Political Theology: Four Chapters on the Concept of Sovereignty,* trans. G. Schwab. Cambridge, MA: MIT Press.

Schmitt, C. 2008. *Political Theology II: The Myth of the Closure of any Political Theology,* trans. M. Hoelzl and G. Ward. Cambridge, MA: MIT Press.

Schneemelcher, W., trans. 1992. "The Acts of Peter." In W. Schneemelcher and R. McL. Wilson, eds., *New Testament Apocrypha,* vol. 2: 271–321. Louisville, KY: Westminster/John Knox Press.

Schoedele, W., and R. Wilken, eds. 1979. *Early Christian Literature and the Classical Intellectual Tradition.* Paris: Éditions Beauchesne.

Schoenebeck, H. von. 1939. *Beiträge zur Religionspolitik des Maxentius und Constantin.* Klio Beiheft 43, n.s. 30. Leipzig.

Schott, J. 2008. *Christianity, Empire, and the Making of Religion in Late Antiquity.* Philadelphia: University of Pennsylvania Press.

Schwartz, S. 2001. *Imperialism and Jewish Society, 200 B. C. E. to 640 C. E.* Princeton: Princeton University Press.

Schwartz, S. 2003. "Some Types of Jewish-Christian Interaction in Late Antiquity." In Kalmin and Schwartz 2003: 197–210.

Scott, R., trans. 2004. "Discovery of the True Cross." In Mullett 2004: 157–84.

Scott, S., and J. Webster, eds. 2003. *Roman Imperialism and Provincial Art.* Cambridge: Cambridge University Press.

Scrofani, G. 2010. *La religione impura: La riforma di Giuliano Imperatore.* Brescia: Paideia Editrice.

Selinger, S. 2004. *The Mid-Third Century Persecutions of Decius and Valerian.* 2nd ed. Frankfurt am Main: Peter Lang.

Sessa, K. 2010. "Exceptionality and Invention: Silvester and the Late Antique 'Papacy' at Rome." *Studia Patristica* 46: 77–94.

Sessa, K. 2017. "Constantine and Silvester in the *Actus Silvestri*." In Bjornlie 2017: 77–91.

Shaw, B. D. 2011. *Sacred Violence: African Christians and Sectarian Hatred in the Age of Augustine.* Cambridge: Cambridge University Press.

Shaw, D. G. 2006. "Modernity Between Us and Them: The Place of Religion Within History." *History and Theory* 45 (4): 1–9.

Shaw, J. 2008. *Miracles in Enlightenment England.* New Haven, CT: Yale University Press.

Shepardson, C. 2009. "Rewriting Julian's Legacy: John Chrysostom's *On Babylas* and Libanius' *Oration 24.*" *Journal of Late Antiquity* 2: 99–115.

Shepardson, C. 2014. *Controlling Contested Places: Late Antique Antioch and the Spatial Politics of Religious Controversy.* Berkeley: University of California Press.

Shiels, W. J., ed. 1984. *Persecution and Toleration*, Studies in Church History 21. Oxford: Blackwell.

Shulman, D., and G. Stroumsa, eds. 1999. *Dream Cultures: Explorations in the Comparative History of Dreaming.* New York: Oxford University Press.

Signer, M. 1999. "Restoring the Balance: Musings on Miracles in Rabbinic Judaism." In Cavadini 1999: 111–26.

Simmons, M. 2006. "The Emperor Julian's Order to Rebuild the Temple in Jerusalem: A Connection with Oracles?" *Ancient Near Eastern Studies* 43: 68–117.

Simon, M. 1979. "From Greek *Hairesis* to Christian Heresy." In Schoedele and Wilken 1979: 101–16.

Singh, D. 2015. "Eusebius as Political Theologian: The Legend Continues." *Harvard Theological Review* 106: 129–54.

Sizgorich, T. 2007. "'Not Easily Were Stones Joined by the Strongest Bonds Pulled Asunder': Religious Violence and Imperial Order in the Later Roman World." *Journal of Early Christian Studies* 15: 75–101.

Smith, C. 1989. "Christian Rhetoric in Eusebius's Panegyric at Tyre." *Vigiliae Christianae* 43: 226–47.

Smith, K. 2016. *Constantine and the Captive Christians of Persia: Martyrdom and Religious Identity in Late Antiquity.* Berkeley: University of California Press.

Smith, M. 1991/1992. "In Search of Santa." *Timeline* 8 (December/January): 28–34.

Smith, R. 1995. *Julian's Gods: Religion and Philosophy in the Thought and Action of Julian the Apostate.* New York: Routledge.

Smith, R. B. E. 2007. "The Imperial Court of the Late Roman Empire, c. AD 300-AD 450." In Spawforth 2007: 157–232.

Smith, R. R. R. 1997. "The Public Image of Licinius I: Portrait Sculpture and Imperial Ideology in the Early Fourth Century." *Journal of Roman Studies* 87: 170–202.

Spawforth, A. J. S., ed. 2007. *The Court and Court Society in Ancient Monarchies.* Cambridge: Cambridge University Press.

Staats, R. 2008. "Kaiser Konstantin der Große und der Apostel Paulus." *Vigiliae Christianae* 62: 334–70.

Stark, R. 1987. "How New Religions Succeed: A Theoretical Model." In Bromley and Hammond 1987: 11–29.

Stark, R. 1993. "Epidemics, Networks, and the Rise of Christianity." In White 1993: 169–75.

Steidle, B. 1956. "'Homo Dei Antonius': Zum Bild des 'mannes Gottes' im alten Mönchtum." In B. Steidle, ed., *Antonius Magnus Eremita, 356–1956 studia ad antiquum monachismum spectantia.* Studia Anselmiana 38: 148–200. Rome: Herder.

Steinbeck, J. 1957. *The Short Reign of Pippin IV: A Fabrication.* New York: Viking.

Stern-Gillet, S. 1997. "Plotinus and His Portrait." *British Journal of Aesthetics* 37: 211–25.

Stewart, C. 2004. "Dreams and Desires in Ancient and Early Christian Thought." In Pick and Roper 2004: 37–56.

Stokes, M., ed. and trans. 1997. *Apology of Socrates.* Warminster: Aris and Phillips.

Storch, R. H. 1970. "The Trophy and the Cross: Pagan and Christian Symbolism in the Fourth and Fifth Centuries." *Byzantion* 40: 105–17.

Stroumsa, G. 2007. "Religious Dynamics Between Christians and Jews in Late Antiquity." In Cassiday and Norris 2007: 151–72.

Sulzberger, M. 1925. "Le Symbole de la Croix et les Monogrammes de Jésus chez les premiers chrétiens." *Byzantion* 2: 337–448.

Sumi, G. S. 2005. *Ceremony and Power: Performing Politics in Rome Between Republic and Empire.* Ann Arbor, MI: University of Michigan Press.

Superbiola Martinez, J. 1987. *Nuevos concilios Hispano-Romanos de los siglos III y IV: la coleccion de Elvira.* Málaga: Universidad de Málaga Press.

Swain, S. 2004. "Sophists and Emperors: The Case of Libanius." In Swain and Edwards 2004: 354–400.

Swain, S. 2013. *Themistius, Julian, and Greek Political Theory under Rome: Text, Translations, and Studies of Four Key Works*. Cambridge: Cambridge University Press.

Swain, S., and M. Edwards, eds. 2004. *Approaching Late Antiquity: The Transformation from Early to Late Empire*. Oxford: Oxford University Press.

Taylor, J. 1993. *Christians and the Holy Places. The Myth of Jewish-Christian Origins*. Oxford: Clarendon Press.

Teitler, H. 2017. *The Last Pagan Emperor: Julian the Apostate and the War Against Christianity*. New York: Oxford University Press.

Thornton, T. 1990. "The Stories of Joseph of Tiberias." *Vigiliae Christianae* 44: 54–63.

Timonen, A. 2004. "Flattering Silence: On the Fear of an Autocrat in the Historians of the Roman Empire." In Timonen, Greisenegger, and Kneucker 2004: 59–70.

Timonen, A., W. Greisenegger, and R. Kneucker, eds. 2004. *The Language of Silence*, vol. 2. Turun Yliopiston Julkaisuia, 271. Turku: Turun Yliopisto.

Tougher, S. 2007. *Julian the Apostate*. Edinburgh: Edinburgh University Press.

Twain, M. 1966. *The Innocents Abroad* (1869). Reprinted in C. Neider, ed., *The Complete Travel Books of Mark Twain*, 2 vols. vol. 1: 369–80. Garden City: Doubleday.

Twelftree, G., ed. 2011. *The Cambridge Companion to Miracle*. Cambridge: Cambridge University Press.

Twomey, V., and M. Humphries, eds. 2009. *The Great Persecution*. Dublin: Four Courts Press.

Ubiña, J. F. 2013. "*Ius et religio*: The Conference of Carthage and the End of the Donatist Schism, 411 AD." In Fear, Ubiña, and Marcos 2013: 47–62.

Uro, R., J. Day, R. DeMaris, and R. Roitto, eds. Forthcoming. *The Oxford Handbook of Early Christian Ritual*. New York: Oxford University Press.

Usener, H., and Societatis Philologae Bonnensis Sodales, eds. 1895. *Marci Diaconi Vita Porphyrii, episcopi gazensis*. Leipzig: Teubner.

Van Dam, R. 1985. "From Paganism to Christianity at Late Antique Gaza." *Viator* 16: 1–20.

Van Dam, R. 2003. "The Many Conversions of the Emperor Constantine." In Mills and Grafton 2003: 127–51.

Van Hoof, L., and P. Van Nuffelen, eds. 2015. *Literature and Society in the Fourth Century AD: Performing Paideia, Constructing the Present, Presenting the Self*. Mnemosyne Supplement 373. Leiden: Brill.

Vanderspoel, J. 1995. *Themistius and the Imperial Court: Oratory, Civic Duty, and Paideia from Constantius to Theodosius*. Ann Arbor, MI: University of Michigan Press.

Verheyden, J. 2008. "Epiphanius of Salamis on Beasts and Heretics: Some Introductory Comments." *Journal of Eastern Christian Studies* 60: 143–73.

Vivian, M. R. 2010. "The World of St. Daniel the Stylite: Rhetoric, *Religio*, and Relationships in the *Life* of the Pillar Saint." In Frakes and DePalma Digeser 2010: 147–65.

Vivian, T. 2002. "Saint Antony the Great and the Monastery of Saint Antony at the Red Sea *ca*. AD 251-1232/1233." In Bolman 2002: 3–17.

Vivian, T. 2005. *Words to Live By: Journeys in Ancient and Modern Egyptian Monasticism.* Kalamazoo, MI: Cistercian Publications.

Vivian, T., and A. Athanassakis, trans. 2003. *Athanasius of Alexandria, The Life of Antony: The Coptic Life and the Greek Life.* Kalamazoo, MI: Cistercian Publications.

Voöbus, A. 1957–1988. *A History of Asceticism in the Syrian Orient, a Contribution to the History of Culture in the Near East.* 3 vols. Louvain: Secrétariat du Corpus SCO.

Walbank, F. W. 1969. *The Awful Revolution: The Decline of the Roman Empire in the West.* Toronto: University of Toronto Press.

Walker, P. 1990. *Holy City, Holy Places? Christian Attitudes to Jerusalem and the Holy Land in the Fourth Century.* New York: Oxford University Press.

Wallace-Hadrill, A. 1981. "The Emperor and His Virtues." *Historia* 30: 298–323.

Wallraff, M. 2001a. *Christus Verus Sol: Sonnenverehrung und Christentum in der Spaetantike,* Jahrbuch für Antike und Christentum, Ergänzungsband 32. Münster: Aschendorffsche Verlagsbuchhandlung.

Wallraff, M. 2001b. "Constantine's Devotion to the Sun after 324." *Studia Patristica* 34: 256–69.

Ward, B. 1999. "Monks and Miracles." In Cavadini 1999: 127–37.

Ward-Perkins, B. 2005. *The Fall of Rome and the End of Civilization.* New York: Oxford University Press.

Ward-Perkins, J. B. 1966. "Memoria, Martyr's Tomb and Martyr's Church." *Journal of Theological Studies,* n.s. 17: 20–37.

Warmington, B. H. 1998. "Eusebius of Caesarea and the Governance of Constantine." In Hillard et al. 1998, vol. 2: 266–79.

Watts, E. 2015. *The Final Pagan Generation.* Transformation of the Classical Heritage, 53. Berkeley: University of California Press.

Watts, W., trans. 2006. *St. Augustine's Confessions.* LCL. Cambridge, MA: Harvard University Press.

Weber, G. 2000. *Kaiser, Träume und Visionen in Prinzipat und Spätantike,* Historia Einzelschriften, 143. Stuttgart: F. Steiner.

Weddle, D. L. 2010. *Miracles. Wonder and Meaning in World Religions.* New York: New York University Press.

Weinreich, O. 1916. "Konstantin der Große als Dreizehnter Apostel und die religionspolitische Tendenz seiner Grabeskirche." In O. Weinreich,

Triskaidekadischen Studien, Beiträge zur Geschichte der Zahlen, 2–14. Giessen: Verlag von Alfred Töpelmann.

Weiss, P. 1993. "Die Vision Constantins." In J. Bleicken, ed., *Colloquium aus Anlass des 80. Geburtstages von Alfred Heuss,* Frankfurter althistorische Studien, Heft 13: 143–169. Kalmunz: M. Lassleben

Weiss, P. 2003. "The Vision of Constantine." *Journal of Roman Archaeology* 16: 237–59.

Wetzel, J., ed. 2012. *Augustine's City of God: A Critical Guide.* Cambridge: Cambridge University Press.

Wharton, A. 1992. "The Baptistery of the Holy Sepulcher in Jerusalem and the Politics of Sacred Landscape." *Dumbarton Oaks Papers* 46: 313–25.

Whitby, M., ed. 1998. *The Propaganda of Power: The Role of Panegyric in Late Antiquity,* Mnemosyne Supp. 183. Leiden: Brill.

White, M., ed. 1993. *Social Networks in the Early Christian Environment: Issues and Methods for Social History.* Semeia 56. Alpharetta, GA: Scholars Press.

Wickham, C. 2005. *Framing the Early Middle Ages: Europe and the Mediterranean, 400-800.* New York: Oxford University Press.

Wienand, J. 2012. *Der Kaiser als Sieger. Metamorphosen triumphaler Herrschaft unter Constantin I,* Klio Beiträge zur Alten Geschichte Beihefte, n.F. 19. Berlin: Akademie Verlag.

Wienand, J. 2015a. "The Empire's Golden Shade: Icons of Sovereignty in an Age of Transition." In Wienand 2015b: 423–51.

Wienand, J., ed. 2015b. *Contested Monarchy: Integrating the Roman Empire in the Fourth Century A.D.* New York: Oxford University Press.

Wilken, R. L. 1983. *John Chrysostom and the Jews: Rhetoric and Reality in the Late Fourth Century.* Berkeley: University of California Press.

Wilkinson, J., trans. 1981. *Egeria's Travels to the Holy Land.* rev. ed. Warminster, England: Aris & Phillips.

Williams, F., trans. 1987–1994. *The Panarion of Epiphanius of Salamis.* 2 vols. Leiden: Brill.

Williams, M. 2008. *Authorised Lives in Early Christian Biography: Between Eusebius and Augustine.* Cambridge: Cambridge University Press.

Williams, R. 2003. "Foreword." In Vivian and Athanassakis 2003: xv–xvii.

Williamson, G. A., trans. *The History of the Church from Christ to Constantine.* Baltimore: Penguin, 1965.

Wills, G. 2012. *Font of Life: Ambrose, Augustine, and the Mystery of Baptism.* New York: Oxford University Press.

Wilpert, J. 1924. *Die römischen Mosaiken und Malereien der kirchlichen Bauten vom IV. bis. XIII. Jahrhundert.* 3rd ed. 4 vols. Freiburg im Breisgau: Herder.

Wilson, N. G., ed. 1975. *Saint Basil on the Value of Greek Literature.* London: Duckworth.

Wilson, S., ed. 1983. *Saints and Their Cults.* Cambridge: Cambridge University Press.

Winkelmann, F., ed. 1975. *Über das Leben des Kaisers Konstantins.* Eusebius' Werke I,1. GCS. 2nd ed. Berlin: Akademie Verlag.

Wood, I. 2008. "Barbarians, Historians, and the Construction of National Identities." *Journal of Late Antiquity* 1: 61–81.

Woods, D. 2006. "Sopater of Apamea: A Convert at the Court of Constantine I?" *Studia Patristica* 39: 139–43.

Woods, D. 2012. "Postumus and the Three Suns: Neglected Numismatic Evidence for a Solar Halo." *Numismatic Chronicle* 172: 85–92 and pl. 6.

Woods, D. 2015. "Gregory of Nazianzus on the Death of Julian the Apostate (Or. 5.13)." *Mnemosyne*, 3 ser., 68: 297–303.

Woolf, G. 2003. "Seeing Apollo in Roman Gaul and Germany." In Scott and Webster 2003: 139–53.

Wortley, J. 1992. "The Spirit of Rivalry in Early Christian Monachism." *Greek, Roman and Byzantine Studies* 33: 383–404.

Wright, F. A., trans. 1980. *Select Letters of St. Jerome.* LCL. Cambridge, MA: Harvard University Press.

Wright, W. C. 1913–1923. *The Works of the Emperor Julian.* 3 vols. LCL. Cambridge, MA: Harvard University Press.

Wright, W. C. 1921. *Philostratus and Eunapius: Lives of Philosophers and Sophists.* LCL. Cambridge, MA: Harvard University Press.

Young, F. 1982. "Did Epiphanius Know What He Meant by 'Heresy'?" In E. Livingstone, ed., *Studia Patristica* 17 (1): 199–205. Oxford: Pergamon Press.

Young, F. 1983. *From Nicaea to Chalcedon: A Guide to the Literature and Its Background.* Philadelphia: Fortress Press.

Zecchini, G. 2011. "Religione pubblica e libertà religiosa nell' impero romano." In Ceccini and Gabrielli 2011: 187–98.

Zelzer, M., ed. 1990–1996. *Ambrose: Epistula et Acta,* Ambrosii Opera 10, CSEL 82.1–4. Vienna: Hoelder-Pichler-Tempsky.

Zenos, A. C., trans. 1890–1900. *The Church History of Socrates Scholasticus.* In Schaff and Wace 1890–1900, 2: 1–178.

INDEX

Acts of St. Silvester. See Silvester, Pope
Acts of Peter, 159, 256n5, 258n30
Adrianople, battle of, 35, 202, 203
Alaric, 199–201, 202–3, 209
Alexander Monachos. 113, 250n52
  See also Legend of the Cross
Altar of Victory, 172–76, 177, 233
  See also Ambrose of Milan;
    Symmachus
Ambrose, bp. of Milan, 3, 32–4, 92, 232
  and Altar of Victory, 172, 174–6
  on Constantine's miracle, 49–50
  and discovery of Cross, 93
  funeral oration of, 28–9, 37, 39–40
  and Helena, 76, 93–4, 107
  and Jews, 45, 127, 129, 132–33
  and miracle language, 159, 177–78
  and miracles, 43–47
  political theology of, 41–43
  silent reading of, 59
  and Symmachus, 176–77
  and Theodosius, 34–35
  on Theodosius's miracle, 29, 40–41
Ammianus Marcellinus, 257n21, 258n50
  and Antioch, 197
  on Jerusalem Temple, 193
  on Julian, 166, 189–90
  on Julian's death, 196, 260n36
  on Julian's school law, 172

anti-Semitism, 122, 132, 250n15
  See also Ambrose of Milan; John
    Chrysostom
Antioch
  and Julian, 197, 260n41
  religions in, 197–98
Antony, Saint, 136, 138–40, 144, 217
  on ascetic training, 145, 154
  debate with philosophers, 155
  and demons, 147, 151, 153–54, 189
  and discourse, 156
  Life of Antony. See Athanasius
  and miracles, 146, 152–53
  his monastery, 140, 253n9
  and monasticism, 139–40
  and St. Martin, 152
  See also Athanasius; monasticism
Arbogastes, 30–31, 184
Athanasius, bp. of Alexandria, 135,
    141, 243n4
  on Julian, 196
  Life of Antony, 5, 137, 140–41, 254n13
Augustine, bp. of Hippo
  on Ambrose, 59, 131, 216
  and Christian identity, 205, 208,
    210, 218
  City of God, 6, 207–8, 210, 214–15, 218,
    223, 229
  and classical learning, 172, 212

Augustine, bp. of Hippo (*Cont.*)
  Confessions, 65, 207
  on Constantine, 215
  and conversion, 65
  on Julian, 215
  on justice, 213
  on *Life of Antony*, 141
  in Milan, 176, 206
  and miracles, 215–17
  and Plato, 212, 214
  sermons on Rome, 205
    quoted, 199
  "the two cities," 211–12

Basil of Caesarea, 171, 258n50
  *Advice to Young Men (On the Value of
    Greek Literature)*, 171
Battle of Adrianople. *See* Adrianople
Battle of Pharsalus. *See* Pharsalus
Baumstark, Anton, 107, 249n39. *See also*
    Holy Sepulchre
bishops, 91, 92, 198, 261n44
  as power brokers, 3, 31, 33
  and Constantine, 75, 85
  and miracles, 6, 16, 103, 113, 218
  and sermons, 38–9
  See also Ambrose; Augustine; Eusebius
    of Caesarea
Book of Job, 154, 217
  and St. Antony, 154
  and St. Augustine, 211
Brown, Peter, 16, 236n12, 237n27, 255n31,
    258n43, 261n44

Callinicum, 34
  Ambrose's use of, 34–35, 44, 127
  See also intolerance
Cameron, Alan, 25, 229–30, 239n8, 258n1
Celsus, 78, 80, 143, 158
Chi Rho emblem, 54–55, 56, 81
  in Lactantius, 52–53, 55–56
  See also Constantine, vision of;
    labarum
Chrysostom, John, 130–31, 154,
    232, 255n43
  and Jews, 127–28, 133
  and monasticism, 147

  and polarization, 129, 197–99
  rhetoric of, 130–31, 251n38
Church and State, 36, 43, 218
  in antiquity, 42, 67–68
coercion, Christian, 14–15, 22, 227
  in Lactantius, 80
  See also intolerance; Julian
coins, 38, 68, 106, 108, 248n20
  as propaganda, 54, 240n24
  of Constantine, 53, 55–56, 61–62, 65
comes ("companion"), 12, 68, 71, 89
  in Eusebius, 91
  imperial rank of, 119
  See also imperial ideology
Constantine I, 11–12, 60, 64, 105, 147, 185
  as bishop, 75–76, 85–87
  in *City of God*, 215–16
  conversion of, 13–14, 57–58, 64–65
  empowers bishops, 33
  and Helena, icon, 107–8
  and Holy Sepulchre, 95, 96, 99–100,
    102, 191, 248n20
  as "Man of God," 4, 76, 243n4
  and miracle, 1, 64
  and Moses, 84–85, 245n28
  Oration to the Saints, 81, 242n33
  "pagan vision" of, 58, 61
  religious policy, 68, 71, 88–89,
    125, 240n2
    ambiguity of, 73, 83, 90
  and St. Paul, 75–76, 84–85
  and Silvester, 157–58, 256n1
  "sincerity," 50
  and True Cross, 102–3, 110–11
  "Vision of the Cross," 3, 10, 51–52
  other visions, 66
  See also Chi Rho; coins; conversion
    models; halo phenomenon;
    Eusebius of Caesarea; imperial
    ideology; Lactantius
Constantius I, 60, 71, 247n4
Constantius II, 102, 161–63, 173, 190
conversion models, 50, 65, 242n21.
    See also Constantine
cosmic order. *See* imperial ideology
Council of Elvira, 15, 249n39
Council of Nicaea, 89, 94

cross. *See* True Cross
Cyril, bp. of Jerusalem, 102, 110–11, 248n25
    Letter to Constantius II, 102

Daniel the Stylite, 219–20, 221, 224–25
    Titus and Daniel, 219, 220–21
demons 104, 131, 136, 146, 151, 153–54,
    222–23, 255n42
    in *City of God*, 215, 217
    in Eusebius, 85, 91–2, 246n44
    and Jews, 128, 133
    See also Antony, Saint
Diocletian, 11, 60, 67–68
    abdication, 11
    Great Persecution of, 12, 69–70
    in Lactantius, 78–79
    See also Tetrarchy
Donatists, 207
Drepanum. *See* Helenopolis

Ebionites, 119, 251n29
economics, religious, 151–52
"Edict of Milan," 67, 72, 187
Elvira, Council of. *See* Council of Elvira
Epiphanius, bp. of Salamis, 118–19, 121,
    126, 133, 251nn30, 32
    Panarion of, 118–19
Eugenius, 30–31, 50, 89, 182, 184, 229
Eunapius of Sardis, 149–50
Eusebius, bp. of Caesarea, 82–83
    on Constantine, 84, 86, 244n23
        criticism of, 87
    on Constantine's Vision, 51–53, 57,
        85, 241n5
        other visions, 66, 242n26
    on chi-rho, 58
    Church History, influence of, 82
    on Galerius, 259n2
    on Helena, 106, 109
    on Holy Sepulchre, 95–96, 99, 102,
        191–9, 248n21
    and imperial ideology, 90–92, 147, 204,
        246nn 40, 44
    on *labarum*, 58, 248n30
    Life of Constantine, 51, 88, 245n34
    on Licinius, 186–87
    on Maxentius, 185

speeches to Constantine, 83–84,
    244n21, 245n32
    and True Cross, 100–1, 103

Flavianus, 30–31, 184
Frigidus River, battle of, 28–29, 30, 31, 202
    See also Ambrose of Milan; Theodosius I

Galerius, 60, 70–71, 78, 182–84
    and Christian identity, 204
Gibbon, Edward, 14, 100, 150, 235n7, 255n33
"good king"
    in Chrysostom, 147
    in Hebrew Bible, 85
    See also imperial ideology
Gratian, 12, 31, 34, 46–47, 173–74, 215
Great Persecution. *See* Diocletian
Grégoire, Henri, 56
Gregory of Nazianzus, 172
    on martyrdom, 188
    on persecution, 187–88
    on Julian, 188, 258n37

hagiography, 5, 140, 146
halo phenomenon, 62–64, 241n18
    See also Constantine
Hammat Tiberias mosaic, 123–24, 125
    and religious identity, 128, 129
Helena, 93–94, 105–7, 109, 112
    and Constantine, icon, 107–8
    and Jews, 115–16, 157
    in Silvester legend, 157
    See also Ambrose of Milan; Legend of
        the Cross
Helenopolis (Drepanum), 148
heresy (*hairesis*), 119, 170, 198, 236n12
    See also Epiphanius
Highest God (*Summus Deus*), 50, 72, 126
    See also monotheism; solar symbolism;
        Sun god
holy man (*theios anēr*), 145
    and demons, 152
Holy Sepulchre, Church of, 98, 100,
    191–92, 248n25
    discovery of, 95–96
    Encainea (Dedication) ceremony,
        96–97, 109

Holy Sepulchre, Church of (*Cont.*)
  hemisphairion, 101, 108
  See also Constantine; Eusebius;
      True Cross
Honorius, 12, 28, 37, 41
  and Sack of Rome, 200–1, 203

imperial ideology, 68–69, 76, 85,
      125, 242n32
  and cosmic order, 19, 90–91, 147, 204,
      222, 235n4, 246n44
  "good king" literature, 90–91, 196
  need for consensus, 89
  See also comes; solar symbolism;
      Sun god
intolerance
  and Christianity, 13–14, 20
  and "sincerity," 50, 198
  See also coercion; Edict of Milan;
      toleration
Isapostolos, 76, 88, 243n5
  See also Constantine; imperial ideology

Jacobus de Voragine, 116–17, 250n3
Jerome, Saint, 77, 148
  and classical culture, 170, 172, 258n34
  on Sack of Rome, 204–5
Job. *See* Book of Job
John Chrysostom. *See* Chrysostom, John
Joseph, *comes*, 119–20, 126
  and Judas Kyriakos, 120–21
Judas Kyriakos, 115–18, 126, 132–33
  See also Helena; Legend of the Cross
Julian "the Apostate," 5, 161–63, 166, 173,
      178, 215, 233, 257n14, 258n50
  Against the Galilaeans, 164–65, 169
  in Antioch, 197
  and blood sacrifice, 166, 204
  The Caesars, 164
  on Christian charity, 166, 167–68
  on Christian coercion, 166
  and Christian organization, 166–67
  on Constantine, 163–64
  and Constantius II, 12, 161–63
  death in Persia, 196
  effect on episcopal control, 198, 261n44
  in Gaul, 163, 195

Misopogon, 197
  and omens, 179, 189, 259n29
  as persecutor, 187–88, 259n16
  Persia campaign, 194–96
  polarizing actions, 171–72, 198
  on priestly behavior, 167
  school law, 168–70, 172, 228
  Temple project, 190–94
Julius Caesar, 178, 184

labarum, 104
Lactantius, 77, 82, 185–86, 188, 259n14
  on Constantine's miracle, 51–52,
      56–57, 63
  on chi rho, 52–56
  Divine Institutes, 79–81
  on Galerius' death, 78, 182–84
  On the Deaths of the Persecutors, 77–78
Legend of the Cross, 112–13
Leo I, 219–20, 224
Libanius
  on monks, 149
  on toleration, 159–61
Licinius, 61, 67–68, 72, 185–87
Life of Constantine. See Eusebius of Caesarea
Life of Daniel the Stylite. See Daniel the
      Stylite

Macarius, bp. of Jerusalem, 96, 103–4, 107
Madaba mosaic, 99, 101
Mark, bp. of Arethusa, 189
Martin, Saint, 151–52
martyrs, 142–43, 146, 165, 188–89, 216,
      230–31, 239n23, 254n13
  See also Ambrose, bp. of Milan; Council
      of Elvira
martyrion, 95, 109, 165
Maxentius, 57, 70, 84, 185
Melania the Elder, 148
Milan, as imperial capital, 32–33
  See also Ambrose, bp. of Milan
miracles, 1–2, 7–9, 10, 16, 28, 30, 64,
      102–3, 165
  and historians, 7, 9, 13, 19–21, 231
  kinds of, 17–19, 135, 210, 222–23
  as discourse, 31, 45, 151–52, 153,
      155–56, 159, 175, 177–78, 181

value of, 231–32
See also Ambrose, bp. of Milan;
Augustine, bp. of Hippo;
Constantine I; Helena; Legend of
the Cross; Theodosius I
monasticism, 138, 147–49
criticism of, 149–50
economic value of, 151
See also Antony, Saint.
monotheism, 18, 23–24, 72, 210, 237n16
Constantine's policy, 89, 125
and intolerance, 14, 238n32
in Eusebius, 83, 246n44
"pagan monotheism," 24–25, 90,
243n36, 244n22
See also Highest God; solar symbolism

Neoplatonism, 144–45, 207, 257n21
Nicholas, Saint, 137
Nock, Arthur Darby, 13, 242n23
numismatics. *See* coins

oracles, 18, 186
Sibylline oracle, 71
Origen of Alexandria, 158
Orosius, 202, 208–9

Pachomius, 148
pagan monotheism. *See* monotheism
paganism, defined, 1, 24–25
and miracles, 18
Panarion. See Epiphanius
panegyrics, how to read, 59–60
XII Panegyrici Latini, 58
(of 310), 60–61, 63
(of 313), 76
Pharsalus, battle of, 184
philosopher-king. *See* Plato
piety, in antiquity, 90–91, 240n27, 246n42
in Ambrose of Milan, 3, 37, 42, 46
in Augustine, 210–11
in Eusebius of Caesarea, 91
in Sack of Rome, 209
pillar saints, 16, 21, 149–50
Plato, 72, 90, 213
Apology of Socrates, 158
and Augustine, 212–14, 262n19

classes of mankind, 214
on justice, 212–13
philosopher-king, 144–45,
213–14, 254n18
The Republic, 212–13, 214–15
theory of ideals, 214
See also Neoplatonism
Platonism, as heresy, 118
Plotinus. *See* Neoplatonism
polytheism, 14
in Eusebius, 83, 92, 246n44
Porphyry, bp. of Gaza, 227–28

religious economics. *See* economics,
religious
rhetoric, 77, 130, 184, 251n38, 257n32
role of, 131–32, 185, 252n44
Rufinus of Aquileia, 107, 148
on Helena, 107
on Theodosius's miracle, 29–30
Rutilius Namatianus, 150

Sack of Rome (in 410), 2, 199–200, 202,
209, 233
and Christian identity, 203–5, 210
and miracle, 218, 222, 229
See also Augustine; Orosius
saint's life. *See* hagiography
Santa Claus. *See* Nicholas, Saint
Santa Croce in Gerusalemme. See Sessorian
Palace
sermons, importance of, 38–39,
128, 240n25
See also Ambrose of Milan; Augustine;
Chrysostom
Sessorian Palace, 109
Silvester, Pope, 178, 256nn1-2
Acts of, 157-9
Simeon Stylites, 149
See also pillar saints
Socrates (church historian)
on Jerusalem Temple, 194
on persecution, 188
solar symbolism, 125
See also imperial ideology;
monotheism
Stilicho, 202–3

Sulpicius Severus, 152
Summus Deus. See Highest God
Sun God, 24, 61–2
  and Jews, 123
  and monotheism, 24, 124
  Sol Invictus, 61
  See also imperial ideology; solar
    symbolism
Symmachus, 160–61, 172, 176
  on Altar of Victory, 174–75
  and miracle language, 177–78
  on toleration, 169

Temple, Jerusalem, 97, 112, 190–91, 193
  See also Julian "the Apostate"
Tetrarchy, 11
  See also Diocletian
theios anēr. See holy man
Themistius, 160, 161, 256n9
Theodoret, 27, 196
Theodosius I, 12, 34, 150, 201–2
  Callinicum incident, 34–35, 45
  and Constantine, 49, 92, 94, 217
  ends subsidies for pagan cults, 14, 31

  his miracle, 27–28, 184, 229–30
  Libanius's plea to, 160–61
  makes Christianity official, 31, 200
  Thessalonika incident, 35–36, 106
  See also Ambrose, bp. of Milan
Titus. *See* Daniel the Stylite
toleration
  as "loser's creed," 15
  Christian arguments for, 15
  edict of toleration (311), 78
  pagan arguments for, 160–61, 174
  See also "Edict of Milan"; intolerance
True Cross
  and boundaries, 111, 133
  identifying, 107, 113, 115
  spread of, 111
Twain, Mark, 98
tyrant, in rhetoric, 184–85

Valens, 12, 34, 203, 209
Valentinian I, 12
Valentinian II, 12, 33–34, 174

XII Panegyrici Latini. See panegyrics